CUES:
Choose, Use, Enjoy, Share

D1518866

Library and Information Problem-Solving Skills Series

Paula Kay Montgomery, Series Editor

CUES: Choose, Use, Enjoy, Share: A Model for Educational Enrichment Through the School Library Media Center. Second Edition. By Phyllis B. Leonard.

Media Skills for Middle Schools: Strategies for Library Media Specialists and Teachers. Second Edition. By Lucille W. Van Vliet. (forthcoming)

Library Information Skills and the High School English Program. Second Edition. By Mary H. Hackman. (forthcoming)

Library and Information Skills Instruction: Applying Research to Practice in the School Library Media Center. By Nancy P. Thomas. (forthcoming)

Beyond the Book: Technology Integration into the Secondary School Library Media Curriculum. By Sandra L. Doggett. (forthcoming)

Learning and Information: Skills for the Secondary Classroom and Library Media Program. Second Edition. By Glen W. Cutlip. (forthcoming)

CUES: Choose, Use, Enjoy, Share

*A Model for Educational Enrichment
Through the School Library Media Center*

Second Edition

Phyllis B. Leonard

edited by

Paula Kay Montgomery

1998
LIBRARIES UNLIMITED, INC.
Englewood, Colorado

LIBRARIES UNLIMITED, INC.
P.O. Box 6633
Englewood, CO 80155-6633
1-800-237-6124
www.lu.com

Production Editor: Kay Mariea
Copy Editor: Louise Tonneson
Proofreader: Suzanne Hawkins Burke
Indexer: Linda Running Bentley
Design and Layout: Pamela J. Getchell

Library of Congress Cataloging-in-Publication Data

Leonard, Phyllis B., 1929-
    CUES : choose, use, enjoy, share : a model for educational
enrichment through the school library media center / Phyllis B.
Leonard ; edited by Paula Kay Montgomery. -- 2nd ed.
    xvi, 209 p. 22x28 cm. -- (Library and information problem-solving skills
series)
    Rev. ed. of: Choose, use, enjoy, share. 1985.
    Includes bibliographical references and indexes.
    ISBN 1-56308-550-X
    1. Elementary school libraries--Activity programs--United States.
2. Media programs (Education)--United States. 3. Library
orientation for gifted children--United States. I. Montgomery,
Paula Kay. II. Leonard, Phyllis B., 1929-   Choose, use, enjoy,
share. III. Title. IV. Series.
Z675.S3L389 1998
027.8'222--dc21
                                                              98-8405
                                                                CIP

Contents

Foreword by *Paula Kay Montgomery* xi

Acknowledgments xiii

Introduction xv

One—Parnassus-in-the-School 1

    References 5

Two—The Shaping of Curriculum 7

    The Process of Education 7

    What Is Intelligence? 9

    Gifted Programs: Theories and Proponents 10

        Differentiating by Curriculum and Instruction 11

            Instructional Models: Information Processing and
Active Teaching 11

            Knowledge As Design 12

            The Subject of Thinking 13

        Differentiating by Grouping 14

            The Revolving Door 15

            Cooperative Learning 15

        Differentiating by Strategy 15

            The Practice of Thinking 15

            The Art of Questioning 16

            Styles and Tricks of Teaching About Thinking 17

            Library Media Program: One Size Fits All 20

    References 20

    Bibliography 21

v

Three—CUES! A Model for a Library Media Centered Curriulum with Books 23

Program Ingredients 24
    Library Media Programs—Officially 25
    The Library Media Center Habit 26
The CUES Interaction 27
Literature Is Curriculum 29
    Literature As Textbook Instruction 30
    Literature Skills 31
    Library and Information Skills 31
        Location and Arrangements 32
        Sources of Information 32
        Information Collection and Retrieval 32
        Communication of Information 32
References 34
Bibliography 34

Four—Portraits and Landscapes for Learning 35

The Collection: Landscape for Learning 36
    Books About Books for Bibliophiles 37
The Art of Teaching 37
    Portraits of Teachers 37
    Teachers at Home: Megaskills 38
    Teachers in Schools: Who Should Teach the Gifted? 39
Portraits of Learners 41
    Checklists 41
    "Quiz Kids" 43
References 44
Bibliography 45

Five—Grouping a Set: Setting a Group 47

Grouping a Set 47
    CUES As Revolving Door 47
        A Longitudinal Group Model: The CPRG,
            a Five-Year Case Study 48
        Independent Study Model I: Research Assistants 51
        Independent Study Model II: Danny Finds Out 53
        Latitudinal Group Model: Topical Units 54
Emotional Intelligence and Setting a Group 55
    Bibliotherapy and Training 56

Affecting a Group, a Progression 57
  Breaking the Ice 57
  Developing Labels, Logos, Rules, and Rituals 57
  Establishing a Sensitivity to Feelings 59
  Toward Global Understanding 61
The Dynamics Duo: Speaking and Group 62
References: Human Relations Resources for Teachers 64
Bibliography 65

Six—Language Arts Unlimited 67
The Gift of Language 67
Wordsmithing 68
  Word Wizardry 68
  Fooling Around with Words 69
  Semantic Strategies 70
    Word Wall 70
  The Structure of Language 71
    Groanless Grammar 72
    Painless Punctuation 72
  The Origins of Language 73
    "What Is the English Language?" 73
    Roots: Other Languages 73
  Painting Pictures with Words 75
    From P→W 75
    From W→P 76
    From W→W 77
Yarnspinning 77
  Reading to Writing to Storytelling 77
    Recesstory 78
    Readers Theatre 78
    Storythinking 79
    Improvisations 79
    Silent Languages and Hidden Languages 80
    Griots, Cochitis, and Speechmakers 80
  Writers' Workshops 81
References 81
Bibliography 82
  For Teachers 82
  For Young Readers 83

Seven—Easy Does It! 87

The Easy Collection 88
  Authors 89
  Narration Teaches 89
  Easy Exposition 93
  Series 95
Snuggle and Read: Connections 95
  Primates for Primaries 97
References 98
Bibliography 98

Eight—Information? Please! But Help Wanted 103

Paths Beyond the Lesson 103
Scope and Sequence for Finding Out 106
What's the Point? 108
  Primarily Fun 108
    Just Open a Book 108
    What Can You Do 109
    How to Find Out 109
  Upper Starts 110
    The 1, 2, 3s 110
    Eric's T-Shirt 111
    . . . And the ABCs, with a Possible D 113
Organizing the Searcher 114
  The Velveteen Catalog 114
  Topicana 115
  Topics by the 000s 115
    A School of Names for the 500s 115
    970 Is a History of US 116
    World History 116
    Countries and *Culturgrams* 117
  Frameworks 117
References 119
Bibliography 119

Nine—Curious? Read! 123

Do You Have a Book About . . .? 123
References Required 124
  Dictionaries 124
  Encyclopedias 125
  Almanacs 127
  Special Reference Books 128

Series Books 129
Miscellany Matters 130
To Bee or Not to Bee 131
    Games and Simulations 131
    Cooperative Competitions 131
Stepping-Stones 132
    Alphabet Antics 132
    Bibliographic Byplay 133
    Calendars and Chronologies 133
    Differentiated Diversions 133
    Lists of Books and Books of Lists 134
    Periodicals and Potpourris 135
    Questions and Quotations 136
    Serendipity Searches and Stone Soup 137
    Wonderful Sevens of the World 138
References 139
Bibliography 139

Ten—Roots and Wings 143
Cultural Literacy Redux . . . Multicultural Literacy 144
Literary Capers 144
    As Transition Curriculum 146
    As CUES Curriculum 146
Cultural Literacy—Literary Capers 148
    The Classics 148
        Media Uses of Classics 149
    Folklore Treasures to Explore 149
Whys of the Storywriters 151
Issues, Issues, Issues 152
Literary Sharings 154
    Pictures, Cartoons, and Web Sites 154
    Penny Theatres, Collages, and Pop-Ups 157
    Curating an Exhibit 158
The Arts Sing Many Languages 160
References 163
    Resources for Planning Multicultural Units 163
Bibliography 164

Eleven—Some Roads to Wham 167
   Seven League Boots 167
      Journals and Journeys 168
      Immigrants All 170
      Bards, Pilgrims, and Troubadours 172
      Arks, Towers, Castles, and Walls 173
   Epics, Epochs, and Eras 174
      Epics 174
      Epoch-ryphal and Era-tic Time Lines 174
      Sweep Across History 175
   Examined Lives 176
      Juvenile Biography 176
      Autobiography 177
      Collective Biography 179
      What to Do with a 92 179
      Side Trips 180
   Mammoths, Museums, and Renaissance Men 182
   Bibliography 188

Twelve—Mindsets to Mindstorms Through Mindscapes 195
   Educational Trends 196
      Paradigms and Protocols 198
      Pendulums 199
   Frontiers 199
      Youth in Action 200
      Wires and Bridges 200
         Wiring the World 200
         Bridging the Centuries 201
   References 204
   Bibliography 204

   Index 205

Foreword

Many bright students excel at whatever they do, especially in school. Whether they encounter a structured academic curriculum or a creative arts program, the students bloom and find ways to express what they learn from what is introduced. Author Phyllis Leonard had those students in mind when she began this book. However, this book is also for those who facilitate learning for all students, including those bright individuals who do not necessarily find their niche while studying within the walls of the classroom. The concepts developed in this book assume that open access to a school library media program is imperative for teaching gifted and talented children. A well-stocked facility and a skilled library media professional are two of the building blocks that support a program for beginning a supportive program for highly gifted youngsters. The author further assumes that there is regular use of carefully selected materials. Students are encouraged to engage their curiosity as they read books, view videotapes, or search Internet sources. A library media specialist is available to motivate interaction with text and to spur children to achieve independence in learning.

The model for the integration of library media and research skills into the curriculum discussed in this book demonstrates that content and skills are not separate, but interwoven. Students "choose, use, enjoy, and share" what they encounter and experience. Library media materials are a regular component of the instructional program. These resources form the basis for generating exploration of content while mastering the skills necessary to understand what is encountered. This CUES model focuses on finding out about all those things that human beings have contemplated, researched, and recorded. The library media specialist is another teacher in the school who coordinates library media and information skills instruction for highly able students in the school.

When Phyllis Leonard wrote the first edition of this book, she was a practicing library media specialist at Belmont Elementary School in Olney, Maryland. She was active in implementing the Montgomery County School Library Media Skills Program. Her involvement as a committee member in the development of library media skills continuum and as a member of gifted and talented teaching programs allowed her to provide meaningful assistance to curriculum documents still used within the school system. Her ideas were tested for many years with elementary children. Her folders are full of success stories and examples of work from children who have now graduated and gone on to rewarding careers in engineering and the arts. Now as a mother, grandmother, and retired media specialist, her ideas are still being tried. She currently serves as a docent at the Corcoran Museum of Art in Washington, D.C. Her experience with gifted students and her knowledge of how to implement successful programs continue to allow her to motivate students.

This book was written initially for library media specialists involved in programs for the highly able. However, the practices might be seen just as easily as classroom initiated activities. The suggestions are also applicable for use with all children. Given the wide variation in definitions of giftedness, it would be easy for library media specialists to apply the methods and ideas for all their classes. After all, all students benefit from the use of library media resources. The meld of content and process can make learning in the library media center a welcome joy rather than a didactic or boring chore.

It is to be hoped that elementary and middle school library media specialists will choose, use, enjoy, and share this book with their teachers.

Paula Kay Montgomery

Acknowledgments

Parnassus on Wheels by Christopher Morley is quoted in Chapter 1 with the permission of Harper & Row (the present copyright holder) and Harper-Collins Publishers, Inc.

Some information in Chapter 2 is taken from *The Process of Education* by Jerome Bruner, copyright © 1960 by the President and Fellows of Harvard College. Reprinted by permission of Harvard University Press.

Some information in Chapters 2 and 4 is taken from *The Art of Teaching* by Gilbert Highet, copyright © 1950 by Gilbert Highet. Reprinted by permission of Alfred A. Knopf, Inc.

Material in Chapter 4 from *Whatever Happened to the Quiz Kids?* is used with permission of the author. © Ruth Duskin Feldman.

Artwork on page 105 is reproduced with the permission of Allied Signal Inc.

Introduction

The ideas expressed in this book evolved from many perspectives on giftedness:

> that of a child who was in separated and accelerated academic programs in the Boston Public School system from second grade through an all-girls high school;

> that of a younger and insecure student in the highly competitive environment of a top university;

> that of a parent who marveled at each day's and stage's unfolding of her baby's and preschooler's language and thinking;

> that of a parent whose children were not in a stimulating or academically differentiated public school environment;

> that of a teacher and writer of curriculum for gifted elementary-age students; and

> that of a library media specialist who believes in the central importance of the school library media center;

. . . . and since 1985

> that of a grandparent observing how gifted programs in different school systems nurture or enrich children's learning;

> that of an adjunct supervisor of school library media specialists in graduate training and practicum; and

> that of a volunteer docent at the Corcoran Museum of Art in Washington, D.C., working with inner city school children.

The ideas for this book began to take shape in the summer of 1977 when I was assigned to a workshop to develop curriculum for gifted students in art, music, literature, social studies, and science. Ten master teachers and one library media specialist (me) responded when asked to develop a list of books for gifted education. Another part of my job was to be a bibliographic resource for the subject teachers. It came as a shock that none of the teachers viewed the library media specialist as a resource beyond that: yet the time and knowledge that would permit them to use literature to implement or create curriculum was limited.

Even more sadly, in the 20 years since, literature as curriculum is everywhere but there is little change in the expectation for and use of library media specialists in gifted programs. Why not? *CUES: Choose, Use, Enjoy, Share* proposes that the perception of library media specialist's role as a vital part of the education of gifted children is long overdue. It is gratifying, however, to note that much that was being quietly done in the Belmont library media center from the 1970s through the early 1990s presaged what is now documented theory, enacted policy (1997), and popularized trend (1998).

One

Parnassus-in-the-School

Once in the days of the Greek deities, Mount Parnassus was sacred to the Muses, the nine sisters who gathered there, along with their supervisor Apollo, in the name of the creative arts. Then the Muses crept away into books on mythology, and no one heard much about Parnassus until Christopher Morley revived the name in 1917 when he wrote *Parnassus on Wheels*. This prophetic novel advocated libraries long before they were widespread. A white horse named Pegasus drew his Parnassus, a blue wagon lined with crowded bookshelves, through the byways of New England. Inside the wagon lived Boccacchio, a sandy Irish terrier, and Roger Mifflin.

Roger was no ordinary itinerant bookseller. Small, wiry, and pugnacious-looking, the owner of this early bookmobile was a man of wit and intelligence. Most of all, he had a fervor for his mission: to bring the message of books to everyone. Roger believed "when you sell a man a book, you don't sell him just 12 ounces of paper and ink and glue—you sell him a whole new life. Love and friendship and humor and ships at sea by night. There's heaven and earth in a book, a real book, I mean" (Morley 1955).

During the seven years he traveled in Parnassus, Roger influenced many people to support his cause, including the governor, who then fought for an appropriation for libraries, and the county sheriff, who decided his prisoners needed books. Roger saw ways to reach even more people with his message. He would sell Parnassus and settle down to write a book—a book, of course, about bringing books to people. So, using his silver tongue and long-range vision, he sold Parnassus—to a most unlikely book gypsy, Miss Helen McGill. Helen, a doughty spinster, had compiled an anthology of her own: She had baked 6,000 loaves of bread in her author-brother's kitchen and gathered 1,300 dozen eggs. These were sold for a profit of $400 she used to buy Parnassus. She then took off on her maiden voyage, with Roger and Boccacchio along to show her the route and the routine. In the sequel to *Parnassus on Wheels*,

Roger and Helen, happily married and retired, live in their Parnassus-at-home, a haunted bookshop in Brooklyn. As the book ends, Roger's dream of having a fleet of 10 Parnassuses-on-wheels is about to come true.

Morley's Parnassus was fiction, but a real one existed. In 1905 Mary Lemest Titcomb, librarian at Hagerstown, Maryland, established "book deposit stations" in general stores and other places accessible to her rural patrons. Then Miss Mary designed and outfitted a horse-drawn wagon to carry books to the people. When the wagon was destroyed at a railroad crossing, its 1912 replacement became the first motorized bookmobile.

School library media specialists are much like Roger, Helen, and Miss Mary. They, too, believe each school library media center is a "caravan of culture"—a Parnassus-in-the-schools that is critically important to all programs. Their dreams about libraries in elementary schools began to come true in the 1960s and 1970s under various titles of the Elementary and Secondary Education Act. This legislation provided seed money for school libraries: for materials, both print and nonprint; for hardware and software; and for personnel. The dusty, understocked classroom-converted-to-library became an instructional materials (or media) center, staffed with library media specialists and paraprofessionals. The school library became more than just a place where curious children could explore their world and the world beyond, or where the book-loving child could read at random. Now, trained personnel were there to guide the child's search and direct the exploration amid an explosion of materials. With the library media center at the heart of the school, the situation seemed ideal.

But flaws were present. Unstructured use of the library media center in the open school with an open library was a problem. During the early 1970s, a library media specialist was likely to face an eager seven-year-old who, by midmorning Monday, had finished classroom centers for the week and was sent to the library media center to "do research on the universe." Later in the day came the confrontation with the entire second grade, assigned to "write a report on an animal" without using an encyclopedia. These reports typically were to be five pages long and to be based on three different books. (Or was it three pages long and based on five books?) Surely lexicographer and literary critic Samuel Johnson's disclosure that his education consisted of being let loose in a library meant something other than this!

School library media programs got their impetus well before demand developed for programs for the gifted. Because of this, school library media centers were often the first and only *de facto* gifted programs in a school—especially for the child who was both bright and an avid reader. Long before procedures or criteria for identifying the gifted had been determined, a child's library behavior was an informal, but accurate, indicator of academic and creative potential. As gifted programs were defined, formal procedures for identification were developed, and program implementation began. Although it seems logical that school library media programs should have been given a key role in gifted program design, this was not usually the case.

In the 1980s an ERIC/DIALOGUE search combining pertinent descriptors showed little in the database about a key role for school library media programs in the education of gifted elementary school children. Despite mention of roles for materials and the library in the vast literature about educating the gifted, very little is explicit. John Curtis Gowan and E. Paul Torrance state that "significant developments in curriculum for the gifted are more likely in out of classroom experiences than in it" (Gowan and Torrence 1971). Expert James Gallagher comments also about learning beyond the walls, writing that "gifted students throughout history have found means of coming into current contact with other great minds through books, and access to a rich library is one of the fundamentals for a good program for gifted students" (Gallagher. 1975). Clearly the notion of how a good library media center can be essential to a unified program for gifted children has been unexplored. This is a startling omission, considering all that has been published in the field of gifted education. The omission is even more amazing when it exists within school systems that are committed to school library media programs. Too often, the role of the school library media specialist is limited to one of compiling lists and collecting materials for curriculum writers or classroom teachers, leaving untapped the library media specialist's experiences with the multifaceted uses of materials in instructional design. This vision also ignores the power of the media specialist's enthusiasm for materials as a motivating force in enticing children to fulfill their learning potential. In the 1990s another library database search still fails to reflect the full significance of the school library media specialist to the education of gifted children.

As educational trends, philosophies, and emphases changed in the 1970s, library media programs adapted. The terminology *school library media center* came to mean a more structured educational environment, one with instructional goals, curriculum coordination, performance objectives, and task assessments. Management by objective often turned teaching and learning in the library media center into a joyless and mechanical scope and sequence that did not include the creative use of literature. Changes in the educational climate continued during the 1980s. Economic realities and budget cutbacks were barriers to goals previously set for library media programs. A more serious obstacle than funding constraints also existed: a change of attitude toward education, which permeated our society. No longer were reading or learning valued for their intrinsic worth. Those who worked with children sensed this phenomenon. The glamour of computers and video made reading for pleasure less appealing to children at the same time that the instructional emphasis on skills devalued *adventuring with books and learning.* Thus, we faced a paradox that greatly affected library media programs. Much money had been spent on building library media collections and facilities staffed with capable and creative teachers, but children, even those who **read well**, were not **well-read**. Nor was helping them become well-read considered a primary goal of either gifted or library media programs.

We found ourselves caught between Bloom and Blume. On the one hand, Benjamin Bloom's taxonomy of thinking levels structured curriculum so that gifted children could exactly identify the level on which they were operating without the substantive knowledge to fulfill a task at that level (Bloom 1956). On the other hand, Judy Blume's popularity as a most requested author typified the one-dimensional aspect of children's reading behaviors. The challenge in providing excellent school library media programs in this climate was to go beyond the Blume/Bloom limits in a framework that would inspire the quest, structure the search, and free the aspiration.

The first chapter of the 1985 edition of this book ended with the suggestion that school library media specialists in elementary schools should assert, even preempt, for themselves a prominent role in the education of gifted children. They expected to accomplish this by expanding the media specialist's role beyond a passive one as selector and keeper of a collection of curriculum-related materials to an active one as a teacher who sets up interactions between teacher, child, and literature. Between 1985 and 1997, many educational trends and practicalities surfaced, or resurfaced, to change or reinforce the thrust of this earlier message. For example, the much imitated Core Curriculum Series Books about what every child should know and the *Reading Rainbow* television series, with its printed Teacher's Guides, gave national prominence to many of this book's themes and suggested titles. "Literacy and Poetry for All" was the message of Robert Hass, recent poet laureate of the United States, as he traveled Main Streets, USA. How will such challenges and revivals affect the role of the school library media specialist?

The rediscovery of the value of literature is a wonderful trend. Not long ago, many educators thought that reading storybooks to a whole class wasted instructional time. Reading teachers worked primarily with remedial groups and chose basals for the school. School librarians were there to teach the card catalogue and other library and information skills, even if they secretly preferred sharing good books with kids.

Then came the changeover to whole language, in which reading is taught through the writing process; the language arts through literature. Reading stories from trade books is an essential daily strategy in the classroom. Basals and textbooks, even those that are literature based, are in disuse, to the chagrin of many teachers. Reading teachers work less with remediation and more with using children's books to present minilessons to launch children's writing workshops. Parnassus moved to the malls, where the 372 section of bookstores (and public libraries) bursts with how-to books for using children's literature to teach—science, multiculturalism, language, math, ecology, and values. Repercussions and reactions have surfaced in the educational establishment. The whole language approach is being blamed for the lack of knowledge of grammar (syntax and spelling), reflected in declining standardized test scores. The long-awaited new national and local subject standards for math, science, history, and language are arguable, as are standardized testing and interpretations.

Many of these changes seem to be diminutions of the media specialist's job. Now a primary class may say to the media specialist, who is about to show them the newer treasures of the collection, "Our teacher read that to us already." Their class library times serve as minilessons for these children, who also ask, "How are you different from Mrs. X (the reading teacher)?" Other things are happening that dilute or change the role of the library media specialist. Many schools have added the curriculum specialist to their support personnel. This often impinges on the library media specialist's role as resource for curriculum implementation through bibliography preparation and unit planning for teachers. At the same time, library media centers are expanding to become communications centers and hubs run by and for new technology with the media staff responsible for the use of computers, television studios, in-school cable, and networks for learning within and beyond one school. The technologies, themselves, have special applications for gifted children, who frequently are technically ahead of media personnel.

Another change became evident in a summer vacation tour group of educators, primarily teachers from California. Their comment to the library media specialist in the group was, "Where we come from, you're an *endangered species*." Endangered—by budget cuts, and through personnel allocation decisions made by school-based site-management committees. Uninformed of the importance of library media programs run by skilled library media teachers, they assume that high technology paraprofessionals alone can staff the media facility.

Belief in school library media programs and library media specialists is the message of this book. Like Roger Mifflin, school library media specialists must hawk their wares to demonstrate that their programs are dynamic, effective, and indispensable elements in educating our ablest students. In Roger's words: "I have no facility in the grand style. I have always suffered from the feeling that it is better to read a good book than to write a poor one; and that I've done so much mixed reading in my time that my mind is full of echoes and voices of better men. But this book I'm worrying about now really deserves to be written, I think, for it has a message of its own" (Morley 1945). That message is no less important for the last years of the 1990s than it was heretofore. As educational trends, philosophies, and emphases follow new directions, so too must school library media programs. Roger Mifflin's recipe for the good life had three ingredients: learning, earning, and yearning. "A man should be learning as he goes; and he should be earning bread for himself and others; and he should be yearning too. Yearning to know the unknowable" (Morley 1945)

Worthwhile goals for the twenty-first century? Yes! A magic carpet still resides in the library media center, but the keepers of the gate are now **cybrarians**. The new call is Ms. Frizzle's "Into the bus, kids!" as the *Magic School Bus* takes off again. Alice no longer goes through the looking glass; she goes through the monitor into cyberspace. Kids thrive on Goosebumps, and the "Web" is no longer Charlotte's—it is a worldwide internet.

REFERENCES

Bloom, Benjamin. 1956. *Taxonomy of Educational Objectives*. NY: David McKay.

Gallagher, James. 1975. *Teaching the Gifted Child*. Boston: Allyn & Bacon.

Gowan, John Curtis, and E. Paul Torrance, eds. 1971. *Educating the Ablest*. Itasca, IL: F. E. Peacock Publishers.

Morley, Christopher. 1955. *Parnassus on Wheels*. Philadelphia: J. P. Lippincott/Harper & Row. (Originally published 1917. Garden City, NY: Doubleday, Page.)

Two

The Shaping of Curriculum

Pragmatic awareness and empirical evidence are not enough foundation from which to develop pedagogically valid programs. The educational establishment requires extensive research and testing as well. This selective overview, based on personal experience and synthesis, summarizes current learning theory and curriculum design, suggesting what factors influence a school system's blueprint for gifted programs. But, according to educational expert Jerome Bruner, action does not always have to wait for research findings.

THE PROCESS OF EDUCATION

Bruner wrote *The Process of Education* in 1960 in response to issues raised by Russia's launch of Sputnik. No better blueprint for curriculum development is available than this brief book, now in its 23rd printing. Bruner's precepts were lost in curriculum trends of the 1970s and 1980s but are renascent and more significant today. The following paraphrasing reinforces the belief that Bruner's theories are essential background for gifted programs.

At the time of his writing, Bruner saw a shift in focus on the learning process: from a production of general understanding to an emphasis on the acquisition of specific skills. He states that this dualism always existed—between what Benjamin Franklin called the useful and the ornamental. Included in the useful category are both skills and understanding. As a result of schooling, each child should achieve optimal skill development and become a better student. But the overall objective of education, he believes, is the cultivation of excellence through understanding.

Bruner develops four themes: structure, readiness, intuition, and interest. He says of **structure** that students need an understanding of the fundamental structure of the subject being taught. Understanding the fundamentals makes a subject more comprehensible, helps with human memory, is more transferable and imitable, narrowing the gap between elementary and advanced knowledge. A specific transfer of learning equals skill; a nonspecific transfer equals understanding. A sharp distinction exists between **rote drill** and **understanding**. "Drill need not be rote and, alas, emphasis on understanding may lead to a certain glibness" (Bruner 1960, 29). Experience with gifted children shows him to be right on both points.

Of **readiness**, Bruner states that one can teach the foundation of any subject to anybody at any particular age in some form. The early teaching of science, math, social studies, and literature emphasizes an intuitive grasp and use of these ideas. Curriculum is a return to and a building upon earlier learning The three factors in readiness are:

1. The process of intellectual development: "The task of teaching a subject to a child at any particular age is one of representing the structure of that subject in terms of the child's way of viewing things" (Bruner 1960, 33).

2. The act of learning, which consists of three almost simultaneous processes: the acquisition of new information; transformation; and evaluation.

3. A spiral curriculum: "A curriculum ought to be built around great issues, principles and values a society deems worthy of the continual concern of its members" (Bruner 1960, 52). Literature is such an example.

Of **intuition** Bruner writes, "Intuitive thinking, the shrewd guess, the fertile hypothesis, the courageous leap, all play a part in learning. The good intuiter may have been born with something special—but his effectiveness rests upon a solid knowledge of the subject, a familiarity that gives him something to work with" (Bruner 1960, 56).

Of **interest** Bruner states, "Somewhere between apathy and wild excitement there is an optimum level of aroused attention" (Bruner 1960, 72). Here Bruner discusses appropriate motivators for long- and short-term attention, points well taken in a library media context. Long-term reliance on high motivators, like television, film, and computers often leads to passivity on the part of the learner. The teacher should increase the inherent interest of the subject being taught while setting the stage for a sense of discovery appropriate for the child. With what Bruner calls teaching devices, the teacher should provide vicarious learning experiences—directly, as with books and media, and virtually—as with computer simulations.

While apparatus and materials help students grasp the underlying structure of a subject, it is teachers, not devices, who are the principal agents of instruction. For Bruner, as with other authorities mentioned herein, the teacher has the role of communicator, model, teaching-learning intermediary, and personal symbol of the learning process. In *The Culture of Education*, written 36 years later, Bruner attributes a greater influence upon children's learning to the environments in which they live: The culture has become the child's teacher (Bruner 1996). Others have seen evidence of this idea. Kindergarten teachers visiting day care centers in China observed that the artistic creations of three-year-olds there were sophisticated beyond any developmental expectations of American children before age seven or eight. They hypothesized that the Chinese culture was the teacher.

Any curriculum plan needs to consider five points about learning:

1. Learning is developmental.

2. Learning is achieved through motivation and purposeful activity.

3. Learning should result in the ability to retain and transfer what has been learned.

4. Learning requires the acquisition of basic skills.

5. The ability to communicate is both an outgrowth and an aspect of learning.

WHAT IS INTELLIGENCE?

In the 1970s the U.S. Office of Education defined giftedness as existing in six general areas: general intellectual ability, specific academic aptitude, creative or productive thinking, leadership, visual and performing arts, and psychomotor. As a practical matter, implementation narrowed to apply to cognitive giftedness only, with a subsequent change of definition.

Frames of Mind, written by Howard Gardner in 1983, propounded the idea of multiple intelligences—separate but not exclusive—that combine to create a mosaic of thinking patterns and learning styles which differ in each child. This pluralistic view of mind must be considered in the identification of gifted children and should exist in all educational programming (Gardner 1983). The following list presents the seven areas of intellectual competence (Winn 1990), similar to the Office of Education definition, along with their personifications. Fifth graders added the names in parentheses.

1. Verbal/Linguistic: sensitivity to the meaning and order of words: poet or translator (Shel Silverstein, Astrid Lindgren)

2. Logical/Mathematical: the ability to handle chains of reasoning and to recognize patterns and order; mathematician, scientist [Einstein] (George Washington Carver)

3. Musical: sensitivity to pitch, melody, rhythm and tone; composer, [Beethoven] (The Beatles)

4. Bodily/Kinesthetic: the ability to use the body skillfully and handle objects adroitly; athlete, dancer, surgeon. [Martha Grahame] (Michael Jordan)

5. Visual/Spatial: the ability to perceive the world accurately and to re-create or transform aspects of that world; sculptor, architect, surveyor [Picasso] (Peter L, age 3)

6. Interpersonal: the ability to understand people and relationships; politician, salesman, religious leader [Gandhi] (Martin Luther King Jr., Thomas Jefferson)

7. Intrapersonal: access to one's emotional life as a means of understanding oneself and others; therapist, social worker [Freud] (school counselor)

Gardner later added an eighth component, the Naturalist/Environmental personified by someone like Rachel Carson.

In the mid-1990s two more intelligences were added by other educational theorists. *Emotional Intelligence* by Daniel Goleman elaborates on the interpersonal and intrapersonal intelligences (Goleman 1995). *The Moral Intelligence of Children* by Robert Coles adds another component to the operating definition of the word *intelligence* (Coles 1996).

GIFTED PROGRAMS: THEORIES AND PROPONENTS

It is an axiom that gifted programs be qualitatively differentiated in three ways: 1) curriculum, 2) grouping arrangements, and 3) teaching strategies. In this area of differentiation, there are theorists and practitioners whose names are synonymous with gifted education. They extensively and pervasively write and lecture on this topic. No state-of-the-art study is complete unless it reflects their influence. These authorities are cited so often in training sessions and in-service handouts that much of what they have contributed seems like public domain. This makes it difficult to attribute specific resources when presenting an overview. Among the names are Sandra Kaplan, James Gallagher, and Joseph Renzulli in the area of research and program design; and Jean Piaget, Benjamin Bloom, J. P. Guilford, Frank Williams, and Calvin Taylor in the area of models of intellect and thinking. *Providing Programs for the Gifted and Talented: A Handbook* by Sandra Kaplan is still a practical and definitive source of instruction and inspiration (Kaplan 1974). Kaplan uses narrative to explain, worksheets to apply, and models to illustrate program prototypes and curricular designs. The frameworks suggested can be tailored for use in a library media-centered, literature-based curriculum. Other names shaping educational practices that also apply to giftedness are Edward De Bono, Seymour Papert, and Madeline Hunter.

Differentiating by Curriculum and Instruction

Instructional Models:
Information Processing and Active Teaching

Several models of instruction differentiate for the gifted. The differentiating feature can be a subject, theme, speed, content level, or best of all, combinations of these elements. It is the artistry of teaching to weave techniques, styles, theories, objectives, and materials into lessons that work. For Gilbert Highet, author of *The Art of Teaching,* the two facets of a teacher's methods are preparation and communication (Highet 1950). Preparation in a dynamic dimension, as opposed to fixed, consists of structure and planning. Communication can be by lecture, by the Socratic method (tutorial and questioning), or by prescribed lesson (classroom study, discussion, and explanation). Highet says, "It is not necessary to glorify a good subject, but you must explain it, fill in a suitable background" (Highet 1950, 73). The teacher should help the student more completely integrate the facts of a lesson to make it more vivid. Highet believes that teachers must "give the students plenty of work and plenty to think about." In addition, he states, "The best way to avoid wasting the powers of a good pupil is to plan his work for him." Highet explains how valuable the "wide reading and accumulated experience of a mature" person can be to a (brilliant) pupil who is "still groping around . . . among untried experiments and unread books. . . . Send him out into the world with a frame of reference suggested by you and tricks of craftsmanship which he could only get from you" (Highet 1950, 45-47).

Highet's language is that of the scholar/poet, but the language of Jean Piaget, the Swiss developmental psychologist, speaks similarly of the way a teacher's presentation can affect the child's developing intelligence: by being a model, by providing occasions and opportunities, and by prescribing tasks for the child at an appropriately high level.

More in the language of the educator, David Ausubel propounds the Advance Organizer. This model is classified among the information processing models summarized in Bruce Joyce's and Marsha Weil's monumental survey-of-the-field book *Models of Teaching* (Joyce and Weil 1980). In Ausubel's model, the teacher develops an organizing concept that is related to the material to be presented but is at a higher level of abstraction, generality, and complexity. With these higher attributes, the Organizer differs from the typical introductory overview or orientation. After the data is presented, the learner relates the material to the organizing concept. The Advance Organizer is effective in presenting information for maximum retention and cognition and serves well the important function of helping gifted children acquire background knowledge. The model is more structured than is usually recommended in literature on gifted education. It is useful for a library media-centered program because teachers and students are processing skill and content information simultaneously.

In 1984, the Maryland State Department of Education invited 24 prominent educators to write and present papers on state-of-the-art issues in gifted education. In response, Florence Pritchard presented a model for the development of curriculum and instruction for academically gifted learners. The model was based on a Theory of Meaningful Learning derived from a synthesis of information processing and transformation studies, primarily by Bruner and Ausabel (Pritchard 1984). Pritchard's list of salient characteristics and capacities of the curriculum developer and implementer of the model, also describes essential attributes of a gifted program.

> This person will have wide general knowledge about knowledge, will be thoroughly grounded in the knowledge base of one or more domains, will be a seeker of knowledge for its own sake, and will be characterized by high cognitive complexity and by exceptional communication skills. Together these capacities will make it possible for this individual to select content appropriate for the gifted and to organize that content so that it will be taught holistically to them (Pritchard 1984).

The Meaningful Learning model is compatible with an important trend in education today—an emphasis on active teaching, strong on content, in effective schools. Widely consulted educators like Madeline Hunter and Thomas Good incorporate factors in learning theory, such as motivation, reinforcement, retention, and transfer, with essential steps in lesson development and presentation. Their sequence for the active teaching of a lesson includes: anticipatory set; instructional objectives; content coverage; modeling; checking for understanding; and guided, then independent practice. What they advocate reiterates Bruner's theories about the structure of a discipline, the spiral curriculum, and his proposition that "when you teach well, it always seems as if 75% of the students are above the median" (Bruner 1960, 9).

Knowledge As Design

Knowledge As Design is an instructional philosophy devised by David Perkins to "make difficult concepts clearer and to integrate critical and creative thinking skills with subject matter instruction." It is suited to any age and ability level, with content both abstract and concrete (Perkins 1986). It addresses what Perkins sees as the problem of teaching "disconnected" knowledge. He suggests four questions to be asked for any learning endeavor: What is its purpose? What is its structure? What examples are there? What are arguments pro and con about the design?

Perkins's snowflake model, connecting creative thinking with subject matter, has as its components an aesthetic orientation to arrange and simplify the complex, the objectivity and motivation needed for an understanding of the nature of a problem, the mobility to move outside the usual to change and reformulate assumptions, and the ability to work at the edge.

The Subject of Thinking

If differentiated instruction has been an axiom of gifted education, then higher-level thinking has been the main postulate. The following four theorems cover the existing ideas about the role of thinking that are relevant to gifted education:

1. Thinking is developmental.

2. Thinking is geometrical.

3. Thinking is teachable.

4. Thinking is everywhere.

Numbers one and two reflect current practices, number three is still today's frontier, and number four is the raison d'être of this book. Numbers three and four will be recurring themes of the CUES interaction.

Thinking Is Developmental

Jean Piaget, the Swiss psychologist, was a pioneer proponent of the idea that intellectual development occurs in an orderly sequence of stages apace with chronological age and physiological growth. Abstract concepts must be concretely introduced with labeling at a later stage so that *doing* leads to *understanding*. He named the stages: Sensorimotor (ages 0 to 2 years); Preoperational (ages 2 to 7-8); Concrete Operations (ages 7-8 to 11-12); Formal Operations (ages 11-12 and up). Four basic conceptualizing levels—seriation, classification, conservation, and number—accompany these stages. These processes occur in a dynamic state called equilibration, which fluctuates between assimilation to and accommodation to the environment. Piaget later reworked his ideas, coming to view thinking as spiral rather than linear in direction. Although Piaget's terminology may require a glossary for the novice, his influence is widely accepted. The educational implications of ages-and-stages theories are clear. Curriculum design and implementation must be based on developmental truths.

Thinking Is Geometrical

Many theories of cognition are illustrated by geometric shapes. For example, Bloom's Taxonomy: Cognitive Domain is depicted as a pyramid or a flower consisting of concentric segments of a circle; Guilford's Structure of the Intellect is a cube; Renzulli's Enrichment Triad involves triangles and intersecting circles; and William's Three-Dimensional Model for Implementing Cognitive-Affective Behavior in the Classroom is a rectangular box. With the exception of Bruner's spiral and Perkins's recent snowflake, these approaches espouse a hierarchic arrangement of thinking as the basis of program planning. The main drawback of this "geometry of thinking" is that the configurations assign the acquisition of knowledge to a lower level. This sometimes leads to a misinterpretation and denigration of the role of knowledge in a thinking school, to the detriment of maximum student learning.

Thinking Is Teachable

An important message about the "teachability of thinking" is that thinking, as much as other subjects and skills, requires 1) systematic teaching, 2) by direct instruction, 3) integrated with other subject areas, 4) infused throughout the curriculum, and 5) developmentally through all grades. This indicates a change in emphasis for some gifted programs that depend more on materials that isolate the skill of thinking from regular curriculum and everyday life.

Challenging children to think critically and creatively has become big business over the past decade. All over the country, commercial after-school, Saturday, or summer camp offerings for gifted children have surfaced, many of which are computer-oriented. Universities offer affiliated programs for gifted children. Typically, programs revolve around an in-depth or accelerated exploration of a subject, topic, or theme. Junior Great Books and Odyssey of the Mind are established programs where carefully thought-out materials are packaged nationally for leaders trained to implement the programs locally. Two other long-available programs may be less known. The Philosophy for Children materials are a "systematic and complete curriculum which fosters the improvement of reasoning skills through the discussion of philosophical topics" (IACP n.d.). The Cognitive Research Trust (CoRT) materials, developed by Edward De Bono, are used in many cultures and ideologies (De Bono n.d.). *On Teaching Thinking* is The Association for Supervision and Curriculum Development's extensive catalog of its materials, including videotapes, audiocassettes, training programs, books, and journals.

Thinking Is Everywhere

Children's thinking occurs everywhere, especially when nurtured by the environment. Adults who work closely with children in any learning environment are intuitively aware of the exciting moment when something clicks—when some new connection is made. A questing and questioning, a sense of wonder, spontaneous problem solving, and an experiment with language are all expressed: the very stuff of which gifted programs are made! Fortunate is the adult who can be part of these special times. Many teachers have witnessed such moments, first, perhaps, as parents marveling at their infants and preschoolers. The best opportunities to infuse thinking into lifetime learning occur in early childhood and the early school years. Primary grades often highlight creative thinking, while problem solving and lateral thinking are the thrusts in the upper elementary grades.

Differentiating by Grouping

Teachers of early childhood and primary grades can identify their abler students from observable language and computational skills plus other anecdotal evidence. This is the basis for informal groupings for classroom instruction. For formal identification, the tools usually are standardized tests of cognitive abilities, a Raven-type test for pattern perception, and personal attributes checklists. The cognitive component has been the most relied-upon criterion and, today, the most debated.

The Revolving Door

Joseph Renzulli and his associates proposed a model for identifying gifted students, called the Revolving Door Identification Model. This uses a more precise characterization of giftedness as an interaction between above average ability, task commitment, and creative/productive performance—a switch in emphasis from giftedness to gifted behavior (Renzulli 1977). This change allows for a flexible and spontaneous participation of more students in selected enrichment activities in environments cooperatively structured by the classroom teacher, resource teachers, and others. These environments can be exclusive and full time, as in magnet schools; more inclusive and part-time, as in pull-out programs within a regular school; or rotating, as within a grade or classroom. Many school systems are adopting policies mandating that gifted students spend a significant portion of the school day in the company of their peers.

Cooperative Learning

Children helping children is the crux of the cooperative learning movement. Group Investigations procedures and Student Team Learning techniques developed at Johns Hopkins are available: Team Games Tournaments (TGT), Student-Teams-Achievement-Division (STAD), and Jigsaw. Many classroom teachers use other simple techniques such as Think-Pair-Share and peer tutoring, for one-on-one learning. Groupings for leadership training are also available. These structured grouping arrangements offer opportunities for all children to perform differently than they may in the traditional whole classroom environment.

Differentiating by Strategy

The Practice of Thinking

American public television introduced audiences to *De Bono's Thinking*, an import from England, consisting of 10 videotaped lessons in front of the same mixed-age audience, hosted with wit and wisdom by Edward De Bono. With little electronic gimmickry other than a magic marker and an overhead projector, De Bono scribbles words and drawings on the screen. Refreshing acronyms, an original vocabulary, and a progression of exercises that relate thinking to problems in everyday living are all part of his performance. He demonstrates how a teacher may draw upon a personal stockpile of visual and verbal materials, including anecdotes, stories, and pictures, to illustrate and explore themes and problems relating to everyday school life (De Bono 1980).

The *De Bono's Thinking* television series, the *CoRT Thinking Program*, and De Bono's many books and speaking appearances make De Bono one of the liveliest advocates for thinking's place in everyday living. De Bono's *Teach Your Child How to Think* may be used as a read-along and read-aloud book. De Bono suggests nine as the lower age limit for his program, unless the child has advanced ability or an adult presents the ideas at the child's level. The ages 9 to

11 (before the right answer becomes all important) are the peak of thinking enjoyment. Lateral (creative) Thinking is an alternative to Vertical (logical, analytic) Thinking. Encourage proactive thinking as opposed to reactive thinking. Teach, De Bono advises, simply with good examples and practice, motivating topics, discipline, and good humor (De Bono 1992, n.d.).

The Art of Questioning

The accepted notion that a higher order question will elicit a higher order response is a corollary of the geometry of thinking. The use of questions, therefore, is a main teaching strategy.

The 5 Ws are sacred for journalists. Who? What? Where? When? Why? These questions are depicted as the logo for the W5 Children's Reference Series published by Henry Holt and are similar to the *4-MAT*'s of Why? What? How? and What If? Series (McCarthy 1980). Lee Bennett Hopkins' *Questions*, an I-Can-Read anthology, adds "how" poems to its poetic 5 W questions. Aileen Fisher gives voice to children's deeper questions about science and feelings in *I Wonder How, I Wonder Why*. Also for younger children are the Owl/Firefly Series of *Question and Answer Storybooks* that ask "Why Is the Soap So Slippery? Do Doors Open by Magic? Why Do the Stars Twinkle?"

More pedagogical ways of classifying questions are to see them as

1. Questions relating to a taxonomy like Bloom's—knowledge, comprehension, application, analysis, and evaluation.

2. Questions from the four categories developed by Gallagher and Aschner—cognitive memory (rote and recall), convergent (analysis and integration), divergent (calling for creative imaginative answers), evaluative (calling for judgment, values, and choices).

3. Questions reflecting properties of thinking—perceptive, associative, conceptual, problem-solving, critical, creative, and adventurous.

The first three classifications are traditional and function apart from the learner and the learning concept.

4. Thesis questions, which have to be framed within the context of the learner's knowledge and the information sources the learner will use to respond. For thesis questions, the answers may be stated intrinsically in the lesson, or may be implied, depending extrinsically on the learner's integration of the lesson with prior knowledge.

5. "Think Trix" is the name invented by Tom Payne for a set of cued thinking process symbols to categorize questions and responses. The symbols represent a questioning sequence that ascends a scale from simple Recall to those that ask about Similarities, Differences, and Causation; that go from Question to Example, from Example to Question; and that ask for Evaluation. The question types are represented in a pictogram form and mounted

on a poster that serves as a giant graphic reminder to students about how to construct questions to elicit higher level responses. When the "Think Trix" framework is distributed to each child as a cue card or bookmark, even first graders get into the habit of analyzing the kinds of questions the teacher asks, and so learn to shape their own questions accordingly.

QUESTIONS about a first-grade year of library media classes, asked, answered, and categorized by Mrs. Frederick's Thinksters:

R   What books did we read together this year?

≡   How are all of the Frog and Toad books alike?

≠   What's different between easy-to-enjoy and easy-to-read books?

↻   Which do you think comes first, the story or the pictures? Of the books we read, which ones were I-Can-Reads?

R   Who wrote some of the animal stories we read?

♡→Ex   What kinds of books did we share?

⚖   Which was your favorite? Which was best?

What if there were no books?

What if there were no shelves?

Regardless of classification system, the use of questions appropriate to the learner and the task is a prime differentiating strategy for instilling higher order thinking into lessons for gifted children.

Styles and Tricks of Teaching About Thinking

1. Thinking Clubs and Thinking Hats

The Thinking Club is an outgrowth of De Bono's *CoRT Thinking Program*. It exists for the practice and enjoyment of thinking as a skill and a hobby, with the formality and discipline that a regular time and place provide. De Bono suggests meeting once every two weeks for one to one and a half hours. With motivation the only qualification, a group of six people, including an organizer/host, timekeeper, and notetaker (keeper of the log book), meet for six sessions. A skill focus is presented first, then a problem focus, then an application focus on current issues, personal problems, books and articles, and television. These meetings present an issue for which group members list the plus, the minus, and interesting/informative points; PMI is the acronym for this exercise. Then an APC analysis of Alternatives, Possibilities, and Choices is followed by CAF (Consider All Factors) and OPVs (Other Points of View).

The Six Thinking Hats are another thinking device (De Bono 1992). The White Hat is worn to deal with matters of facts, figures, and information. The Red Hat is for emotions, feelings, hunches, and intuitions of the moment. The Black Hat signifies caution, truth, and judgment, and the Yellow Hat focuses on advantages and benefits—both are logical, requiring reasons. The Green Hat represents a freedom of thinking, creativity, and new ideas. The Blue Hat is metacognitive, providing an overview, a summary, control, and direction. Full spectrum thinking requires changing or combining hats as needed to solve daily school "problems."

2. Designs for Knowledge

Curriculum writers and teachers use Venn diagrams. These patterns help analyze and interrelate the parts of a learning task by fitting them into a schema for information gathering and reporting. The conventional Graphic Organizers (GO) are intersecting, adjoining, or appending circles, rectangles, and ovals. But any way of patterning a child's search for information becomes a GO for David Perkins, who assigns design analysis for "seatwork" or homework. The designs for analysis may be concrete, like a tool, or abstract, like a poem or the Dewey decimal system. Designs may be unintentional, improveable, or invented.

Designing or finding literary GOs is especially appropriate for library media instruction. An "I HAVE A QUESTION ABOUT THE MEDIA CENTER" form left on a circulation desk encourages children to ask questions that the library media specialist never knew needed to be answered, a reminder that effective teaching requires clear communication.

3. PMI, Metacognition, and Think Trix—A Triptych for Thinking

A trio of techniques builds thinking into all learning tasks. They are PMI for problem analysis, Think Trix for questioning and answering, and Metacognition for awareness of what we know, how we know it, and what more we need to know. The three processes are formulae, tools for task analysis, which become staples of classroom protocol. De Bono's PMI analyzes an issue for decision making and problem solving by having group members list the pluses, minuses, and interesting or informative points. For example, in an analysis of the issue that "Schools should abolish homework," a P statement is shown as a smiley face, an M as a frowning face, and an I as a lightbulb icon. Metacognition is a current educational term. The teacher helps students articulate the three steps in metacognition: planning, monitoring, and evaluating the learning process. Children are able to answer these questions: What did you already know? Where did you start on this research? How did you go about it? What did you learn? What do you know now?

The three techniques combine into a thinking triptych distributed to students on a bookmark or enlarged to poster size for display in classrooms and library media center.

PMI

is a way of analyzing an issue for decision making and problem solving.

P
PLUS (positive)

M
MINUS (negative)

I
INTERESTING & INFORMATIVE

Metacognition

means knowing **WHAT** you know **&** **HOW** you know it.

IT HAS 3 PARTS:

Planning
+
Monitoring
+
Evaluating
=
Metacognition

THINKTRIX
for Thinksters
THINKING
Through Question/Response Cues

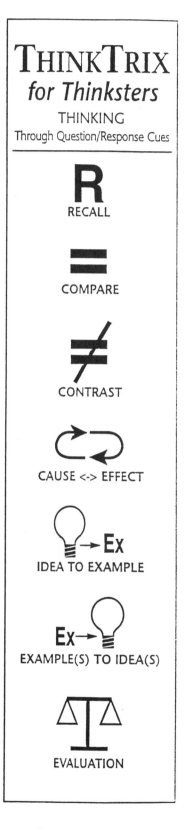

R RECALL

= COMPARE

≠ CONTRAST

CAUSE <-> EFFECT

IDEA TO EXAMPLE

EXAMPLE(S) TO IDEA(S)

EVALUATION

Fig. 2.1. Triptych for Thinking.

Library Media Program: One Size Fits All

A library media program that is attuned to what stimulates and supports thinking is the embodiment of the thinking school. It is content, technique, and framework. The program's mission is to direct children to the road not taken and set the stage for meaningful discovery. More knowledge than any school jurisdiction calls curriculum dwells in the library media center. It is where "the strangest and best thing about teaching is that a seed dropped into what looks like rocky ground will often stick and take root gradually, and spring up years later, sometimes in a bizarre form and oddly hybridized, but still carrying the principle of life" (Highet 1950).

REFERENCES

Bruner, Jerome S. 1996. *The Culture of Education.* Cambridge, MA: Harvard University Press.

———. 1960. *The Process of Education.* New York: Vintage/Random House.

Coles, Robert. 1996. *The Moral Intelligence of Children.* New York: Random House.

De Bono, Edward. n.d. *CoRT Thinking Program.* Elmsford, NY: Pergamon Press.

———. 1980. *De Bono's Thinking.* Television Series. London: BBC, Lionheart.

———. 1992. *Teach Your Child How to Think.* New York: Viking.

Gardner, Howard. 1983. *Frames of Mind: The Theories of Multiple Intelligences.* New York: Basic Books.

Goleman, Daniel. 1995. *Emotional Intelligence.* New York: Bantam.

Highet, Gilbert. 1950. *The Art of Teaching.* New York: Vintage/Random House.

Institute for the Advancement of Philosophy for Children. n.d. *Philosophy for Children.* Upper Montclair, N.J.: IACP, Montclair State College.

Joyce, Bruce, and Marsha Weil. 1980. *Models of Teaching,* 2d ed. Englewood Cliffs, NJ: Prentice Hall.

Kaplan, Sandra. 1974. *Providing Programs for the Gifted and Talented: A Handbook.* Ventura, CA: Office of the Superintendent of Schools.

Lyman, Frank. 1986. *THINK TRIX.* Maryland: Howard County Public Schools Staff Development Center, 1986.

McCarthy, Bernice. 1980. *The FourMat System: Teaching to Learning Styles with Right-Left Mode Techniques.* Why? What? How? and What If? Series. Arlington Heights, IL: Excel, 1980.

Perkins, David. 1986. *Knowledge As Design.* Hillsdale, NJ: Lawrence Erlbaum Associates.

Pritchard, Florence Fay. 1984. *A Meaningful Learning Model for the Design and Development of Curriculum and Instruction for Academically Gifted Students.* Baltimore, MD: Maryland State Department of Education.

Renzulli, Joseph. 1977. *The Enrichment Triad: A Guide for Developing Defensive Programs for the Gifted and Talented.* Mansfield Center, CT: Creative Learning Press.

BIBLIOGRAPHY

I Wonder How, I Wonder Why? Aileen Fisher. New York: Abelard-Schuman, 1962.

"New Views of Human Intelligence" from the *New York Times* Magazine/Part 2 *The Good Health Magazine.* Marie Winn. April 29, 1990, p. 16.

Questions: Poems. Lee Bennett Hopkins, sel. New York: HarperCollins, 1992.

Taxonomy of Educational Objectives: The Classification of Educational Goals. Benjamin Bloom, ed. New York: McKay, 1956.

W5 Children's Reference Series. New York: Henry Holt Reference Books, 1996.

Three

CUES! A Model for a Library Media Centered Curriculum with Books

A second-grade class was in the library media center for its weekly literature and skills visit. The library media specialist had chosen *Space Case* by Edward Marshall, a story to delight all. Matias commented that the book was science fiction. Philip asked what science fiction was, triggering a discussion about science fact and science fiction. Karen spoke up emphatically, "I'll tell you what science fiction is: Matias said the world was going to end today and it didn't, so that's science fiction." Steven and Michael both chimed in, "Well the paper said that Jupiter . . .", and the children began a debate about the validity of the so-called Jupiter effect and the prediction of cosmic catastrophe that very day that had not come true. Clearly they had been disturbed by newspaper and other media coverage. The library media specialist then showed the class that day's newspaper article, as well as the current issue of *Odyssey* magazine. The lesson ended. As the class left, Brian confided to the media specialist, "That story could keep on going with another adventure." It did, as author Edward Marshall wrote more than one sequel about his beguiling character. Kids, themselves, have written about *Space Case*'s returns.

Later that day, as the same class passed through the library media center which doubled as the main corridor of the school, Matias was overheard saying, "It didn't happen, but according to Einstein . . ." Karen, Matias, Michael, and Steven were part of a group of eight second graders identified as gifted who met weekly with the library media specialist in what they called the "Comfortable Polite Research Group" or CPRG.

Thirteen identified gifted students who had completed either fifth or sixth grade were enrolled in an area summer institute for the cognitively gifted, taught by the same media specialist. The class met for three hours each weekday for a month. The course title was *Story-Ways, Story-Wise: A Literature Sampler*. The literary form being discussed was science fiction. Since one of the course objectives was a Penny Theater production of a picture storybook, a teaching strategy was the use of high quality picture books to introduce a literary genre. *E.T.—The Extraterrestrial* was the movie of that summer, ripe for comparison with *Space Case*—the "text" for the day. Although the students were at an age where they were cynical and disparaging about anything beneath their level, Mike, the biggest, oldest, most trying, brightest, and certainly the most well informed, murmured, "That's just like E.T." "How?"

asked the teacher; the discussion began. They noted the similar way the artists and writers depicted the alien in both screenplay and trade book, even though the formats required different conceptualizations; the world into which each character was thrust and the contact through a child or children; and the indifference of the adults as a theme in both. The class was critical of the ending of *E.T.* when fantasy superseded science-fiction as all of the children's bikes rose into the air. Surprisingly, the picture book rated well against the multimillion dollar screenplay as both creative effort and effective story.

The material of instruction in both of these cases was the same—an easy trade book that became the springboard for a learning experience beyond its apparent application. For the younger class, it had been an adventure in curiosity, science, and sequeling. For the older group, it was a spontaneous expedition into higher level thinking and beyond, when it was transformed into a clever Penny Theater production.

These anecdotes illustrate the basic premise of this book: that any school with a library media collection, a library media specialist (in collaboration with classroom and subject teachers), and bright children has the essential ingredients for a qualitatively differentiated program for the gifted. The planned interaction between these variables—children, teacher, and materials—becomes a curriculum model compatible with programming recommendations for educating gifted children. As a bonus in this time of limited resources, an appealing presentation of subject matter, in addition to higher expectations, usually brings out the intellectual responsiveness in every child (the so-called Pygmalion in the Classroom effect).

PROGRAM INGREDIENTS

CUES, which stands for Choose, Use, Enjoy, Share, is a program designed to take into account the intellectual and behavioral characteristics of elementary age, able children. The CUES approach is open-ended, cross-disciplined, and multigraded. It addresses the cognitive, affective, and psychomotor needs and abilities of students. It combines the teaching and use of library and information skills with language skills in a way that invites higher order thinking and student involvement in the creation of a product. Taking a cue from De Bono, it acknowledges the importance of the learner's perceptions, emotions, feelings, and values, using shorthand devices, rituals, and activities in its instructional bag of tricks. Such a course may be defined as a "loose-leaf curriculum with books" based on children's literature and emanating from the library media center. Loose-leaf implies a flexibility and never-ending supply of materials that allows substitutions for out-of-print and unavailable titles and the addition of newly published books. The goals of this curriculum are to:

1. impart knowledge in interesting and challenging ways.

2. stimulate the student's pursuit of information, required or random.

3. sharpen the student's skills in the collection, organization, retrieval, and presentation of data.

4. encourage the interpretation and transformation of information via a productive or creative activity.

5. capitalize on curiosity and whet the student's appetite for further knowledge.

All of this takes place in the context of "Worthwhile Activities" described in a paper by James Rath. "A large part of every child's day should include participation in activities that

1. allow him to make choices,

2. provide opportunities for sharing,

3. involve him in the consideration of profound ideas, and

4. include the application of rules, standards, and disciplines that can be made meaningful to him" (Rath 1969).

To these may be added a few ingredients supplied by the teacher who:

- arranges feasible groups for bringing children together,

- establishes realistic expectations for behavior and preparation,

- selects and collects assorted materials and ideas of personal appeal, and

- relates these themes and topics to curriculum areas.

We need look no further than a library media-centered program to meet these specifications.

Library Media Programs—Officially

The school library media center as the heart of a school is a vision grounded in steps for achievement. Like all elements of school curricula, school library media *programs* evolve from content area *standards*, a national ideal of goals and objectives. These are translated into a state mandate, which is applied to a local school system's *curriculum* for implementation by teachers in ways that best meet the needs of that system and each of its individual schools.

Information Power is the guidelines statement of the American Association of School Librarians (AASL) and the Association of Educational Communications and Technology (AECT), published in 1988 and currently under revision. With this as a foundation, the State of Maryland, for example, has published its own *Standards for School Library Media Programs in Maryland*. Within the state, each county school system has developed its own standards for school library media programs. Highlights of the AASL/AECT blueprint include:

"The mission of the library media program is to ensure that students and staff are effective users of information."

"The challenge is to provide equal access to knowledge for diverse populations in a changing world for young people at all ages and stages."

"The school library media program that is fully integrated into the school's curriculum is central to the learning process" (AASL/AECT 1988).

The school library media program should be a partnership "dependent upon the collaborative efforts of all responsible for student learning." Within this framework, the library media specialist fulfills three roles: that of teacher, information specialist, and instructional consultant (AASL/AECT 1988).

The ideas described in the CUES constellation are based on existing standards. Most official documents do not relate the school library media program to such specific populations as the gifted, but they express high expectations of the school library media program's role in quality learning for all children.

The Library Media Center Habit

Official mission and vision statements for a school library media program are important but are not likely to be achieved unless an entire school population acquires the media center habit implicit in the words Choose, Use, Enjoy, Share! The use of the school library media center should be second nature for students and teachers. Children should have the habit of visiting the library media center by second grade, or it will likely be lost to them in upper grades. Their introduction to the library media center as they begin their school years is crucial to starting the practice. Teachers need to know how preschoolers have experienced books, first at home, at day care or nursery school, and at the public library. For many children, the introduction to books is electronic, via television series such as *Sesame Street*, *Reading Rainbow*, and *Wishbone*. Preschoolers should visit the school library as part of "kindergarten roundup." The media center should be included in kindergartners' first field trip around their new school. Is the center an enticing place sure to make young eyes grow wide with anticipation? Will it be a place where readers and nonreaders alike can browse freely and have questions answered? Will it be an authority—a database for verifying information? Does the library media center encourage the teacher advocacy and cooperation necessary for success? Without teachers no program can evolve. With them, a strong partnership is formed that affects student use of the center.

Children have three reasons for using the library media center on their own: to satisfy curiosity, as they browse for quick answers to their own questions; to fulfill curriculum requirements, as they research and report on content area subjects; and to read, as an activity of personal choice. The library media center habit becomes essential to curriculum. For the gifted student, it becomes a course of study enriched and extended above and beyond the usual. For the teacher, it sets in motion a system for differentiating classroom instruction. For the library media specialist, it establishes conversations with children about books as a teaching strategy. Once the classroom teacher has identified subjects to be differentiated for abler students, the library media specialist can devise ways to introduce materials that will

1. provide initial knowledge about a subject or add to prior knowledge.

2. use thinking and library and information skills.

3. lead students to a clearer understanding of the process of collecting information.

4. allow the exploration necessary to continue the spiral of learning to a higher level.

5. enable students to translate their learning into a product for passing on information.

A similar statement of procedure is now part of the mandate for gifted education in many school systems.

The library media specialist sets the stage, after which the teacher carries on the instruction in the classroom. This is happening more often as teachers become aware of the value of this process. Ideally, the library media specialist may work on a continuing schedule with instruction weekly, daily, or even after school. Depending on the time allocation and the size and age of the group, the library media specialist assumes the role of tutor, mentor, or teacher. The goals and objectives for the group expand or contract according to time and content variables. Once the teacher establishes regular visits to the library media center for students to browse, research, or read for pleasure, the stage is set for students to

- Choose materials appropriate to the designated use,

- Use the materials effectively and efficiently,

- Enjoy the process, and

- Share the product with others.

The hope is that for some of the children, an additional dimension—learning—will be experienced. From CUES to CLUES—every teacher's dream.

THE CUES INTERACTION

The CUES interaction is a continuum in which the child's own motivation and the teacher's assignment combine to create the desire or need to use the library media center. The CUES involvement of the library media specialist makes the child's efforts easier, more informed, and more successful. This reinforces the library media center habit, which becomes identified with the successful application of skills for curriculum implementation. The interaction is shown in Fig. 3.1.

Library Media Specialist Will Help Student

Student Uses Library Media Center for	CHOOSE (materials)	USE (skills)	ENJOY (affect)	SHARE Media Center (product and format)
CURIOSITY	Browse through new and misc.	Locate answers, whet appetite	Personal satisfaction	Quiz, exhibit, display
	Explore	Think and question	Challenge, interest, and fun	
CURRICULUM	Content area, formats	Reference and research	Academic success	Depends on assigned specifications, reports
	Print, nonprint			
CHOICE	Quality, popular items, appealing items	Evaluation, judgment, summarizing skills	Broadening horizons	Reviews, recommendations, bibliographies
			Appreciation, developing taste	

GOAL = a new dimension
CUES transforms to CLUES as **learning** takes place

Fig. 3.1. CUES Interaction.

CUES is an example of the Revolving Door Identification Model in action. It adapts to most recommended instructional settings and delivery systems. In practice, it works with groups as enrichment and acceleration, in a pullout program or inside a magnet school or regular classroom. It serves an individual child or a small group of children from kindergarten or first grade (when their potential is first recognized) through grades three to six (when they participate in more formal programs). Other children or groups only participate for a specified unit that is set up within the course objectives for a particular subject and grade. Some groups meet weekly throughout the semester or year; sometimes the same material is covered more thoroughly on a daily basis during the summer.

Book publishers and booksellers, alike, used to promote their wares primarily to libraries. Now in shopping malls, the super bookstores such as Borders and Barnes and Noble are wonderlands of children's books, videos, software, CD-ROMs, and literary happenings. Enterprises, like Discovery Zone, Imagination Place, and public television's affiliate, The Store of Knowledge also offer stimulating materials and activities. Book publishers have assumed the role of educational experts, using consultants, seminars, and curriculum guides to advise teachers directly about teaching with trade books. Dell's Laurel-Leaf and Yearling books provide teacher's guides for using selected books to teach gifted children. Puffin Books offers The Circle of Literacy thematic program for K-12 teachers. Richard C. Owens Publishers' has Teacher Notes for "Creating a classroom of writers using their Meet the Author Collection." The new periodical, *Online-Offline*, presents itself well in its introductory issues as "the first resource guide linking themes with Web sites and other media." The American Association of School Librarians publishes *Book Links* and presents "Curriculum Connections on the 'Net" through its ICONnect (AASL 1996). Bantam Doubleday Dell invites teachers to browse their new website, "Teacher's Resource Center." Houghton Mifflin's website features "Education Place," "Classroom Connections," and an interactive "Author Spotlight." Great resources all, but the idea is not new.

The school library media center through its staff and materials has always offered teachers and children these same services and invitations to learn and enjoy in a place available to all—their school. Motivating children to savor learning through reading would not be necessary if all of our children were like Pulcifer who resisted efforts by his parents, his teachers, and his therapist to divert him from reading to watching television. Today's diversions are less television and more video and computer, but Florence Heide's satirical depiction of a society where reading and love of books are out of step with accepted practice is an idea too imminent to be amusing. Pulcifer, with all of his motivation, would benefit from a creative introduction to the world of children's literature.

LITERATURE IS CURRICULUM

It seemed for a while that booktalks and story hours were en route to extinction . . . at least in schools. Despite the lamentations of library media specialists, there was no room for nostalgia about pleasant pastimes such as these as we megatrended our way from the industrial into the information society. In this educational milieu of accountability, assessment, and achievement, there was no room for unmeasurables such as enrichment, enjoyment, excitement, and exploration. These goals did not justify the expensive existence of school library media centers. Only when the affective instructional goals that these words represent are absorbed into achievable performance objectives can teachers and library media specialists afford to spend time on them. Yet, few who have grown intellectually from these pursuits can deny that they are valuable educational tools. When a definition and library information skills objectives are specified, **literature** becomes **curriculum**.

Literature is defined in the third edition of *Webster's Unabridged Dictionary* as "writings in prose or verse having excellence of form or expression and expressing ideas of permanent or universal interest; the body of written works produced in a particular language, country, or age." Literature clearly is content to be considered with children in the context of its traditional home—the library media center.

In the book, *Beyond Fact: Nonfiction for Children and Young People*, compiler Jo Carr laments the omission of nonfiction from consideration as literature. Her collection of beautifully written essays on the literature of fact makes an excellent case for nonfiction literature as curriculum, and even begins with a reiteration of Bruner's spiral, Piaget's idea that children's learning should be an outgrowth of their interests, and Bloom's taxonomy (Carr 1982).

Other curricula based on literature were locally written and implemented. Beginning in 1981, Montgomery County, Maryland, has continuously developed a reading language arts curriculum based on literary discourse for narration, exposition, and writing, with special units for the gifted and talented (MCPS 1982). The California State Department of Education published two curriculum guides for the teaching of literature to gifted children in grades one to three and four through six (CSDE 1978 and 1978a). Nancy Polette has written several books with the same purpose (Polette 1982). These efforts were bridges from research findings and educational theory to the practical job of reaching children. Little acknowledgment of literature as mainstream curriculum was seen until the publication by the College of William and Mary of units for grades three to six. The literary thread is the idea of change and its expression through the example and practice of persuasive writing (College of William and Mary 1994). This is a curriculum for the language arts that is literature based, researched, field tested, and ready made for classroom implementation. The reception has been enthusiastic. Because the units were developed by the College of William and Mary under federal grants, reproduction and dissemination of the materials is permitted, an important budgetary consideration.

Literature As Textbook Instruction

The acceptance of literature as curriculum opened an inexhaustible and inexpensive resource to teachers and library media specialists. Even as textbook series became more like literary anthologies, trade books became textbooks for teaching library and information thinking and learning skills. They also became the textbooks for reading and language instruction. Whole Language as the current canon for teaching reading may be in question, but literary materials have always been the domain of a library media center.

The ability to read well is prominent on every list of characteristics of gifted children. While it is less true now, it is also characteristic that gifted children **like** to read. Many such children come to school already reading, sometimes self-taught. Others, fluent in language and rich in knowledge, are not reading when they start kindergarten and first grade, but quickly and easily learn to read. Reading instruction is necessary for both kinds of children, but the focus should be less on *learning to read* than *reading to learn*—by reading more widely, creatively, and critically.

Literature Skills

An element in reading instruction is story grammar, which provides a schema for comprehension. By analyzing the parts of story structure—character, plot, setting, theme, conflict and resolution, and climax—even beginning readers are given the tools to arrange stories into meaningful patterns. When children have the vocabulary, they hear stories in a different way, eagerly anticipating, predicting, and evaluating the outcomes. *Story grammar*, together with *knowledge of literary forms* or *genres*, composes the *literature* element in a CUES curriculum. These literary skills, combined with thinking and library information skills, are the variables with which the teacher or library media specialist (even if a novice at gifted programming) can operate.

Library and Information Skills

In isolation, the four library media skills, now called library and information problem-solving skills, may seem utilitarian and routine. They include

1. the location and arrangement of information within the library media center and within specific resources,

2. the use of basic sources of information and the various formats in which information is organized,

3. the retrieval of information from these sources, and

4. the communication of information to others.

Teaching such skills sometimes seems to be on the lowest level of Bloom's pyramid—hence, unworthy of inclusion in a curriculum for the gifted. Yet, without these skills, the most gifted of students cannot function effectively as an explorer, interpreter, and producer of information. A library media-centered program that combines these basic skills with thinking skills through a vehicle of excellent materials creates an effervescence that puts zing into a gifted program.

Location and Arrangements

Beginning with the location and arrangement of information, this first set of skills addresses the arrangement of materials common to all library media centers, as well as the location of these materials within a particular library media center. Since this information is ordered in several ways—alphabetical, numerical, chronological, and random—the interactions must be explained and explored. Access to information within the library media center depends on familiarity with an alphabetical system—a holdings catalog, whether card or computer—and a numerical system—like the Dewey decimal classification. The interrelationships between these and other classification and indexing tools can be concretely demonstrated to children at any age with tasks that generate the challenge of a puzzle and the thrill of the hunt.

Sources of Information

The second set of skills involves the basic sources of information. Many materials are included in the modern collection with its own distinctive vocabulary. Print materials consisting of easy books, fiction, nonfiction, reference, and periodicals, as well as nonprint formats, consisting of audiovisual and video equipment, and computer hardware and software are elements of the entity, the library media center.

Information Collection and Retrieval

The third set of skills involves the collection and retrieval of data from appropriate sources. Planners and teachers often operate on the assumption that gifted children must use the most difficult sources in order to differentiate the assignment properly. This results in teachers and students ignoring or deprecating some of the most appealing, interesting, and valuable resources. This issue of visual literacy and the proper use of graphic materials is important for curriculum design. As children increasingly rely upon computers for researching, reporting, and writing, keyboarding emerges as another desirable media skill.

Communication of Information

The set of skills that should most emphasize differentiating for giftedness is the fourth: The communication of information to others via a product that can either be a restatement or new information. It is in this last area of production—be it an electronically sophisticated multimedia presentation, a computer program, a piece of writing, or a modeled or otherwise graphic summation—that gifted children can amaze with products that surpass all expectations. It is because gifted children are so adept at this transformation and manipulation of information that teachers must provide a rich background and database whereupon the creative process can feed.

All children need practice with library and information processing skills, as well as familiarity with the specialized vocabulary of the information world. Such practice is adapted to the abilities of gifted students by the introduction of the skills at an earlier age, by the speed with which the students comprehend the skills, and by the level at which they apply the skills. The most exciting differentiation is in the form of the products by which able children demonstrate the application, transformation, and synthesis of the information collected and retrieved through their mastery of library media skills.

Librarian's Enthusiasm Contagious . . .

This headline from a local newspaper captures the essence of the library media specialist who has three indirect roles:

1. to supply resources for the classroom that stimulate thinking

2. to evaluate and select materials for the school

3. to collaborate in the planning of instruction to promote thinking

It is not enough when the library media center is merely a place for teaching skills. The satisfying occasions are during the library media specialist's direct interactions with students—those times when literature is shared, a new idea is discussed, or some questions are raised or answered. The challenge is selecting the language of the lesson and the learning task, each having the potential for expanding the students' thinking capabilities. Literary activities, concrete and sensory, impart language that builds vocabulary, one of the best indicators of giftedness. The library media collection respects multicultural values and speaks to multiple intelligences. The library media specialist in a teaching role has at his or her fingertips an atmosphere to make learning experiences vivid, memorable, and relevant.

The library media environment, created from facility and people, has a dynamic of its own, one that welcomes a thinking and questioning attitude. Sometimes, on their own, children ask questions. At other times, the setting invites inquiry about artifacts and shelf teasers. The moments for imparting knowledge are there to be seized. The library media center environment contains the summary of humankind's recorded thinking. Today, in its electronic incarnation it is called The Hub, from which there is global access. De Bono often suggests wandering around a stimulating setting, like a library or an exhibit, as a technique for generating and intertwining ideas. Beyond the classroom, the library media center offers a risk-free environment, the perfect place to explore the road less traveled, to stir intellectual juices before roll call, and to set the stage for meaningful discovery. These are the reasons children remember their library media specialist's name, as did Beverly Cleary, or count them among the teachers who influenced their intellectual development.

Literature is not an abstract science to which exact definition can be applied. It is an art the success of which depends on personal persuasiveness, on the author's skill to give as ours to receive (Sir Arthur Quiller-Couch 1913).

REFERENCES

AASL. 1996. *Curriculum Connection on the 'Net*. Chicago: American Library Association.

AASL/AECT. 1988. *Information Power: Guidelines for School Library Media Programs*. Chicago: American Library Association.

California State Department of Education. 1978. *Literature: Curriculum Guide for Teaching Gifted Children Literature in Grades One to Three*. Sacramento: CSDE.

———. 1978a. *Literature: Teaching Gifted Children Literature in Grades Four Through Six*. Sacramento, CA: CDSE.

Carr, Jo, comp. 1982. *Beyond Fact: Nonfiction for Children and Young People*. Chicago: American Library Association.

College of William and Mary. 1994. *Changing Ideas, Changing Perspectives: What Is the Role of Persuasion and Argument in Our Lives?* Williamsburg, VA: College of William and Mary, Center for Gifted Education.

Montgomery County Public Schools. 1981. *Instructional Guide for Exposition*. Rockville, MD: MCPS.

———. 1981a. *Instructional Guide for Narration*. Rockville, MD: MCPS.

———. 1982. *Program of Studies: English Language Arts*. Rockville, MD: MCPS.

———. 1983. *Instructional Guide in Reading Language Arts*. Rockville, MD: MCPS.

Polette, Nancy. 1982. *Three R's for the Gifted: Reading, Writing, and Research*. Littleton, CO: Libraries Unlimited.

Rath, James. 1969. "Worthwhile Activities." Mimeographed.

BIBLIOGRAPHY

The Problem with Pulcifer. Florence Parry Heide. New York: J. B. Lippincott, 1982.

Space Case. Edward Marshall. New York: Dial Press, 1980.

Four

Portraits and Landscapes for Learning

One day when Sam was in grade three, he told his mother about a poem his librarian read to the class. "It was called *Sam at the Library*," he marveled, "and it tells how the kid and the librarian talked about books, and he never chose what she recommended." When Sam was in grade four, he told his mother, "The teacher says that *I* have intelligence but *she* has knowledge." Then he added, "You know Samuel Johnson (he wrote a dictionary) said there are two kinds of knowledge: we know about a subject ourselves or we know where we can find information about it. That's our library." He smiled. "There sure are a lot of smart Sams." When Sam was in grade five, he stated sadly, "I told my teacher I had scientifically solved the question of which came first, the chicken or the egg. But I don't think my teacher likes me to ask questions."

CUES suggests that a powerful interaction occurs between the dynamic triad of collection, teachers, and learners. The catalyst is the elementary school library media center, a learning environment far greater than the sum total of these parts. The ideal center is like a pleasant teacher and taskmaster, urging students to continue in the study of human experience. It is a database ripe for accessing and networking. It is a commitment to the past as prologue, and to the present and future of the world's cultures, civilizations, and societies. It is an important setting for students' school time quest for knowledge. It is a comfortable, yet challenging, landscape that encourages the exploration of ideas in a kaleidoscopic fashion: the systematic acquisition of information, with the translation of the learning into a new creative dimension. The school library collection is the CUES first ingredient.

THE COLLECTION: LANDSCAPE FOR LEARNING

Grahame Green said, "The influence of early books is profound. So much of the future lies on the shelves." In his 1978 Nobel acceptance speech in Oslo, Isaac Bashevis Singer said, "I am not ashamed to admit that I belong to those who fantasize that literature is capable of bringing new horizons and new perspectives." Ralph Waldo Emerson once wrote, "When I read a good book—I wish that life were three thousand years long." These are but three of the testimonials from great writers to the fundamental importance of books and library collections. In their autobiographies, children's authors such as Beverly Cleary, Cynthia Rylant, and Lee Bennett Hopkins write of the titles and libraries that nurtured their creativity. A multiskills bibliographic research project for fourth or fifth graders would have them list, try to locate, then comment on the influential titles cited by these and other authors.

Most elementary school library media collections are based on a core list of books and materials recommended by a recognized selection authority, such as Brodart's perennial, *The Elementary School Library Collection: A Guide to Books and Other Media,* familiarly known as ESLC, now in its twentieth edition and also available on CD-ROM. This guide allows for priorities and choices of books and other media in the nonfiction, easy, and fiction areas (The Elementary School Library Collection 1996). In addition to the core list, each collection should contain materials that support the subject goals of a school system's curriculum. The collection should also reflect the ranges of abilities, performance expectations, and flux of an individual school's students. A library media collection extends curriculum implementation beyond sole dependence on textbooks, as it adds a tempting array of materials for learning. This basic collection, updated through constant addition and weeding, becomes the first element of differentiation in the CUES program for the gifted—not because the collection consists of gifted materials, but rather, because the materials selected lend themselves for use with gifted children.

To be compatible with learning characteristics of gifted children, the materials should

1. provide information in a challenging, open-ended, and imaginative style;

2. encourage questioning;

3. foster divergent thinking;

4. stimulate creative expression;

5. deal with content in an interdisciplinary context;

6. appeal to students' natural curiosity; and

7. represent the versatility, attractiveness, and quality of tradebook publications.

Books About Books for Bibliophiles

Since a collection, to which the best of new materials is regularly added, is a foundation of the CUES program, some further mention about the art of choosing books for children may be helpful. The professional shelves of libraries abound with books about books. From books by Huck and Arbuthnot, the standbys devoured in children's literature courses, to the classic *Bequest of Wings*, these run the gamut from pedagogical to practical to inspirational. In tying the use of children's books to the teaching of gifted children, some resources offer a skills approach and others offer a literary one.

A plethora of clever workbooks guaranteed to challenge and sharpen thinking abilities through books is available. The problem for the teacher or school library media specialist becomes one of choice, given much overlap and funding limitations. These workbooks concentrate on the development of specific thinking skills via worksheets based on Bloom, Guilford, or Renzulli teaching models. Goodyear, D.O.K., Good Apple, Incentive, Creative Teaching, Book Lures, and Midwest are among the publishers of excellent resources of this kind. Such materials are useful adjuncts to any program, serving as warm-up exercises, challenges, sponges, and fillers. They are a popular way to connect books and gifted children.

With the success of *The Read-Aloud Handbook* in 1982 came an explosion of books advocating the use of tradebooks for children starting at infancy. Most of these books about books are delightful reading. While they may be a busman's holiday for librarians, these books help the less-practiced teacher weave literary knowledge and allusion into classroom assignments. Taken as a whole, these books provide guidance for teachers who wish to incorporate literature into all of their lessons. One of the newest, *Children's Books and Their Creators* (Silvey 1995), is "an invitation to the feast of twentieth-century children's literature." It describes authors and illustrators, history, genres, and children's literature issues of the last 50 years. With encyclopedic arrangement, extensive bibliographies, and a special feature, "Voices of the Creators," this anthology is an outstanding resource. However, the book has a telling shortcoming: an article on books in classrooms is included, but none for a school library media collection.

THE ART OF TEACHING

Portraits of Teachers

In Chapter 7 of her autobiography, Helen Keller writes about Annie Sullivan, her teacher:

> Everything Miss Sullivan taught me she illustrated by a beautiful story or poem. Whenever anything delighted or interested me she talked it over with me just as if she were a little girl herself. . . . We read and studied out of doors. . . . All my early lessons have

in them the breath of the woods. . . . Seated in the gracious shade of a wild tulip tree, I learned to think that everything has a lesson and a suggestion. Indeed, everything that could hum, or buzz, or sing, or bloom, had a part in my education.

Our favorite walk was to Keller's Landing. . . . There we spent many happy hours and played at learning geography. I built dams of pebbles, made islands and lakes and dug river-beds, all for fun, and never dreamed that I was learning a lesson. . . .

Thus I learned from life itself. At the beginning I was only a little mass of possibilities. It was my teacher's genius, her quick sympathy, her loving tact which made the first years of my education so beautiful. It was because she seized the right moment to impart knowledge that made it so pleasant and acceptable to me (Keller 1961).

Gilbert Highet was a scholar, lecturer, professor of the classics, and lover of language and languages. Unable to find a book about the art of teaching, he wrote his own. In the preface, he describes teaching as an art, not a science, because it is "not like inducing a chemical reaction, it is more like painting a picture or making a piece of music, or on a lower level, like planting a garden or writing a friendly letter. You must throw your heart into it, you must realize that it cannot be done by formulas, or you will spoil your work and your pupils and yourself" (Highet 1950). He writes of the influence of great teachers of the past and those in everyday life, who are often unaware that they are teaching.

Of the reciprocal process of teaching and learning, Highet states: "There are thousands of different things to learn and teach. . . . all these subjects and many more are taught in schools. But a great deal of teaching is done outside school. . . . Wherever there are beginners and experts, old and young, there is some kind of learning going on and some sort of teaching. We are all pupils and we are all teachers" (Highet 1950).

Teachers at Home: Megaskills

Parents and families as a child's first teachers in everyday life is the message of *MegaSkills*. A landmark book, written by Dorothy Rich, funded in part by a "genius grant" from the MacArthur Foundation, *MegaSkills* describes how to help children succeed in school and beyond (Rich 1988). In workshops all around the country, Rich turns insights from child development into "home-learning recipes" for children of all ages beginning with infancy. Rich helps parents and teachers alike become attuned to "teachable moments" that occur each day. The 10 MegaSkills, "the inner engines of learning" are:

1. *confidence* — feeling able to do it
2. *motivation* — wanting to do it
3. *effort* — willing to work hard
4. *responsibility* — doing what's right
5. *initiative* — moving into action
6. *perseverance* — completing what is started
7. *caring* — showing concern for others
8. *teamwork* — working with others toward a common goal
9. *common sense* — using good judgment
10. *problem solving* — putting knowledge and ability into action (Rich 1988)

This early framework for reading, writing, and math comes from common-sense experiences with everyday activities. These experiences must tie into school work, be serious yet fun, and have a teachable focus:

For ages 4-6—getting ready for school by counting, sorting, and reading

For ages 7-9—getting organized, building study skills, and developing solid work habits

For ages 10-12—gaining understandings—about themselves, friends, and families; and greater self-reliance and career awareness (Rich 1988)

Among other important suggestions in *MegaSkills* is that teaching should take place in manageable bites, within time limits, and provide positive feedback to the child. In addition to their own home teaching roles, parents of gifted and talented children have formed vocal advocacy groups to advise and monitor school systems on curriculum and its implementation.

Teachers in Schools: Who Should Teach the Gifted?

What should the teacher of gifted children be expected to do? Should they have special characteristics, training, or a particular personality? Can the required attributes or skills be learned? Highet's list of qualities exhibited by a good teacher includes:

- The teacher must know the subject and continue to learn it. Teaching and learning are inseparable.

- The teacher must like his or her subject.

- The teacher must like his pupils and enjoy their company in groups. This includes knowing the pupils—developmentally as a group—and, in a tutorial situation, each pupil's name.

- The teacher must have a sense of humor, needed to keep the students alive and attentive.

With great insight, Highet further describes the good teacher as a person of exceptionally wide and lively intellectual interests. The job involves understanding a large and important area of the world's activity and achievement and making it viable for the young. The teacher's professional function is to make a bridge between school and the world, youth and maturity. Essential abilities for a teacher are creative memory, kindness, and the willpower to overcome the resistance of the young to learning (i.e., resistance to work, to authority, and to concentration) (Highet 1950).

An official documentation of the qualities of a competent teacher of the gifted may be found in the Pennsylvania state model guidelines. Desirable qualities include:

- understanding academic giftedness;

- awareness of the needs of the gifted arising from their developmental tasks;

- ability to teach at the level of inspiration;

- flexibility in classroom management;

- superior intellectual ability;

- broad cultural interests and enthusiasm;

- skill in stimulating students' independent study and creativity;

- sound mental health and the capacity to deal with groups of varied personalities, opinions, and interests;

- competency in classroom teaching at the gifted child's threshold of learning;

- skill in coordinating programs and services for the gifted with other aspects of the school program (Clendening and Davies 1980).

These portraits of teaching translate well into past, current, and emerging definitions of a library media specialist's job. They justify a past role most dear to library media specialists—the guide to an exploration of ideas through books. The other traditional role—that of evaluator, selector, and custodian of a library media collection—sometimes limits how teachers and administrators view library media specialists vis-à-vis gifted programs. Since library media specialists know materials and their use, others may only see them as resource organizers. Too often overlooked is the library media specialist as a teacher beyond skills—as mentor, model, tutor, and motivator. For example, in one large suburban school system, an annual summary questionnaire about programs for the gifted distributed to each school requests the job titles of those who teach gifted students. The form lists classroom teacher, reading teacher, and so forth, but not library media specialist. Library media specialist involvement has to be inserted on the line marked "Other." Another school system, which prides itself on innovative programs for the gifted, no longer employs library media specialists in all of its schools.

PORTRAITS OF LEARNERS

The third component of a library media-centered program for the gifted is the students themselves. As many descriptions of gifted children exist as do articles, research studies, or school system reports on the subject. Some of these descriptions are statistical, some narrative, some anecdotal, and some autobiographical, but all have some commonalities. Assembled, these observations and trait lists paint a realistic picture of gifted students.

Checklists

Most in-service training for teachers who work with gifted children begins with a discussion of the characteristics of giftedness. In conjunction with cognitive and perceptual abilities tests, lists such as the Renzulli-Hartman Behavioral Scale are used for identification, curriculum design, and implementation. The scale evaluates children on learning, motivation, creativity, and leadership characteristics. Among the traits most often appearing on all of the lists are:

- curiosity and imagination;
- ability to observe, organize, and abstract;
- ability to learn and memorize quickly;
- wide interests and background;
- longer attention span;
- capability for independent work;
- many interests and hobbies;
- early and rapid reading and computing (Renzulli and Hartman n.d.).

Programs should be designed to capitalize on the potential inherent in these characteristics.

Some of the most practical advice on gifted children for teachers and administrators was given by Sandra Kaplan in an October 1978 workshop. Four basic realities that have to be considered when designing effective programs are 1) giftedness is progressive and developmental; 2) gifted students are variable; 3) gifted students are not homogeneous; and 4) giftedness is only one aspect of the total development of a child (Kaplan 1978).

While gifted children will learn faster, they still need to be taught in basic areas. They need varying levels of activities and kinds of experiences. The most important of Kaplan's four points is to "start with the child's world," something parents, teachers, and planners often forget. Each teacher's experiences abound with case studies.

At noon, Anthony, a kindergartner, asked the school secretary to call his home so he could find out whether he was to go there or to computer class after school. She agreed to call and asked for his number. "I don't know it," he said. She got the number and talked to Anthony's mother, who informed her that computer class had ended several weeks before.

Stewart, an extremely advanced first grader, came to school knowing a great deal about maps and their use. He was always talking about geography books and atlases. Stewart's specialty was longitude and latitude. Yet, he was unfamiliar with the term *intersection,* either by itself or in relation to his home, suburb, or school.

Alan, a kindergartner, could read better and with more expression than most fifth graders, yet he could not fold a piece of paper lengthwise. When tested for placement at the beginning of first grade, he topped the fourth grade basal assessments. The comprehension question involved the story, "Mrs. Dunn's Lovely Farm," which was about how Mrs. Dunn's life in New York differed from her life in Dublin, Ireland. After pondering for a minute, Alan asked, "Could you give me a clue?" The reading teacher referred to a previously shared story about feeling different in a strange place. He then commented, "In New York, not all the people had Irish names."

A teacher in a summer institute for the gifted made exciting plans for her second graders to study animals through puppetry, fairy tales, plays, field trips and more. After the first week, she confided to her colleagues during a progress reporting session that she had not reckoned with the fact that the children lacked note-taking speed and skills. She had to backtrack and teach the skills before she could continue with her agenda, which was probably a lost cause. Her realization was not unique. Many enthusiastic teachers plan beyond the level of their students—not cognitively, but developmentally.

A library media specialist in the same summer program took her class of third and fourth graders to the National Geographic Society's Explorers Hall in Washington, D.C. The children sat spellbound as the docent turned a giant 30-foot globe upside down, free from its axis, and moved continents and countries. The class amazed the adults with their perceptions and knowledge about geography, a subject never studied as a discrete entity. As the demonstration showed the strategic importance of the future ownership of Antarctica, one child whose family had fled Cuba asked soberly, "Does this mean there will be wars?" The group moved on to the other purpose of their field trip—a visit to the magnificent three-room exhibit of toy soldiers from Malcolm Forbes' great collection. A window looking into Robert Louis Stevenson's "The Land of Counterpane" opened into a stunning series of dioramas presenting the pageantry and horror of famous battles and the history of tin soldiers. The children raced through the displays with little interest, much to the media specialist's chagrin. Then she saw them begin to look at the displays again, this time with great concentration. She was pleased until a chaperone explained that someone had discovered that pennies and gum paper had been thrown into one of the display cases. The children were trying to see if the coins were retrievable, and if any other cases contained money.

Two second graders were solving a complex longitude/latitude problem in the computer lab where they worked daily before school. One anxiously asked the other whether it was time to go to class. His coworker pointed to the wall clock: "Not yet. We don't have to leave until the big hand gets to the 1."

Start with the child's world—advice not to be ignored.

"Quiz Kids"

Ruth Duskin Feldman, a veteran "quiz kid," wrote a revealing book, *Whatever Happened to the Quiz Kids?*, on growing up gifted. She wrote from her point of view as one of the "quiz kids" who were part of American life for 13 years beginning in the 1940s. They were radio stars, exemplars, entertainers, war bond sellers, and product endorsers. A few excerpts from her book corroborate characteristics of gifted children found on formal lists of traits.

- Those with the most staying power had a fund of general information plus a general interest or talent.

- Helpful assets were a diversified portfolio, a test-taking knack, a venturesome spirit, ability to think on one's feet.

- [Each was] early readers either on their own or with the help of parents and siblings.

- [Each had] flypaper memories for things of so-what value.

- [Each had a] headful of trivia (Feldman 1982).

Feldman also mentions the lasting effects of motivation, inspiration, and self-discipline. She recounts how some of the "quiz kids" got their knowledge in those pre-high-tech days. In the 1990s, their comments read like a book publisher's blurb for *A First Dictionary of Cultural Literacy.*

Gerard: "Well, you go to the library and ask for a lot of books, and you take them home to read them all and go back for more."

Joan: consumed two newspapers daily and took an encyclopedia to bed. "When it came time for schooling, her parents gave her a globe, an atlas, a dictionary, and a blackboard and let her go her own way."

Jack:	read three newspapers a day, along with *World Book*, Mark Twain, Rudyard Kipling, and Robert Louis Stevenson.
Dick:	was given an atlas at seven. This book started him on geography and the world.
Naomi:	lived in the library. Her department was literature: *Little Women*, Shakespeare, *Tom Sawyer*, the Bible, and mythology.
Harvey:	specialty was animals in general, dinosaurs in particular. These interests had been kindled by a museum trip (Feldman 1982).

"Most of the former Quiz Kids say that they were merely bright, poised, curious youngsters who were given extra doses of cultural exposure." Several of those Feldman surveyed commented on the lack of depth of the education they felt their own kids received, an effect of watching too much television. What would they say today about the hours children spend on-screen and online? "Quiz kid" Richard Williams found "no incompatibility between independent thinking and the glorification of the remembered fact. In those days, everybody knew more facts than anybody does now" (Feldman 1982).

Whatever Happened to the Quiz Kids? provides valuable insights into the characteristics of these gifted children—how they learned, and the roles played by adults in their unfolding. Of the latter, Feldman states that in each case, there was "at least one parent who shared enthusiasm with the child, who watched for areas of interest, who gave encouragement and praise for achievement, who made a game of searching out answers to questions, who went out of his way to supply the tools of learning." She also claims that a "memorable teacher is worth more than the best curriculum guide." About the children themselves, she generalizes that the "typical Quiz Kid had a near photographic memory, an adult vocabulary, a vivid imagination, lots of hobbies and collections, and an insatiable curiosity about just about everything" (Feldman 1982).

In a 1996 book, Ellen Winner explores further the myths and realities of *Gifted Children*. The children themselves, the materials that nurture their intellectual growth, and the adults who coach them—the same three components interact to create a library media program for the gifted.

The whole art of teaching is only the art of awakening the natural curiosity of young minds. . . . (Anatole France n.d.)

REFERENCES

Clendening, Corinne P., and Ruth Ann Davies. 1980. *Creating Programs for the Gifted: A Guide for Teachers, Librarians and Students*. New York: R. R. Bowker Company. Citing from *The Guide for Organizing and Operating Programs for the Mentally Gifted*. Harrisburg, PA: Pennsylvania Department of Education, 1979.

The Elementary School Library Collection: A Guide to Books and Other Media. 1996. 20th ed. Williamsport, PA: Brodart.

Feldman, Ruth Duskin. 1982. *Whatever Happened to the Quiz Kids? Perils and Profits of Growing Up Gifted.* Chicago: Chicago Review Press.

Highet, Gilbert. 1950. *The Art of Teaching.* New York: Vintage/Random House.

Kaplan, Sandra. 1978. Workshop for Montgomery County Maryland Public Schools library media specialists, 24 October. Rockville, MD.

Keller, Helen. 1961. *The Story of My Life.* New York: Dell.

Renzulli, Joseph, and Robert Hartman, et al. n.d. *Renzulli-Hartman Behavioral Scale.* Mansfield Center, CT: Creative Learning Press.

Rich, Dorothy. 1988. *MegaSkills.* Boston: Houghton Mifflin.

Silvey, Anita, ed. 1995. *Children's Books and Their Creators.* Boston: Houghton Mifflin.

Winner, Ellen. 1996. *Gifted Children: Myths and Realities.* New York: Basic Books.

BIBLIOGRAPHY

A sampling of books to help relate literary trade books to teaching concepts.

A to Zoo: Subject Access to Children's Picture Books. 2nd ed. Carolyn W. Lima. New York: R. R. Bowker, 1986.

The Arbuthnot Anthology of Children's Literature. 4th ed. May Hill Arbuthnot. New York: Lothrop, Lee & Shepard, 1976.

Bequest of Wings: A Family's Pleasure with Books. Annis Duff. New York: Viking, 1944.

Beyond Fact: Nonfiction for Children and Young People. Jo Carr, comp. Chicago: American Library Association, 1982.

Books for Children to Read Alone: A Guide for Parents and Librarians. George Wilson and Joyce Moss. New York: R. R. Bowker, 1988.

Books for the Gifted Child. Barbara Baskin and Karen H. Harris. New York: R. R. Bowker, 1980.

Children and Books. May Hill Arbuthnot and Zena Sutherland. Glenview, IL: Scott, Foresman, 1972.

Children's Literature in the Elementary School. 3d rev. ed. Charlotte S. Huck. New York: Holt, Rinehart & Winston, 1979.

Children's Literature in the Elementary School. 5th ed. Charlotte S. Huck, et al. New York: Harcourt Brace Jovanovich, 1993.

Choosing Books for Children: A Commonsense Guide. Betsy Hearne. New York: Delacorte Press, 1981.

Choosing the Right Book for the Right Child at the Right Time. Joanne Oppenheimer, et al. New York: Ballentine Books, 1986.

Creative Connections: Literature and the Reading Program Grades 1-3. Mary Lou Olsen. Littleton, CO: Libraries Unlimited, 1987.

E Is for Everybody: A Manual for Bringing Fine Picture Books into the Hands and Hearts of Children. Nancy Polette. Metuchen, NJ: Scarecrow Press, 1976.

The Elementary School Library Collection: A Guide to Books and Other Media. 20th ed. Lois Winkler. Williamsport, PA: Brodart, 1996.

Exploring Books with Gifted Children. Nancy Polette and Marjorie Hamlin. Littleton, CO: Libraries Unlimited, 1990.

Eyeopeners! How to Choose and Use Children's Books About Real People, Places and Things. Beverly Kobrin. New York: Viking Penguin 1988.

For Reading Out Loud! A Guide to Sharing Books with Children. Margaret Mary Kimmel and Elizabeth Segal. New York: Delacorte Press, 1983.

The New Read-Aloud Handbook. Jim Trelease. New York: Viking, 1989.

The New York Times Parents' Guide to the Best Books for Children. Eden Ross Lipson. New York: Times Books, 1988.

Picture Books for Gifted Programs. Nancy Polette. Metuchen, NJ: Scarecrow Press, 1981.

The Read-Aloud Handbook. Jim Trelease. New York: Penguin Books, 1982.

Through the Eyes of a Child: An Introduction to Children's Literature. Donna E. Norton. New York: Macmillan, 1991.

Five

Grouping a Set:
Setting a Group

Mrs. Olinski's four sixth graders seemed an unlikely combination to beat out seventh and eighth graders from around the state. She herself cannot give the conventional rationales for choosing these four participants to represent Epiphany Middle School in the Academic Bowl competition, yet together they go on to win the Newbury Award for their creator, E. L. Konigsburg. *The View from Saturday* tells how the Souls evolve as a winning team. Starting as four offbeat young people whose lives strangely intertwine, they meet weekly at a Mad Hatter's Tea Party, where they emotionally and intellectually coalesce. A fortuitous grouping indeed, for Epiphany and for story lovers! Alistair Griddle, Archibald Frisbee, and Meg Wallace are other bright loners from the pages of children's fiction. How does a teacher group a bunch of one-of-a-kind kids?

GROUPING A SET

CUES As Revolving Door

A cornerstone of a gifted program is the way participants are grouped. Such groupings may be revolving doors, magnets, pull-outs, charter schools, special schools, and affirmative action. A retrospective look at how gifted programs patterned themselves over the years in a typical suburban school reveals three informal groupings—all adaptations of the Revolving Door Identification Model (RDIM) (Renzulli 1981).

1. Longitudinal model—the library media specialist follows a group over a period of several years, from kindergarten through the sixth grade.

2. Independent study model—a group of top children are assigned to work with the library media specialist in the general area of library media research and production.

3. Latitudinal model—a teacher or grade team and the library media specialist start a group for a specific duration and instructional focus that provides for kids to move in and out of the program.

Some case studies illustrate how these differing groups operate whether the giftedness is in the nurturing or identified stage. *Terman's Kids* (Shurkin 1992) continues the longitudinal study of how the gifted grow up. Shurkin follows up on Lewis Terman's groundbreaking work begun in 1921. Terman's "Termites" provided 1,500 life histories, the longest ranging life study. Literary loners in children's stories do a lot of independent study. Konigsberg's fictional Souls fit this model until they were grouped latitudinally to become a winning academic team. Together since preschool, the intrepid First Grade Class members from Miriam Cohen's books learn to read, worry about school, go on field trips, then continue on to second grade adventures together.

A Longitudinal Group Model: The CPRG, a Five-Year Case Study

The kindergarten class of 1979–80 included five children who stood out because they were advanced in reading, thinking, and computing. Three others showed gifted characteristics but were not reading. In first grade, the original five became the first-grade component of a grade one/two combination class. Their teacher asked the library media specialist for a one-hour-per-week enrichment group. The other three students, now in first grade, also joined the group. Of the eight, five were accelerated in math, two were musically amazing, two more were artistically exceptional, two had broad general knowledge, and one was worldly wise. The gamut of multiple intelligences was represented here. In addition to the library media center enrichment and subject area acceleration, the children met weekly for one semester with a mentor from the university, herself a gifted student. By the second grade, most of the little group were together for accelerated math. Another university student worked with them in the fall semester to create an original Readers Theatre production that included an improvisational instrumental ensemble. They met each week with the library media specialist for an hour and a half and by this time were calling each other not by name, but by initials. They named their library media group CPRG, the Comfortable Polite Research Group. Their thinking soon outdistanced the speed of their pencils, so sessions were recorded on audio or videotape. A summary of their accomplishments (see fig. 5.1) was written at the end of the year to provide feedback to the classroom teacher and parents and to combat the "What-did-you-do-today-in-class?—Nothing!" communication syndrome. Many library media and thinking skills were slipped into the group's lexicon.

Second Grade Summary:
What the CPRG Did This School Year.

We have explored the library, language, and literature in the following ways:

- We were introduced to *Scienceland* and other interesting periodicals.

- We have read several series of nonfiction books on many topics.

- We planned and performed in a music and mime play of *Hansel and Gretel.*

- We chose a name and a logo for our group.

- We learned about researching and reporting starting with the book *How Can I Find Out?*

- We worked with thinking and poetic patterns.

- We acted out *Hildilid's Night,* an alliterative story, then drew the verbs.

- We asked questions, questions, questions—for curiosity and browsing.

- We read *The Silver Pony,* a book-length story without words. We described, summarized, predicted, changed, took notes, and titled the chapters.

- We used reference books like *Nelson's Encyclopedia, Compton's Precyclopedia,* and the *Wonderful World of Knowledge.*

- We learned how to do biographical research and reporting.

- We read about Helen Keller's life in her own words, then studied the topic Women in American History.

- We solved mysteries.

- We worked with interviews, questionnaires, and surveys.

- We discussed and compared science books, science fiction, and mythology.

- We read *Pickle Creature,* then wrote and illustrated sequels.

Our goal was CURIOSITY, CURRICULUM, and SERENDIPITY learning through the library. We used all of the components of language—reading, listening, writing, and speaking, as well as of creative thinking and problem solving.

Fig. 5.1. Second Grade Summary: What the CPRG Did This School Year.

By the third grade, several children had moved out of town and several new children had replaced them. All of the gifted students were in one class under the tutelage of an imaginative and strong teacher experienced in teaching the gifted. Ten of her 22 students qualified as gifted. The whole class performed on a high academic level in science projects, media productions, and creative writing—all direct outgrowths of the curriculum. In the second half of the year, six children were selected to attend a one-day-a-week gifted "cluster" program at another school. The entire group that had started together in kindergarten were recommended for this pullout program. The teacher asked the library media specialist to provide computer instruction for the three strongest of the students left out of the pullout program.

In the fourth grade, two of the original kindergartners were chosen to attend a special fourth-grade class scrupulously selected from more than 125 finalists areawide within the school system. One of these students had attended the once-a-week gifted pullout in third grade. The new program would carry them through the sixth grade. The students left at the home school were assigned to a total class of capable students. Eight students participated in the weekly cluster pullout—five continuing, and three additional students. Through formal channels, all of the original early-identified children were served by special programs. Still, highly able students remained in the fourth grade class, not served by any formal programs, for whom the teacher sought differentiation and enrichment. Within her classroom, some of the curriculum extensions included:

- *Immigrants All*—literature and social studies
- *Maryland Adventures*—history through field trips, slide tapes, and videos
- an Apple Logo pilot unit—geometry and language
- *Writers' Workshop*
- Kinder-German

All of these programs were joint efforts between the classroom teacher and the library media specialist using the CUES configuration.

A review of the local school's 11-year history before the systemwide adoption of special programs for the gifted showed a similar pattern of formal and informal grouping for acceleration and enrichment affecting the same children from a grade level for some part of each year, K–5. Most groups started as a custom-designed outgrowth of the reading language arts curriculum. The library media specialist was the instructional constant following along with each group.

As each group graduated, another came spiraling along. One group of five reading kindergartners who had other intellectual strengths in first grade, joined the library media specialist to enjoy Pets and Apples, the computer frontier at the time. They went on to do "different and difficult things" connected with books and information, hence the choice of their name, *Different and Difficult Research Group*, or DDRG. In second grade, two more children joined the group. Notetaking was their delight and talent, so the teacher planned for a series of reporting activities that combined fiction and FACTion, their word to connote nonfiction books.

The children who participated in these *ad hoc* groups are now college graduates. Their personal frames of giftedness—in math, computers, science, music, art, and human relations—continued to stand out. By the time they left elementary school, well-defined formal programs for the gifted were in place for them. Some attended an International Baccalaureate high school; others the math/science or communications magnet high schools. In most of these programs, no formal role for the library media specialist is in place, other than as the selector, gatherer, and custodian of resources.

Independent Study Model I: Research Assistants

The "research assistants" were fifth and sixth graders working independently on library media-centered projects chosen by students in consultation with the library media specialist. The projects had to serve two purposes: to help the students become more adept library media center clients, while introducing such advanced concepts as project design and data arrangement for retrieval; and to help the library media center serve the informational needs of the school through student-prepared materials. For simpler tasks, junior research assistants were recruited from lower grades.

The first research assistants group consisted of top readers in the school who were receiving accelerated reading instruction from the reading teacher. When she realized the group could handle more work, she subcontracted with the library media specialist for an independent study program. The group was a mixed bag. All were advanced readers, yet some were mature, leaders in school activities, while a few were "itchy," incapable of listening or following through on anything. Billy, new to the area, had been in isolated gifted classes during all his school years. Like *Henry 3*, he, too, did all he could to hide his capabilities from his new schoolmates (Krumgold 1969).

The group responded well to guidance that kept their feet on the ground with firm expectations and accountability. They were a prototype for similar groups in later years. Some of their products lasted for many years.

To start a research assistants group,

the classroom teacher selects students to participate in projects to help them learn more about the library media center, so that they can help others do the same;

the students explore the facility, enumerating and classifying everything they see;

the library media specialist offers a catalog of serviceable projects;

after each student makes a choice, an initial planning conference with the library media specialist to design a project takes place;

the student contracts for assigned and free work periods, logging time and progress; and

finished products are cataloged into the library media collection. The products may be vertical/picture file items, bulletin boards, centers, exhibits, publications, or statistical surveys.

An inventory of original products shows the diversity of topics that familiarize youngsters with such information processing skills and formats as databasing, indexing, selecting and evaluating materials, and whetting curiosity. Most activities fit in the CUES category of working with miscellany, described in Chapter 9.

A Strange Phenomenon Center—containing articles, clippings, questions about this high interest topic. (The first center included a weekly issue of *The Nessie News Bulletin,* with articles solicited from students and containing the advice column, "Dear Drac.")

Thinking Bulletin Board for posting challenges, contests, and questions.

Book reviews and other promotional items.

Clipping service for vertical and picture file topics; especially a file of imagination and creativity pictures to trigger thinking.

A listing similar in format to *The Abridged Readers' Guide,* indexing useful topics from such periodicals as *Cobblestones, National Geographic World, Cricket, MiniPage, Odyssey, Owl,* and *Scienceland.* These skillfully produced magazines are excellent curriculum resources, especially when articles are cross-referenced to grade level units of study.

A shelf reading service for keeping the shelves in order and getting to know the collection and the Dewey decimal system. (First grade classes are the Easy Shelf Readers.)

A taped tour of the artifacts, models, realia, and shelf teasers, as well as the print and nonprint collections of the library media center.

Minute Biographies of famous women, modeled after the now-out-of-print book of brief text-and-sketch lives.

Study boxes containing realia, samples, and articles related to a topic:

Museum Boxes, containing diagrams, maps, postcards to introduce each museum in the Smithsonian complex.

Trees, for use as a field guide, with wood samples, illustrations of leaves, fruits, and basic facts.

Fifty Nifty—a spiral-bound book about the 50 states, containing a page for each state with graphic summaries of facts and statistics.

Collection-building and evaluation advice via book reviews and other bibliographic activities:

Do We Own This Book?—checking bibliographies against holdings;

Shall We Buy This Book?—a packet of blurbs and other promotional literature collected from publishers' catalogs, book reviews, and so forth, evaluated and arranged as a file for possible purchase.

Independent Study Model II: Danny Finds Out

Sometimes in kindergarten, just one child reads so well that it is impossible for the Language/Reading Arts time in the regular classroom to suit that child's needs. Danny was such a student in Mrs. Tanner's class during her first year. Without reading peers in his class, she had the option of pushing him up to read with higher grades, despite his typical six-year-old maturity level or having him spend time each day with the reading teacher and the library media specialist. Danny came to the library media center for his extended classroom. Here is what Danny found out.

The Plan: Danny and Mrs. Leonard work together on Danny's list of activities.

1. Read *Magic School Bus Inside the Earth,* then borrow the book to take home.

2. Find more books about the inside of the earth.

3. Read *How Can I Find Out?*, a book about doing "research."

4. Concentrate on topics that interest Danny: Earth, questions and answers, trains, paper planes, rocks, and *Guinness*-type records.

5. Work in his special place, a carrel.

6. Keep a log of what he learns this year.

Some things that happened:

1. Danny and his dad read the book, *Easy Answers to Hard Questions*. Danny wrote down some questions and answered them with information from the book and his own thoughts, about health, babies, how things around the house work, pets, and weather.

2. He used an unabridged dictionary to look up new rock words: sedimentary, igneous, metamorphic, shale, limestone, stalagmite, and stalactite. He also looked up the word unabridged.

3. Danny toured the Belmont School building to find that it is made of cement, brick, some marble, and cinderblock.

4. Danny at work became a familiar sight to all who passed through. Age and grade were no barriers to the many learning conversations that took place.

Latitudinal Group Model: Topical Units

Mrs. Caruso wanted to extend the vocabularies of the 13 gifted readers in her third-grade class. She asked the library media specialist to meet with them for about six sessions to help them enjoy word resources, dictionaries, thesauri, and other materials. Mr. LaRue wanted to improve his fifth graders' research and reporting skills, while he was offering them a minicourse in video production. He and the library media specialist devised a unit that combined both sets of skills, with a rotation of students between research and production, splitting the teaching needed for each facet of the program.

These are examples of latitudinal groups set up for a period of time or unit of study. Each is a vehicle for differentiation: the first specifically designed for gifted students, apart from their classroom activities; the second includes the whole class—the product being the differentiating factor. Such groups begin in several ways:

1. A classroom teacher or grade team asks the library media specialist to offer accelerated or enriched content for a top reading group; or in the case of first graders, for curious not-yet-readers; or

2. Individual children in a grade or class who have become independent library media center customers, either on their own initiative (free time and curiosity use) or at teacher request, ask to be helped or to be helpers; or

3. The library media specialist contacts the teacher about the possibility of composing a group of children who stand out because they display more background knowledge, respond on a higher level, or seem capable of working on a topic at greater depth.

A variable shaping the direction of such groups is the amount of involvement the teacher wishes to have in student work time and choice of content. When the teacher offers little input about the content, as with the CPRG second-grade group, the result is more eclectic or episodic than when the teacher requests a curriculum focus. Either way, the spiral is in motion for a trip to guided discovery via the library media center. Such matching of the learner and the learning is an idea now suggested for gifted programs.

The choice and treatment of a topic for a specific group of able children depends on an alignment of their developmental level, the curriculum requirements for their grade, and their interests. For example, when the CPRG discovered Helen Keller, they wanted to branch out in several directions. Some wanted to find out more about women in American history by following a time line of women from the MiniPages; some were more interested in Braille and nonverbal communication; and others wanted to study about children with disabilities. All of these interests were accommodated; and each topic stretched the students to find and interpret information.

EMOTIONAL INTELLIGENCE AND SETTING A GROUP

It is not often that books about educational philosophy turn into best sellers, but in 1995-96, *Emotional Intelligence* by Daniel Goleman did. Following up on Gardner's theory of multiple intelligences, Goleman elaborates on aspects of personal intelligence that are indicators of success beyond the school years. While IQ (Intelligence Quotient) and EQ (Emotional Quotient) are separate, they are not opposite. Goleman claims that *metamood* and *metacognition*, together, comprise *self-awareness*. Personal intelligence consists of the ability to know one's emotions; manage them; motivate oneself; recognize emotion in others; and handle relationships. Emotional self-control often requires the stifling of impulsiveness and delaying of gratification. Contained in the November 1995 issue of *The UTNE Reader* is an article by Goleman, "EQ, What's Your Emotional Intelligence Quotient?" The article has an EQ test consisting of "case studies" of everyday human relations on which to rate oneself. Appendix D of Goleman's book lists "Key Ingredients of Effective Programs." He enumerates many well-known ideas to clarify for children: the "inner dialogue" of self-talk; reducing stress; knowing the difference between feelings and action; anticipation of consequences; reading and interpreting social cues; understanding the perspectives of others; and knowing behavioral norms (Goleman 1995). This echoes Dorothy Baruch's long-ago statements that discipline consists of knowing that it is all right to have feelings, whatever they are, but behavior needs to be controlled. Once children become comfortable with Goleman's ideas, they, too, can devise EQ questionnaires. What situations will they set up to study? Will they find literary examples?

Goleman cites several programs that operate well in the area of emotional and social skills. Book characters like Arnold Lobel's Frog and Toad introduce words for feelings and emotions. Other packaged materials promote self-awareness in a self-science curriculum.

However in-school groups are structured, the teacher's purpose is to provide an intellectually stimulating experience with peers in an environment conducive to learning. But grouping a set is not synonymous with setting a group into harmonious operation. This is true of children from the same class. It is even truer when the children are pulled together from different grades or schools or geographic areas. Some of the problems to be anticipated include:

- children who are sensitive about disabilities, observable or not, that affect their being comfortable in a group;

- cliques that come ready-made into a new situation;

- best friends who compete with each other to be "in" with the new group, often cruelly;

- the child who has always been top dog and has to reassert that position with each new teacher and group; and

- children who do not perform because they are not going to get a grade or otherwise be held accountable.

Affective problems have to be resolved before gifted groups can perform intellectually. Solutions come when teachers and students cooperate with the problem-solving process as part of the curriculum. Setting a group requires an accepting climate created from the establishment of rules and rituals and an examination of people's feelings, moods, and behaviors. Overall, the larger theme of human relationships ought to be treated in an ongoing curriculum emphasis. The progression runs from concern for oneself to responsibility for one's actions, to respect for and responsiveness to others (sympathy), to an understanding of the words empathy and altruism.

Bibliotherapy and Training

The term *bibliotherapy* has long been used to describe the strategy of encouraging good human relations through literature. While the realm of feelings is the area being explored, the strategies and materials involve problem-solving and production skills. For children in kindergarten through the second grade, reading or telling stories about friendship and getting along with others sets the stage. Share *Feelings* by Aliki, or the chapter "Anna and I Make People Happy" from Astrid Lindgren's *Children of Noisy Village*. *The Little Brute Family* is a sure-fire resource here, especially if children get to guess the family's new name. Judith Viorst combines her poetry and therapy skills to write *If I Were in Charge of the World* and *Sad Underwear*. How do *The Cut-Ups*, like *Otis Spofford*, affect the classroom? Middle graders sympathize with the narrator of *Henry 3* who hides the numbers of his IQ, or the eccentricities of some of E. L. Konigsberg's characters, or the hurt of many fictional outsiders. Introduce "psychology" to elementary graders with Joy Wilt Berry's Let's Talk About . . . Series—whining, tattling, and other annoying everyday behaviors. Tracking characters and behavior and the books in which they dwell is a possible assignment for some book sleuth. Educators, themselves, need to deal with the "learned incompetence" some children develop as a coping device.

For educators and young people alike, training programs and bibliographies provide guidance in dealing with daily dilemmas and climate. Students learn "talking-it-out," peer mediation, conflict resolution, and leadership skills. The seminars take place in educational settings, summer camps, and other positive environments. Books and settings teach techniques for global understandings, circles of learning, service learning, and discipline with dignity.

Affecting a Group, a Progression

A homegrown set of lessons for effectively setting a group, grades three to six, might include: Breaking the Ice; Developing Labels, Logos, Rules, and Rituals for the Group; Establishing a Sensitivity to Feelings; and Toward a Greater Understanding. This sequence of lessons involves different data collection techniques such as inventories, surveys, and interviews, which lead to collating and publishing data, ranging from simple pencil-and-paper formats to the most sophisticated online and database computer applications. At the same time, students are practicing their human relations skills.

Breaking the Ice

As a first lesson, the teacher distributes the questionnaire, "Ice Breaker and Literary Quotient (LQ)" (fig. 5.2). Students then embark on a literary scavenger hunt. Responses are collated and analyzed to give a class profile. Then the class discusses the items, relating each to an area of literary knowledge.

Developing Labels, Logos, Rules, and Rituals

After a group's focus has been established, whether it is to sharpen media skills, to select books more wisely, or some other goal, the members suggest appropriate names for the group from which the members choose. Each student designs a logo. All of the logos are projected from an overhead transparency for better judging. Once the names and logo are selected, these symbolize the group on any of its products or presentations.

Able students are fully aware of proper group behavior. It is counterproductive for the teacher to have to belabor the standards; nonetheless, some restatement of ground rules for acceptable behavior is necessary. "The Schoolroom," chapter 12 in *Stuart Little*, belongs in every teacher's repertoire for setting climate and rules.

"Do you think you can maintain discipline?" asks an anxious but desperate superintendent of schools in response to Stuart's offer to fill in for the ailing Mrs. Gunderson. Stuart reassures him that interesting work makes discipline take care of itself.

In the classroom, Stuart makes short work of attendance, arithmetic, spelling, writing, and social studies in order to *talk* about what is important and some rules for behaving. As Chairman of the World, Stuart asks for suggestions for good laws for the world. After making the distinction between friendly advice and "law," which is more "solemn than advice," Stuart helps the group define two laws: "Nix on swiping anything" and "absolutely no being mean" (White 1945).

Ice Breaker and Literary Quotient (LQ)
(for intermediate groups)

Everyone in this group is a *good reader*. But are you all avid readers? Ask around the group until you find someone who

- enjoys the online card catalog
- has read all of *The Narnian Chronicles*
- has read a book by flashlight under the covers after bedtime
- has the same favorite book as you
- likes science fiction
- has acted in a play
- can quote the first line of the poem *The Midnight Ride of Paul Revere*
- can tell for whom the Peanuts gang waits on Halloween
- can name two Charlottes in children's literature
- usually wins at Scrabble
- writes Haiku
- reads two magazines a month and names them
- recites a nursery rhyme
- uses an unabridged dictionary
- reads an atlas for the fun of it
- browses in an encyclopedia
- describes the Dewey decimal system
- can name three sections of a newspaper besides comics and sports
- enjoys trivial pursuits
- would rather read a good book than watch television
- names a film based on a book seen either in a theater or on TV
- (invent your own question and ask it here)

Bonus Questions

- has worn "seven league boots"
- met the Muses
- trod the boards
- studied a battledore
- bopped around with Punch and Judy

Fig. 5.2. Questionnaire for Breaking the Ice Lesson

What rules would a 1997 class make? Bring Stuart Little, Miss Viola Swamp (the dreaded fill-in when *Miss Nelson Is Missing),* and Mrs. Mallyho (*The Substitute Is Me* with the grand piano in her bag of tricks) into the classroom to launch a discussion of personal feelings and group rules. Before or after opening the topic for group brainstorming, the teacher suggests a list of 10 key words relating to behavior in a group: 1) Conversation; 2) On-Task?; 3) Responsibility; 4) Movement; 5) Cooperation; 6) Evaluation; 7) Sharing; 8) Listening; 9) Self-Discipline; and 10) Respect. The students—separately, in pairs, or in groups of five—examine what the words imply. Then the words are posted and need only be referred to by number when infractions occur. Jefferson (Oregon) Elementary School devised a program to turn students into self-managers, which included a personal rating sheet on classroom management skills; respect for property, self, and others; and helping others. This Positive Action Plan not only improved behavior, it improved test performance as well. The best-selling *The Children's Book of Virtues* is a collection of stories and poems from Aesop to Robert Frost, which teach compassion, courage, honesty, friendship, and faith, albeit with didactic intent.

Chants originally were brief choral elocutions taken from poetry or folk tale anthologies. Then Mary Carter Smith, who performs in schools as the *griot* from Baltimore, charmed students with her chant beginning, "When you have something to say, open your mouth." Fifth graders who were having trouble listening to the ideas of others or blurting out, developed their own metacognitive chant. The reminder worked!

When you're working by yourself, use your brain.
When you're working by yourself, use your brain.
Thinking problems out quite logically
Makes answers come more easily.
When you're working by yourself, use your brain.
When it's a time to listen, close your mouth.
When it's a time to listen, close your mouth.
Directions that get lost, your good grades may cost.
When it's a time to listen, close your mouth.
When you're learning in a group, be polite.
When you're learning in a group, be polite.
Good discussion depends on listening to your friends.
When you're learning in a group, be polite.

Establishing a Sensitivity to Feelings

A third step in setting a group is opening positive channels for expressing feelings. Mood indicators such as PMIs, Clouds, and Emoticons are unusual teaching ploys that help improve classroom climate.

A typical De Bono PMI statement is: "Everyone should wear a badge showing his or her mood." This is a coincidental parallel to an old Chinese tale, "A Visit to the Land-of-Great-Men," a place reputed to have no silly quarreling, a place where people were kind to each other (Fahs 1948). In this land, everyone walked on a small colored cloud that hovered a foot above the ground. The cloud colors ranged from rainbow to yellow to red and green and blue to grey or black. The color of the cloud revealed its owner's disposition for all to see. It was impossible to hide or change it, except by what the person felt inside. Wealth, occupation, intelligence, or status mattered not. So, when a noble gentleman passed in procession along the main street with a red satin curtain covering his cloud, he fooled no one.

After presenting the story and the PMI to the group, the teacher asks what color each would choose for his or her personal cloud; whether one's cloud can change from moment to moment during the day—and with what provocation; or how one's own perception of the color of his or her cloud may differ from the way others see it at any given time. Each student makes a "mood indicator" to show his or her prevailing mood during class time. Given only this direction and some simple art materials, classes of third through sixth graders have come up with an amazing array of mechanical devices, no two alike, to measure moods. It becomes part of the group's daily ritual to have the indicators on view. It is revealing to see the indicators change unobtrusively during the course of the class's interactions with each other and the lesson. An observer from China visiting one summer literature group told how the color red was the Chinese symbol of happiness. The group took off on a discussion of the scientific concept of change: of color, as with a chameleon (camouflage); and of form, as with a caterpillar (metamorphosis). Ever-changing moods can be graphed for an individual or for the class. As swings and fluctuations are observed, hypotheses can be made about the causes. Do moods relate to weather or holidays? What is the folklore of weather?

Emoticons send mood messages throughout the online world. The word is part of the new vocabulary of the Internet, where brevity and clarity are important. Emoticons are clever combinations of letters and keyboard symbols to form icons that communicate *feelings*. Not all emoticons are the "smileys" of approval that teachers have long stamped on children's work; creating emoticons is becoming a thinking challenge.

:-D   :-)   ;-)   :-/   :-[:-X   :-0   :-<   %-)   >:-<   <*>   :-(

Rules, rituals, mood indicators, and chanting all lessen bickering and confrontation, affording an improved climate for learning. They are a channel for maintaining decorum, as they minimize the chaos of transitions. They occur within the metacognitive framework of what a school system requires, what teachers expect, what the group understands, and what parents want. For each session, the rituals might include 1) an opening—a chant for younger groups, a browsing activity, or an agenda cryptically stated; 2) a calendar—for showing cumulative course content; and 3) a closing—logs, study journals, or a rating of the session. Rituals for reporting help eliminate the indefinite and vague "we did divergent thinking today" summary sentence, an easy out that gifted students quickly discover. Rituals facilitate opening and closing sessions; keeping to schedules and objectives; and recording and evaluating progress.

Since gifted groups tend to present an irrepressible and irreverent facade, the real key to turning these characteristics to beneficial use is the teacher's good nature and adeptness at human relations, both needed for crisis intervention and prevention. Sometimes it is edifying for adults to survey how they, as teachers, parents, and school officials, are portrayed in childen's stories, usually as examples of irony or satire in the genre called humor. How would Mr. Fairbain, the Assistant Superintendent for Curriculum, and Dr. Rohmer, the Superintendent of Schools, the overseers of Konigsburg's competition, rate in a peer evaluation?

Toward Global Understanding

A more important need exists for developing a group's sensitivity to and appreciation of the efforts, feelings, and needs of other people. When a class of fifth and sixth graders were chided for their consistent pattern of discourtesy and inattentiveness to guest speakers, bus drivers, and others who gave of their time, as well as their rough treatment of prized objects on a museum table, their response was: "We're cut from a different mold." Most teachers do not feel that this exempts the kids from societal rules for polite behavior. This elan, frequent among gifted groups, is difficult for teachers to counteract in positive ways. One such way is to build into any course of study materials that address universal experiences and problems. Such materials are readily available on the shelves of the library media center, from *Manners* to conflict resolution to *Peace by Peace* through peer mediation from talking it out in multicultural classrooms to community service learnings to global understandings.

An expanded unit on sensitivity themes could include:

- "What If You Couldn't . . . ?" (about disabilities);
- illness, death, and dying;
- cautionary and morality tales;
- comeuppances in fiction and folklore;
- "Against All Odds" (about personal shortcomings);
- cooperation, instead of competition; and
- the cosmic theme of good and evil.

Going beyond the first steps of consciousness raising and creating empathy, the ultimate reason for all human relations curriculum is understanding. In this area of coping and caring, some human relations advocacy groups publish book lists that help in planning. Many of the trade books listed, both fiction and fact, treat contemporary problems sensitively, poignantly, and candidly. Whether it is the etiquette of eating when *Soup Should Be Seen, Not Heard*, or Netiquette of the web, what do you do when a pesky little brother turns his older sibling into a *Toy Brother*?

According to Compton's on America Online, the ancient Egyptians called the library "a healing place for the soul," a natural hub for today's affective learning. It is full of case studies, real and vicarious, humorous and sad, to help kids develop the skills they need to resolve conflicts at home, at school, and within themselves.

THE DYNAMICS DUO: SPEAKING AND GROUP

Yarnspinners were 10 second graders, seven boys and three girls, who met weekly for literary enrichment in the library media center. They liked reading stories and wanted to tell stories like the storyteller who had come to school one day. He was a giant of a man, and when someone asked, "How tall are you?" he answered, "Oh, about seven stories high." After they probed the metaphor of yarn-spinning, their first assignment was to spin a yarn one story high about when they were very young. They went on to telling favorite tales from the shelves, solo or in chorus, then to dramatic presentation and video production. To help them become better tale tellers, the library media specialist devised Speaking Dynamics, a system for evaluating and improving oral skills. Three sets of words were related to speaking: HIGH—LOW, FAST—SLOW, and LOUD—SOFT, with MEDIUM in all ranges. The children latched on to this device, coopera- tively designing a card with a spinner to encourage the variety in their speaking. The speaking improved, but the group's progress was hindered by a clash of personalities within. What followed was a perfect case study that could be called "Emotional Intelligence and Metacognition in Seven-Year-Olds."

Paul opted to leave the group "because he was bored and tired." Stephanie was his replacement. This made a better gender balance and added a catalyst personality. In the daily lesson log, it is noted that "Tommy was in tears because he had to be LOW and it hurt his throat . . . he could only be MEDIUM." Mark explained that Jeff had assigned the voice parts. Scott showed his elaborate plan for marking the scripts for pitch, speed, and tone. Good will was restored as the group used crayons to draw their own dynamics charts. As the boys worked at a table, Mark asked, "Where's the gold?" Jeff replied, "You can use it after me." at which Robby exclaimed, "Finally, something you two agree on!" In the lesson evaluation, Mark said, "It was great at the end, but the middle was terrible." Why? "The arguments," was the unison reply.

Mrs. Rivers, their teacher extraordinaire, and the library media specialist were enrolled in an in-service course about Higher Order Intellectual Skills, with a video of classroom application as homework. They chose to work together on the group dynamics of the Yarnspinners. At the next session, the children were asked to characterize some literary friends:

Winnie the Pooh: happy, good-natured, prancing, hungry

Piglet: squeaky, bright, scared, worried, nervous, stammer

Eeyore: lazy, not energetic, curious, gloomy

Kanga: cooks well, serious, motherly, maternal

Tigger: energetic, unusual, bouncy, doesn't listen, doesn't let people get a turn

Christopher Robin: regular

Then they were introduced to "Types in a Group," caricatures from a handout distributed in the teachers' workshop. The types were The Boss, The Clown, The Me-First-Side-Tracker, The Needler, The Icicle, The Fence-Sitter, The Silent or Invisible Member, and The Dark Cloud. Jeff illustrated and described his own group types—The Time Taker, The Computer User, The Smarty Pants, and The Hand Raiser. They prepared a packet called "How Do *You* Behave in a Group?" Little did they know that they were in the footsteps of the *Four and Twenty Watchbirds*, first created by Munro Leaf in 1939 to teach that *Manners Can Be Fun.*

Again from the daily log:

As the Clown was discussed, Robbie commented, "I think every-one here but Stephanie knows what it's like to be in a group with a clown." The climate was comfortable, so the teacher/library media specialist risked telling Samantha that she was miffed when Samantha acted like a Me-First-Side-Tracker by diverting everyone to a dead cricket in the ceiling light. The child was taken aback and said, "Oh, I didn't *mean* to spoil the lesson. Are you mad at me?"

Since the group had some very recognizable types, it was important not to let labels become too personal. They wanted to characterize people in their families. The log again:

Robbie mentioned that his cousin was a Fence-Sitter, so he said "I always ask him to give an answer first." Tommy's brother was a Needler and Dark Cloud. Then Scott spoke up: "How come this is talking about the things that go wrong instead of what's right with a group?" Here is their idea of a "best group":

- smart, nice listeners
- attentive, cooperative
- not yelling
- respond to direction
- always wait patiently
- have good handwriting
- teachers' helpers: paper filers
- imaginative, bright ideas, thinking caps on

They rated themselves as having only one flaw—yelling out responses. They knew why the teacher introduced the type models: "To tell kids what behavior causes problems so they can be better." After they discovered that decision making about their production was difficult—"Jeff spoiled our group by being too bossy" and "Samantha decided what our group should do and the others just let her"—they appointed Mark as their group process observer who reported that "boys split 3/3, couldn't agree; girls 4-0, unanimous." A few commented on Mark's observations: "I had no idea we acted like that at first"; "No one liked Jeff's idea but we did it."

They were learning the act of cooperation and the art of compromise. Ever after, the Yarnspinners rated themselves on content, the lesson, process, and behavior. Their emerging self-awareness enabled the group to finish the video, which they invited the Administrator of Higher Order Thinking to view. She loved it and them!

REFERENCES: HUMAN RELATIONS RESOURCES FOR TEACHERS

Adams, Barbara. 1979. *Like It Is: Facts and Feelings About Handicaps from Kids Who Know.* New York: Walker.

ASCD. 1997. *New Mandates, New Methods, New Books.* Publications for 1997. Alexandria, VA: Association for Curriculum Development.

Barker, Dan. 1992. *Maybe Right Maybe Wrong.* Buffalo, NY: Prometheus Books.

Dreyer, Sharon S. 1977. *The Bookfinder: A Guide to Children's Literature About the Needs and Problems of Youth, Aged 2-15.* Circle Pines, MN: American Guidance Services.

Educators for Social Responsibility. Publications and Workshops. Cambridge, MA.

Fahs, Sophia. 1948. *From Long Ago and Many Lands: "A Visit to the Land-of-Great-Men."* Boston, MA: Beacon Press.

GCFP. n.d. *Peacemaking ABC's for Young Children: A Guide for Teaching Conflict Resolution.*

Goleman, Daniel. 1995. "Key Ingredients of Effective Programs." In Appendix D of *Emotional Intelligence.* New York: Bantam.

——. 1995. EQ, What's Your Emotional Intelligence Quotient? *The UTNE Reader*, November 12, 74–76.

Kamien, Janet. 1979. *What If You Couldn't...? A Book About Special Needs.* New York: Charles Scribner's Sons.

Krumgold, Joseph. 1969. *Henry 3.* New York: HarperCollins.

Lantieri, Linda, and Janet Patti. 1996. *Waging Peace in Our Schools.* Boston: Beacon Press.

McCormack, Sammie. 1981. To Make Discipline Work, Turn Kids into Self-Managers. *The Executive Editor*, November.

National Conference of Christians and Jews. n.d. *The Human Family. Understanding Other People: Books for Children and Young Adults.*

Renzulli, Joseph S., et al. 1981. *The Revolving Door Identification Model.* Mansfield Center, CT: Creative Learning Press.

Schmidt, Fran, and Alice Friedman. 1993. *Peacemaking Skills for Little Kids,* 2 vols. Miami, FL: Peace Education Foundation.

Shurkin, Joel N. 1992. *Terman's Kids.* New York: Little, Brown.

Stone, Karen F., and Harold Q. Dillehunt. 1973. *The Subject Is Me.* Santa Monica, CA: Goodyear.

Tway, Eileen, ed. 1981. *Reading Ladders for Human Relations.* 6th ed. Washington, DC: American Council of Education and National Council of Teachers of English.

White, E. B. 1945. *Stuart Little.* New York: Harper & Row.

The WISH List: World Information Shapes Harmony. n.d. A Bibliography. Hammond, IN: Hammond WAND.

BIBLIOGRAPHY

Children of Noisy Village. Astrid Lindgren. New York: Viking Press, 1988.

The Children's Book of Virtues. William Bennett. New York: Simon & Schuster, 1996.

The Cut-Ups. James Marshall. New York: Viking Press, 1990.

Feelings. Aliki. New York: Greenwillow Books, 1984.

Four and Twenty Watchbirds. Munro Leaf. 1939. Reprint: Hamden, CT: Linnet Books, 1990.

Frog and Toad. Arnold Lobel. New York: HarperCollins, 1972.

If I Were in Charge of the World and Other Worries. Judith Viorst. New York: Atheneum, 1981.

Let's Talk About . . . Series. Joy Wilt Berry. Chicago: Children's Press.

The Little Brute Family. Russell Hoban. New York: Macmillan, 1966.

Make Someone Smile and 40 More Ways to Be a Peaceful Person. Judith Lalle. Minneapolis, MN: Free Spirit Publications, 1996.

Manners. Aliki. New York: Greenwillow Books, 1990.

Manners Can Be Fun. Munro Leaf. 1939. Reprint: New York: HarperCollins, 1985.

Miss Nelson Is Missing. Harry Allard and James Marshall. Boston: Houghton Mifflin, 1977.

Sad Underwear: And Other Complications. Judith Viorst. New York: Atheneum, 1995.

See You in Second Grade. Miriam Cohen. New York: Greenwillow Books, 1989.

Soup Should Be Seen, Not Heard: The Kids' Etiquette Book. Beth Brainerd and Sheila Behr. New York: Dell, 1990.

Toy Brother. William Steig. New York: HarperCollins, 1996.

The View from Saturday. E. L. Konigsburg. New York: Atheneum, 1996.

What Do You Think? A Kid's Guide to Dealing with Daily Dilemmas. Linda Schwartz. Santa Barbara, CA: Learning Works, 1993.

Six

Language Arts Unlimited

At the center of a language arts curriculum is the triumvirate of grammar, rhetoric, and logic, the three-fold way to eloquence during the Middle Ages. The language path wends through the library media center where, shelved among the 400s, 800s, 398.6s, and the 745s, is a motherlode of books guaranteed to imbue students with language. The books present the history of language, elementary foreign languages, hidden languages, figurative language, literal language, and the sound and sight of language. To supplement the trade books, reproducible workbooks, and magazines about language, a library media specialist usually keeps a personal data bank of word challenges, activities, articles, bibliographies, and cartoons.

THE GIFT OF LANGUAGE

Fluency in language is discernible at an early age in many highly able children. These 10 characteristics on a language arts checklist developed by Montgomery County, Maryland, Public Schools are observable. A child with the gift of language

1. has an extensive vocabulary;

2. shows great interest in the derivation of words;

3. shows ability to classify and divide information;

4. has the following writing skills: organization, ability to support a generalization; and basic mechanical skills such as writing complete sentences and using appropriate capitalization and punctuation;

5. generates many ideas or solutions to problems, fantasizes and imagines, and offers unusual and unique responses;

6. is able to compare and contrast; perceives analogical relationships;

7. reads a variety of materials (e.g., novels, biographies, nonfiction, and magazines) beyond level of peers;

8. has developed areas of special depth and interest;

9. is able to comprehend, interpret, and evaluate literature; and

10. uses colorful and imaginative figures of speech, such as puns and analogies, and appreciates irony and satire.

Because children identified as gifted commonly exhibit many of these behaviors, teachers and planners often forget that this language potential needs to be stretched beyond any student's entry level. When one kindergartner saw Gail Haley's calabash in *A Story, A Story*, he exclaimed, "It's a gourd-jeous." About a guitarlike African gourd instrument show during the same lesson, he asked, "Where do you plug it in?" A second-grade class viewed the cover of *Cross Country Cat* and was asked to predict the story. Brian, the only identified gifted member of the class and a nonskier, suggested, "He's going across the country." How? "By foot," was Brian's response. Of the then-new *Magic School Bus Inside the Waterworks*, Greg marveled, "It's scientific fiction."

WORDSMITHING

Reading, writing, speaking, and listening—the four components of the language arts—are addressed by library media resources through

1. word wizardry (vocabulary);

2. the structure of language (grammar);

3. the origins of language (etymology and foreign languages);

4. painting pictures with words (writing); and

5. storytelling (speaking and listening).

The library media specialist can provide, adapt, and combine the best of the language sections of the collection to extend and enrich students' personal vocabularies in any subject, with special attention to items 1, 2, 4, 6, and 10 of the checklist.

Word Wizardry

An acquired skill, growing out of and expanding on prior knowledge, vocabulary is both a strength and deficiency of many capable students today. Many studies agree that a large vocabulary is a factor in all career success, but this is only one reason why the cultivation of excellence in language is important to differentiated instruction. The statement, "The limits of my language mean the limits of my world," suggests that expanding a child's words opens the child to a larger world. New studies in 1997 reinforce the old notion of how important early exposure to language is to the intellectual development of infants. The data indicates that babies are receptive to all languages, and the selection of one early in life inhibits the ability to know others. If early childhood is the time when minds are most ripe for learning all languages, how will this idea affect school foreign language curricula?

Fooling Around with Words

A first step to language mastery is the manipulation of words. The list of wordplay challenges is long. Some activities are loftier than others, but all are enjoyable diversions whether used to fill a lesson block of time or to serve as a filler or warm-up. Some include:

Alliterative Alphabets	Parodies
Body Language	Patterned Prose
Codes and Ciphers	Pictonyms
Daffynitions	Plays on Meanings
Flytings and other poetic constructs	Portmanteaux
Hinky-Pinkies	Prime Rhymes
Homophonic Homophones	Pun Fun
Idioms	Rebuses
Improbable Opposites	Terse Verse
Invented Names	Tom Swifties
Jokes and Riddles	Wordoodles
Palindromes	

Some additional word games and activities include:

Acronyms	Lists, Lists, Lists
Acrostics	Naming
Anagrams	Neologisms
Analogies	Pictionary
Balderdash	Scrabble
Boggle	Turnabouts
Chants	Upwords
Charades	Word Finds
Fictionary	Word Scrambles

Among popular tradebooks, *Andy That's My Name* is a caper in phonics with "learning-to-readers," and Amelia Bedelia always misinterprets word meanings "as we would never do," laugh the children. Andy and Amelia highlight the teaching potential of humorous wordplay. Even the youngest scholars ask for joke and riddle books to "make me laugh." For older humorists, Alvin Schwartz's anthologies of folklore fun put witcracks, whoppers, tomfoolery, superstitions, twisters, and tanglers into oral and written language lessons. Codes, ciphers, and rebuses scramble the ingredients for brewing a *Humbug Potion* from an abundance of word recipes. *Let's Find Out About Names* is a perennial request. A report on the origins of *Names, First, Last, Middle, and Nick* is always a challenge.

Comprehensive bibliographies of children's books for playing with language appear regularly in issues of *Language Arts* and *Reading Teacher* magazines. Such lists, a personal data bank, and trade books are the core around which to build and update a language curriculum. *Fooling Around with Words*, sparked by books like *"I Can't," Said the Ant, Teapot Switcheroo,* or *The Whatamacallit Book,* are first steps on the road to Word Wizardry as students savor and experiment with words.

Semantic Strategies

In addition to commercial and personal materials, simple generic techniques for vocabulary development may be less familiar to teachers. They are open-ended and require no purchase of materials. They also accommodate any number of participants at any grade level in any subject area. Sometimes the processes are called semantic association, semantic mapping, or semantic feature analysis, but the basic form is the word web, relating to and emanating from a class's experience. Examples show up in unlikely places:

A graphic in a publisher's catalog was a science glossary. Boxed in black and randomly arranged around a balance scale were chemistry words. Isaac Asimov wrote a glossary series of books on the vocabulary of each physical science.

A small challenge from the newspaper is to present, in a sentence, two words probably never thought of for the same sentence.

Thirteen authors of adult mysteries wrote a round robin novel, a technique adaptable for young writers.

Word Wall

A word wall is like a bulletin board on which to post words chosen by participants according to some given criteria. Word walls are built from words chosen for the way they sound, the way they look, or because their meaning is unknown. The teacher suggests a word wall and lists words that have appeal for one of these reasons. Students are to search daily—through newspapers, magazines, and other sources—for personal lists of words in each category. Part of wall building is the identification procedure. When this is completed, each student posts his or her words on the wall, properly categorized under Sound, Look, or Unknown Meaning categories. Once the idea catches on, nonstop use of dictionaries and thesauri begins. The wall words can be used for alphabetizing, classifying, chanting, illustrating, making mobiles, and dramatizing.

After Mrs. Root attended a workshop on how to enrich language in the classroom through poetry and drama, she assigned 10 fourth graders to the library media center to learn to "let language leap from our lips." They built a wall of words gathered from everyday sources. Some examples of their words: to look at—hadrasaur, sassafras, atmosphere, professional, and xylophone; to say—lugubrious, ooze, and archeopterix; to find the meaning—serendipity, knowledge, gory, science, camera, and hydrogen. From his grandparents' trip "down under," Jimmy contributed some Australian words that had look, sound, and meaning appeal: pommy, furphy, and whinge. Stacy mentioned that word walls were like the petroglyphs of the Anasazi she had seen in New Mexico. Diane brought in a magazine issue all about hieroglyphics. After their start as word clippers, they moved to analyzing words in sentences, inspired by David McCord's *Take Sky*. They looked at Leonardo's sketchbooks, then they went on to become "commonplacers." The commonplace book, an idea from earlier times, is "a book of literary passages, cogent quotations, occasional thoughts, or other memorabilia" (*Webster's Unabridged Dictionary*, 3rd edition). The commonplacer copies whatever fascinates, then responds to it in the same style, e.g., a four line verse for a four line verse. When these commonplacers became comfortable with an unabridged dictionary, they changed their name to Noah's WWWebsters. They compared Random House and Webster's unabridged dictionaries. They recalled the invented spelling of their earlier years, even as they laughed about the signs on Owl's house, WOL, as spelled and written by Christopher Robin. "PLES RING IF AN ANSR IS REQIRD" and "PLEZ CNOKE IF AN ANSR IS NOT REQID". They read the story of the dictionary and held spelling bees for the class based on words from Noah Webster's 1783 blue-backed speller of the American language.

All of the children at Maryvale Elementary contributed to a word wall that their artist-in-residence helped them transform into a work of art. Each child wrote an important word about learning or school on a 3 x 6 card, using acrylics, colored pencils, or oil pastels. The finished wall was 36 feet long and displayed 700 items. The project reached out to the larger community, involving everyone who entered the building. A local newspaper photographed the story. The words included parents' names, favorite subjects, other languages, and such cosmic ideas as understanding, power, share, and create. The popular Magnetic Poetry for Children moves the word wall into the home and onto the 'fridge, where the magnetism of words in flux is apparent.

The Structure of Language

Grammar is ". . . lovely, exciting, irresistible . . . a kind of magic lens, a secret thinking method to peek inside our own minds and detect the designs of our own ideas . . ." claims the author of *Inspecting Our Own Ideas* (Thompson 1994), a grammar self-study program for high-ability students. Teachers have long been urged not to bog down gifted students in the drill associated with grammar, or learning the mechanics of English, such as syntax, punctuation, parts of speech, sentence structure, and spelling. This fear of boring children with endless workbook exercises shortchanges many who require dexterity in these skills. Instead of textbook lessons, why not use a few trade books that delight as they reinforce learning about the complex, but routine, aspects of our language?

Groanless Grammar

Mary O'Neill, Richard Armour, Eve Merriam, and David McCord are authors who poetically sneak in syntax. Groanless grammar springs fully blown from *Words, Words, Words* by Mary O'Neill. Richard Armour packages punctuation in *On Your Marks*, while Eve Merriam advises that *There Is No Rhyme for Silver*, and *It Does Not Always Have to Rhyme,* books in which she elaborates on figurative language and the idiosyncrasies of spelling. David McCord teaches how to "Write Me a Verse" in *Take Sky*. The title poem, by itself, is a course in creative writing. Students join Word Detectives as they sleuth for parts of speech in books such as the *Amazing Pop-Up Grammar Book*. Ruth Heller's ingenious images of prepositions are *Behind the Mask*, adverbs are *Up Up and Away*; adjectives are *Many Luscious Lollipops*; and *Kites Sail High*, as verbs; and nouns are *Cache of Jewels* on a *Merry Go Round*. In her word picturebook series, Joan Hanson draws antonyms, synonyms, homonyms, possessives, and similes to impart linguistic information.

Painless Punctuation

In a sequence for teaching painless punctuation to fifth and sixth graders that refreshes punctuation skills, uses library media reference and literary sources, and encourages higher-level thinking in order to communicate the basics of punctuation to others, the teacher asks questions to elicit summary statements about each punctuation mark. After students discuss their knowledge and its sources, they turn to a grammar reference, like *Harper's English Grammar* for verification. In a lighter vein, the teacher introduces equivalent punctuation poems by Mary O'Neill and Richard Armour. Students then read selections from other poems about punctuation marks. The teacher poses the problem of succinctly and vividly communicating grammatical information with two examples. The first, an easily achievable product, is an activity called "play with punctuation," wherein students design and cut out all sizes and shapes of each punctuation mark. These are moved around—on a game board or overhead projector. The second, the animated film *On Your Marks,* based on the book of the same name, sets their sights on a higher and more expensive kind of production. A comparison of the two projects can trigger a discussion of cost and energy effectiveness given the time constraints and how a product will be used. When students are assigned to design their own grammatical expression, a range of creativity is identified—in ingenuity, in care of execution, and in levels of effort.

A similar pattern applies to other syntactical topics. All this proves that *Grammar Can Be Fun*, even if a collection lacks Munro Leaf's 1934 text to teach it.

The Origins of Language

"What Is the English Language?"

"What Is the English Language?" is the title of a poem from Mary O'Neill's *Words, Words, Words*. In 50 lines of polished verse, O'Neill covers all of the languages upon which English is based, combining supposition and fact about its origins. Another excellent resource on the origins of our everyday language is *Words* by Jane Sarnoff and Reynolds Ruffin. This book synthesizes many of the standard references in the field of etymology with a writing style as appealing as it is informative for the middle-grade reader. These two books combine for a literary start to a study of languages covering such topics as

Where Did It All Begin?

Borrowed Words

People and Place Names

Digging for Roots (Latin and Greek)

The Tree of Languages

Families of Words

Communicating Without Words

Statistical Data About Languages in the United States

Bibliography of Language Reference Books

Roots: Other Languages

To answer the question *Why Do You Speak As You Do?* a next etymological step after studying the origins of the English language is getting acquainted with some of the root languages named in O'Neill's poem. They include: Latin, Greek, German, French, Sanskrit, and Celtic.

A practical reason for embarking on a foreign language course with gifted children in the intermediate grades is the fact of bilingualism, even multilingualism, in many areas of the United States. This occurs as more and more children come to English as a second language from Russian, Hebrew, Vietnamese, Cambodian, and Spanish. Spanglish, Ebonics, and Esperanto are polyglots whose use is debated. The study of Latin and Greek is also back. In language immersion programs, elementary schoolers start in kindergarten to learn totally in French or Spanish or Chinese, even when English is their first language. How does this affect their contacts with the library media specialist and collection? New on the language shelves are other bilingual books such as *Arctic Memories* with Inuit/English text for its art. *A to Zen* is an alphabet book of Japanese culture.

Another reason to explore foreign languages is the opportunity for thinking and learning that comes from the lighthearted treatment afforded by many materials. Most basal language series deal with root words. Foreign language dictionaries are part of the reference collection. Other trade books introduce several languages in "see and say" fashion. Children are familiar with novels and picture storybooks translated from other languages and to other languages. See beloved *Spot* in Chinese and many other languages!

Even with all of this advance organizing, such a unit imposed on a group out of context probably would not fly. Put in a proper framework, as in the following case study, a unit can take off.

The example begins with a set of coincidences. Eswar, newly arrived from India, joined Mrs. Taylor's highly able fourth-grade class. He was shy and silent as the class gathered around him, exuberant, boisterous, and eager to make him feel at home. They assumed he spoke no English, so a two-way picture-drawing, labelling, pointing communication began. He drew and named, until they had the beginnings of a picture dictionary, including the words boy, girl, teacher, flower, house, and book. Excitedly, two students rushed to the library media center for word books. While the class took the scheduled standardized achievement tests later that morning, Eswar visited the library media center. After he relaxed a little, he spoke—in English with a clipped accent and style. He browsed and experimented with filmstrips, all the while expressing his pleasure. The class, delighted with their diversion, were disappointed when they found out that they did not have to teach him their language.

A few months later, the class read *Snow Treasure*, a novel included in their reading/language arts curriculum. They wanted to learn more about German. Several students who had lived overseas brought in German picture books. German language tapes were added. The library media specialist provided additional resources and ideas, and the Kinder-German project was born.

In the first visit to the center, the class was surveyed to see how many spoke or were familiar with another language. Korean, Spanish, Czech, Polish, French, Hebrew, and Hindi were the responses. The students were asked how many of these used the Roman alphabet, readable by most regardless of comprehension or pronunciation. What languages used a different alphabet? "Hebrew, Greek, Russian, Chinese, Korean, Japanese, and German (a little)" were the answers. The library media specialist then displayed and described language books and records from the 400s. Only two titles specifically included German: Lee Cooper's *Fun with German* and Richard Scarry's well-known *Best Word Book* (in three languages: French, German, and English) entitled *Mein Allerschönstes Wörterbuch*.

All the resources displayed were trade books. Some were in different languages: *Fun with Spanish* (also Italian and French); *The Chinese Language for Beginners*; *See and Say*; *At Home*; *In School*; *In the Park* (each in four languages); *Babar's Spanish Lessons* and *Babar's French Lessons*; *The Prancing*

Pony: Nursery Rhymes From Japan; Chinese Mother Goose Rhymes; Mother Goose in French (also Spanish). Some were easy books, well-known stories translated into French, Spanish, and German. Most interesting to the class was *Puh der Bär*. Some were foreign-language-to-English picture dictionaries; others were English picture dictionaries. The Count Your Way series introduces number words in 13 languages spoken around the world. *Moja Means One* and *Jambo Means Hello* teach children words in Swahili. *Alphabet Times Four* is an international ABC lesson in English, Spanish, French, and German.

The next day, the library media specialist visited the classroom where the materials were now displayed. She explained that the materials showed the gamut of projects for students to develop. The catalog of possibilities included: 1) *See and Say*—adding German to the languages in the Frasconi or Hautzig books; 2) *Babar's German Lessons*—to accompany Babar's other language lessons; 3) picture dictionaries—German to English and English to German; 4) a simple dictionary of foreign words; 5) a list of English words of foreign origin; 6) alphabets or scripts of other languages. Student projects could be in the format of learning centers, picture books, charts or posters, or audio tapes. Students made choices of content, product, art materials, and working groups. They were able to apply the background information to a complex task, with unique results. Michael added Czech to his German-English word book because he had always wanted to talk with his grandparents in their native language. Jenifer and Heather decorated a heart-shaped German valentine book for presentation to the library media center's language section.

On a subsequent visit to the classroom, the library media specialist read Marilyn Hirsch's *Tower of Babel* to open a discussion about "Would the world be a better place if we all spoke the same language?" Using the end papers *From Long Ago and Many Lands*, class calligraphers reproduced the saying "Under the Sky All Men Are Brothers" in 12 scripts. The next novel the class studied was *Landslide* by Veronique Day from which came a consideration of works in translation. Whose language are we enjoying—the author's or the translator's?

Painting Pictures with Words

Good writers are artists who paint with words. The sample lessons that follow develop this idea as they introduce gifted students to authors, genres, and the crafts of writing and illustrating books. Each day, the teacher begins with an equation: The first is a cliché, one picture equals a thousand words, posed as a question, "Does 1 P = 1000 W?" The debate concerning the efficacy of the visual over the verbal is ongoing.

From P →W

The formula is strategically displayed to start the session. Also posted are assorted thought-provoking pictures: larger mounted pictures from *New Yorker* and *Booklist* covers; smaller pictures cut out from cartoons, wordless books, and publishers' catalogs. Pictures should have enough ambiguity to evoke more than one interpretation. Students question the formula until someone figures it out. They write a brief composition to describe or explain a particular picture and read the essays aloud to compare and contrast their interpretations. Their assignment is to find other samples to share.

From W→P

In a switch of direction, the teacher reads selected fiction excerpts describing a character or setting. Students translate the descriptions into pictures without the benefit of seeing the original illustrations until after they have finished their illustrations. Basal excerpts and paperback versions often change the pictures from the original hardcover editions. These differences may be evaluated later. A stroll through the literary portrait gallery reveals many unmistakable friends.

> Miss Pippi Longstocking: "hair, the color of a carrot, in tight braids that stuck straight out. Freckled nose shaped like a small potato . . . atop a wide mouth with strong white teeth. Homemade dress, mostly blue, with little red pieces here and there. Long thin legs sporting a pair of mismatched stockings, one brown the other black, wearing a pair of black shoes twice as long as her feet" (Lindgren 1950).

> Mrs. Mae Tuck: "a great potato of a woman; of a round sensible face and calm brown eyes, gray-brown hair wound into a bun; wearing a rusty brown skirt with one enormous pocket worn over three petticoats, an old cotton jacket and a knitted shawl pinned with a tarnished metal brooch; thin age softened leather boots on her feet; and on her head, a blue straw hat with drooping brim" (Babbitt 1975).

This description inspired Julie to create a mixed media paper sculpture of Mrs. Tuck with detachable cape and hat, hinged arms and legs.

> The Hairy Man: "a-coming through the trees . . . ugly . . . eyes burning like coals . . . spit drooling all over his big, white, sharp teeth . . . swinging a sack . . . feet like a cow" (Bang 1976).

Alongside this portrait is Brian Pinckney's embodiment of the conjure man in his Alabama swamp setting. The next space on the wall is blank, to be filled by a portrait of Hairy Man from *Wiley and the Hairy Man*.

> Pickle Creature: "looked like a very large pickle attached to a sort of creature. But the pickle was really the tail. It looked like a pickle, but also a dinosaur, a big dog, a crocodile . . . nearly as big as Conrad" (Pinkwater 1979).

The people from "The Planet of Mars," who have much the same features as ours, but not in the same places, contains a surprise from Shel Silverstein.

In the landscape room are hung the settings from the planet Shine in *The Green Book*; the bat cave, underhung cliffs, and salt licks from *Old Yeller*; and the great storm that portends the arrival of *The Moonball*. Illustrator Ruth Brown paints Yorkshire to life in the animal stories of veterinarian James Herriot. Julie and Kelly reconstructed a tabletop village of Treegap and its environs from Natalie Babbitt's poetic description in *Tuck Everlasting*. Matt drafted the floor plan of M. Nortier's house that was destroyed in a *Landslide*. When a setting is worded more vaguely, like *The Bridge to Terabithia*, interpretations will vary more than when an author describes it in detail. Students can discuss how this factor might shape an illustrator's task. Do this, and *voila!* Some children discover the kinship between the elements of fiction: character, setting, and plot; and the types of painting: portraits, landscapes, and genre (scenes from everyday life). Some may even be able to present this insight as an analogy.

From W→W

In this transformation exercise set, the teacher reads excerpts that can be translated into other word patterns, prose, or poetry. Using the previous examples, students can write a cinquain or other poetic form describing the character or place. They can title each chapter in a novel without chapter titles, comparing the group's creations. Students can turn a descriptive passage or familiar fairy tale into conversation, dramatic dialogue, letter, or journal form. They can write limericks for science, math, or history concepts.

Exercises in visual and verbal literacy are preludes, jumping back and forth between figurative and literal language, between narration and exposition. After this practice in exploring language, the next step is to begin to weave with one's own language through a storytelling seminar or writers' workshop. These may be beyond the time and mandate for a library media specialist to conduct with a gifted group, but they can be extras worth planning with a teacher.

YARNSPINNING

Reading to Writing to Storytelling

When Writers First Learned to Read is the story of the way writers began their work. Eloquently told, their personal narratives provide children with role models for learning and self-knowledge. Unlike her novels, where her experiences appear in pieces, *A Girl from Yamhill* is Beverly Cleary's own story.

We now had a school library with a librarian, Miss Smith . . .
who also taught reading. She taught us how to use the library
and once made us line up alphabetically by our last names, as if

we were books on the shelves. After that, I found a place on the shelf where my book would be if I ever wrote a book, which I doubted" (Cleary 1988).

Some of the not-typical-for-the-times ideas introduced by Miss Smith were 1) allowing reading in the classroom, with standards—"must read good books, not cheap series" 2) unusual assignments—"pretend you live in George Washington's time and write a letter to someone describing an experience," and use your imagination; and 3) original homework—write an essay about a favorite book character. Miss Smith's recommendation was that "when Beverly grows up, she should write children's books." To this Beverly's mother added that Beverly needed a steady way of earning a living, so she became a librarian. Along the way from reader to writer, Cleary learned to avoid writing description, thus endearing her books to young readers.

Recesstory

Indoor recess was always a drag, for teachers and kids alike, until some fifth graders from the *Impressions,* Houghton Mifflin basal, top reading group had a great idea. As a spin-off after reading *The Great Gilly Hopkins* with the library media specialist, they advertised a drop-in story time after lunch. Just a few came to the first recesstory, but as the demand for lunchtime stories increased, different days were set aside for primaries and intermediates, and early and late lunchers. The library media specialist was the first to read aloud, gradually to be replaced by individual children who brought their own selections, chosen from best and best-selling books. The library media center was located in a heavily trafficked open area, and nonparticipating students were often spied on the fringe of the storytelling area. Like *Leo the Late Bloomer*'s parents, they pretended not to be watching yet they really were.

Readers Theatre

The Gobble-uns'll Get You, an adaptation of James Whitcomb Riley's story poem "Little Orphan Annie," is an appealing recitation for a second-grade voice chorus, as is *In a Dark, Dark, Dark Wood.* Other reprises to chant are culled from catch tales like John and Jane of "The Yellow Ribbon" and the Snook family from folklore anthologies like *Juba This and Juba That.* Selected poems from *Good Books, Good Times* or *Whiskers and Rhymes* or *Blackberry Ink* also make enjoyable chanting.

"High in the hills near Hexham" lived Hildilid, who hated the night, and how many were her attempts to thwart its coming! Cheli Durand Ryan's book, *Hildilid's Night*, is an example of how effective a picture storybook can be in the teaching of language to enrich curriculum, encourage performance, introduce children to several instructional media, and explore the relationship between fiction and drama. First and second graders savor the nuances of each verb as they delve into artistic interpretation, readers theatre, book making, and video production. In the lesson sequence, the library media specialist or teacher reads the story, after which the children retell the story in several ways. Narrators can retell the tale, as some of the group act out Hildilid's antics to the accompaniment of Orff instruments. Children can draw their interpretations of Hildilid as she *swept* and *scrubbed* and *scoured* and *whisked* and *sewed* and *wadded* and *pushed* and *crammed* and *ladled* and *simmered* and *sheared* and *ducked* and *singed* and *spanked* and *spat* and *dug a grave* and more—all to get rid of the night (Ryan 1986). If a videotape is made, the children can dub in the narration and music. The experience of seeing themselves and critiquing their own efforts is always valuable. Selected drawings can be bound into a class version of Hildilid's story then cataloged into the library media collection.

Storythinking

As part of her mastery teacher training workshops, Dr. Madeline Hunter asks teachers whether their words are think starters or think stoppers. Rather than directive words that tell the student, she suggests that teachers use indirective words that require active thinking from the student. Speaking and thinking skills come into play kinesthetically whenever children respond to literature with language: by chanting, by patterned speech and movement, and by choral reading. Children of any age or grade can start with a simple retelling of a familiar folktale, weaving in both narration and original dialogue. From personal and literary experiences, gather "Think-Abouts," "Used-to-Thinks," and "What-Ifs." There are *Stories*—and *More Stories to Solve.* Better endings may be written for favorite stories or senseless rhymes. Whatever the trigger, encourage children to be choosers, collectors, and tellers.

Improvisations

Telling stories is often less forbidding than play acting. To lead older students to Ruth Sawyer's classic *The Way of the Storyteller*, start with improvisations from story starters from a picture file full of "Creativity-Imagination-Paradoxical" items. Book publisher's catalogs are an inexpensive source of story-starters for collecting into a tell-a-tale notebook. Sometimes only a picture is put on a page or the title and one or two sentences from the blurb are included; othertimes the illustrator or the book itself are recognizable. The same picture evokes different responses: perhaps a short poem, an essay, or a humorous, fantastic, or realistic vignette. The different genres are identified as students compare and evaluate their interpretations. Students may practice sharing personal anecdotes as well. Those who move on to traditional storytelling gain experience in selecting appropriate stories or authors, synopsizing and adapting stories from narrative to dialogue for acting out, choosing props, and deciding between projected or live performance options. These activities offer an alternative to the "Do you have a book of plays?" approach to dramatic exercise.

Silent Languages and Hidden Languages

The signing of the hearing impaired enables them to communicate with each other and the hearing world just as the dots of Braille spell out stories for the sightless. Stories are told in the mime of *Shadowplay*. Fingers fly in *A Show of Hands* as they tell *Mother Goose in Sign* at the *Handtalk School*. Concerts by an elementary school signing chorus are emotional and aesthetic experiences. Historically *Indian Sign Language* enabled tribes who spoke different languages to speak with each other. Several trade books relate how the Navaho language became the basis of the unbreakable American codes during World War II.

Griots, Cochitis, and Speechmakers

The words, "I do not mean, I do not really mean . . ." and "This is my story. If it be sweet or not sweet, take some and let the rest come back to me" are beginnings and endings for African folk tales. Carrying on ancestral tradition, the African Griot travels from village to village, wearing a story-teller's hat with *A Story, A Story* to tell about any of the articles dangling from it. "That's not really how we got stories," said the young listener. "Why the hat?" asked another. "It's an ozone layer protecting the world," affirmed a third grader. Then the teacher's large brimmed straw hat was perched atop the round head of the globe to symbolize the world of stories.

The *Pueblo Storyteller* enveloped by *Children of Clay* emerged from the story tradition of southwest Indians. These Cochiti dolls, stylized storyteller and children figures, are a valued art form and a worthy project for art classes. Each year, third- to fifth-grade classes fired the kilns of Belmont Elementary with hundreds of dolls, some to decorate the media center as its symbol. Storytelling was such an important part of daily life among the "First Nations" children of the earth in the Canadian province of Saskatchewan, that the storyteller could only tell tales in the winter lest he entice people away from their tasks in the good weather seasons.

For some children, the silver tongue that enables its owner to speak well in formal contexts is a gift; for others, speechgiving is a formidable experience. But oral fluency is a necessary skill and is demonstrable. Early in their school careers, most students will speak on camera, run for school office, or present their oral reports. Fourth graders filled a ditto outline profile of Abraham Lincoln with the words of the Gettysburg Address from the encyclopedia. *"You Can Speak Up in Class,"* they reassured each other. The Address had to be delivered, but by whom? They resolved the argument of who would be Lincoln—"Not a girl"—by having each member deliver the speech in turn. They went on to Martin Luther King's "I Have a Dream," then to Chief Seattle's message, *Brother Eagle; Sister Sky.* The Gettysburg Address and Martin Luther King's speeches are familiar, but more oratory to read and originals to hear are housed with the 800s.

Writers' Workshops

The importance of the art of conversation and the craft of writing shows in disparate sources. Robert Frost asserted that good writing must be as clear as a voice. Technical writers increasingly seek brevity and clarity in their burgeoning genre. Whole language, the prevailing philosophy for teaching reading for the past decade, returned writing to the curriculum. Writers' workshops, a major component of whole language, provide a differentiated method for encouraging children to write. Underlying all efforts to teach language is the idea that clear writing follows clear thinking.

As a beginning, share with students what writers say about themselves, especially about how and why they write. In *Books Are by People*, Lee Bennett Hopkins presents interviews with children's authors and illustrators. Publishers' catalogs and articles in children's magazines are also sources from which to collect similar information about the creative process of writing.

Style in both narrative and expository writing is another avenue to explore. *The First Book of Creative Writing* is a compact introduction to the kinds of writing most required for school assignments—the essay or composition, the book report, and short stories; the differences in style and expression; grammar; and vocabulary. *The Young Writer's Handbook* is subtitled a practical guide for the beginner who is serious about writing. Eve Merriam's poem, "What Is a Cliche?" calls attention to the overuse of tired words. Beverly Cleary's *Dear Mr. Henshaw* exemplifies epistolary style in fiction, while Laura Ingalls Wilder's *West from Home* are the author's real letters. Has the advent of e-mail made "Dear Sir," *Sincerely Yours,* and other conventions of friendly or business letter writing unnecessary? Point of view in autobiography, whether in real or fictive journals like the "Dear America" Diary Series, or in first person narratives, is an acceptable way to show writer's bias. By analyzing categories of writing and distinguishing between literary forms, children begin to learn *How to Write a Story* "in their own words." Writers' Workshops afford insights into books, authors, choice and evaluation, and production, to say nothing of the publishing possibilities for children's writings.

Whether the technique is wordsmithing or yarnspinning,

"Literature is a transmission of power. Text books and treatises, dictionaries and encyclopedias, manuals and books of instruction—they are communications; but literature is a power line, and the motor, mark you, is the reader" (Curtis 1957).

REFERENCES

Babbitt, Natalie. 1975. *Tuck Everlasting*. New York: Farrar, Straus & Giroux.

Bang, Mollie, adapter. 1976. *Wiley and the Hairy Man*. Brian Pinckney, illus. New York: Macmillan.

Cleary, Beverly. 1988. *A Girl from Yamhill.* New York: Morrow.

Montgomery County Public Schools. n.d. *MCPS Resource Handbook for Elementary Identification Procedures for Gifted and Talented.* Rockville, MD: MCPS.

Pinkwater, Daniel. 1979. *Pickle Creature.* New York: Four Winds Press.

Ryan, Cheli Durand. 1986. *Hildilid's Night.* New York: Macmillan.

Sierra, Judy, reteller. 1996. *Wiley and the Hairy Man.* Lodestar/Dutton.

Thompson, Michael Clay. 1994. *Inspecting Our Own Ideas: A Grammar Self-Study Program for High Ability Students.* The Center for Gifted Education, College of William and Mary.

BIBLIOGRAPHY

The suggested resources for language instruction and extension are arranged alphabetically by title in two sections, those for teachers and those for young readers, with enough titles listed to offer alternatives for out-of-print or unavailable titles.

For Teachers

The American Reader: Words That Moved a Nation. Diane Ravitch. New York: HarperCollins, 1990.

A Book of Puzzlements: Play and Invention with Language. Herbert Kohl. New York: Schocken Books, 1981.

Chalk in Hand: The Draw and Tell Book. Phyllis Pflomm. Metuchen, NJ: Scarecrow, 1986.

Clear and Lively Writing: Language Games and Activities for Everyone. Priscilla Vail. New York: Walker, 1981.

The Concise Dictionary of 26 Languages in Simultaneous Translation. Peter Bergman, comp. New York: New American Library, 1968.

From Plays into Reading: Plays to Read in the Classroom. Gerald C. Glass. Boston: Allyn & Bacon, 1939.

Harper's English Grammar: A Complete Guide to Modern English Usage. John P. Opdyke. New York: Harper and Row, 1966.

The Language Book. Franklin Folsom. New York: Grosset & Dunlap, 1963.

The Magic Lens: A Spiral Tour Through the Human Ideas of Grammar. Michael Thompson. Unionville, NY: Trillium, 1991.

The Oxford Guide to Word Games. T. Augarde. London: Oxford University Press, 1984.

The Penguin Dictionary of Confusibles. Adrian Room. New York: Penguin Books, 1979.

Playing with Words. Joseph T. Shipley. Englewood Cliffs, NJ: Prentice-Hall, 1960.

The Way of the Storyteller. Ruth Sawyer. New York: Viking, 1962.

When Writers First Learned to Read. Ed Gilbar, ed. New York: Godine, 1989.

Word Wizardry: An Enchantment of Word Games, Puzzles, and Activities. Linda Shevitz. Chicago: Goodyear, 1982.

You Be the Author! Beginning Writers: Twenty Exciting Mini Books Kids Love to Write and Read. Jill Hauser. Columbus, OH: Good Apple, 1994.

For Young Readers

Books to use for language exploration with Young Readers. Not all of these titles are cited in text, nor are all titles used in activities listed here.

A to Zen: A Book of Japanese Culture. Ruth Wills. New York: Simon & Schuster Children's, 1992.

Add It, Dip It, Fix It: A Book of Verbs. R. M. Schneider. Boston: Houghton Mifflin, 1996.

Alphabet Times Four: An International ABC. Ruth Brown. New York: Dutton, 1991.

The Amazing Pop-Up Grammar Book. Jennie Maizels and Kate Petty. New York: Dutton Children's Books, 1996.

Andy That's My Name. Tomie dePaola. New York: Simon & Schuster, 1991.

Arctic Memories. Normee Ekoomiak. New York: Henry Holt, 1988.

At Home: A Visit in Four Languages. Esther Hautzig. New York: Macmillan, 1968.

Babar's French and English Word Book. Laurent DeBrunhoff. New York: Random Books for Young Readers, 1994.

Babar's French Lessons. Laurent DeBrunhoff. New York: Random House, 1963.

Babar's Spanish Lessons. Laurent DeBrunhoff. New York: Random House, 1963.

Behind the Mask: A Book About Prepositions. Ruth Heller. New York: Grosset & Dunlap, 1996.

Blackberry Ink. Eve Merriam. New York: Morrow, 1985.

Books Are by People. Lee Bennett Hopkins. New York: Citation Press, 1969.

Brother Eagle; Sister Sky, adapted from Chief Seattle. New York: Dial, 1991.

Cache of Jewels and Other Collective Nouns. Ruth Heller. New York: Grosset & Dunlap, 1989.

The Cat's Elbow and Other Secret Languages. Alvin Schwartz. New York: Farrar, Straus & Giroux, 1981.

Children of Clay. Rina Swentzell. New York: Lerner, 1992.

A Children's Almanac of Words at Play. Willard Espy. New York: Crown, 1983.

The Chinese Language for Beginners. Lee Cooper. Rutland, VT: Charles E. Tuttle, 1971.

Chinese Mother Goose Rhymes. Robert Wyndham, ed. and comp. New York: Sandcastle/Putnam, 1989.

Count Your Way Through. . . . Series. Minneapolis, MN: Carolrhoda Books, 1989.

Cross Country Cat. Mary Calhoun. New York: Morrow, 1979.

Dear America Diary Series. New York: Scholastic, n.d.

Dear Mr. Henshaw. Beverly Cleary. New York: William Morrow, 1983.

The First Book of Creative Writing. Julia C. Mahon. New York: Franklin Watts, 1968.

The First Book of Words. Sam Epstein and Beryl Epstein. New York: Franklin Watts, 1954.

Fooling Around with Words. Ruthven Tremain. New York: Greenwillow Books, 1976.

From Abenaki to Zulu: A Dictionary of Native American Tribes. Evelyn Wolfson. New York: Walker, 1988.

From Long Ago and Many Lands. Sophia Fahs. Boston: Beacon Press. 1948.

Fun with French; Fun with German; Fun with Italian; Fun with Spanish. Lee Cooper. Boston: Little, Brown, n.d.

Good Books, Good Times. Lee Bennett Hopkins, ed. New York: Harper & Row, 1990.

Grammar Can Be Fun. Munro Leaf. Philadelphia: J. B. Lippincott, 1934.

The Great Gilly Hopkins. Katherine Paterson. New York: Thomas Y. Crowell, 1978.

The Green Book. Jill Paton Walsh. New York: Farrar, Straus & Giroux, 1982.

Handtalk School. Mary Beth Miller and George Ancona. New York: Simon & Schuster, 1991.

How to Write a Story. Bentz Plagemann. New York: Lothrop, Lee & Shepard, 1971.

"I Can't," Said the Ant: A Second Book of Nonsense. Polly Cameron. New York: Coward, McCann & Geoghegan, 1961.

If You Were a Writer. Joan Nixon. New York: Simon & Schuster, 1988.

In a Dark, Dark Room and Other Scary Stories. Alvin Schwartz. New York: HarperCollins, 1984.

In the Park: An Excursion in Four Languages. Esther Hautzig. New York: Macmillan, 1968.

In School: Learning in Four Languages. Esther Hautzig. New York: Macmillan, 1969.

In Your Own Words: A Beginner's Guide to Writing. Sylvia Cassedy. New York: Thomas Y. Crowell, 1990.

Indian Sign Language. Robert Hofsinde. New York: Morrow, 1956.

It Does Not Always Have to Rhyme. Eve Merriam. New York: Atheneum, 1964.

Jambo Means Hello: Swahili Alphabet Book. Muriel L. Feelings. New York: Dial, 1974.

The Jolly Postman and Other People's Letters. Janet Ahlberg and Allen Ahlberg. Boston: Little, Brown, n.d.

Juba This and Juba That. 2d ed. Virginia Tasjian. New York: Little, Brown, 1995.

Kites Sail High. Ruth Heller. New York: Grosset & Dunlap, 1958.

Let's Find Out About Names. Valerie Pitt. New York: Franklin Watts, 1971.

Magic School Bus at the Waterworks. Joanna Cole. New York: Scholastic, 1986.

Many Luscious Lollipops: A Book About Adjectives. Ruth Heller. New York: Scholastic, n.d.

Mein Allerschönstes Wörterbuch. Richard Scarry. Stuttgart and Zurich: Delphin Verlag, 1971 (ABC, 1995).

Merry Go Round: A Book About Nouns. Ruth Heller. New York: Grosset & Dunlap, 1990.

Moja Means One: Swahili Counting Book. Muriel Feelings. New York: Dial 1971.

More Stories to Solve: Fifteen Folk Tales from Around the World. George Shannon. New York: Greenwillow Books, 1991.

Mother Goose in French. Hugh Latham, trans. New York: Thomas Y. Crowell, 1964.

Mother Goose in Hieroglyphics. Boston: Houghton Mifflin, 1962.

Mother Goose in Sign. S. Harold Collins. Eugene, OR: Garlic Press, 1992.

Mother Goose in Spanish. Alistair Reid and Anthony Kerrigan, trans. New York: Thomas Y. Crowell, 1964.

Names, First, Last, Middle and Nick: All About Names. Barbara S. Hazen. Englewood Cliffs, NJ: Prentice-Hall, 1979.

The Nonsense Book of Riddles, Rhymes, Tongue Twisters, Puzzles, and Jokes from American Folklore. Duncan Emrich, comp. New York: Four Winds Press, 1970.

On Your Marks: A Package of Punctuation. Richard Armour. New York: McGraw-Hill, 1969.

101 Words and How They Began. Arthur Steckler. New York: Doubleday, 1979.

"The Planet of Mars" from *Where the Sidewalk Ends.* Shel Silverstein. New York: Harper & Row, 1974.

The Prancing Pony: Nursery Rhymes from Japan. Charlotte B. Deforest. New York: E. P. Dutton, 1968.

Pueblo Storyteller. Diane Hoyt Goldsmith. New York: Holiday House, 1991.

Puh der Bär. E. L. Schiffer, trans. New York: E. P. Dutton, 1968.

A Scale Full of Fishes and Other Turnabouts. Naomi Bossom. New York: Greenwillow Books, 1979.

See and Say: A Picture Book in Four Languages. Antonio Frasconi. New York: Harcourt Brace Jovanovich, 1975.

Shadowplay. George Mendoza. New York: Holt, Rinehart & Winston, 1974.

A Show of Hands. Mary Beth Sullivan and Linda Bourke. New York: J. B. Lippincott, 1980.

Simple Pictures Are Best. Nancy Willard. New York: Harcourt Brace Jovanovich, 1977.

Sincerely Yours: How to Write Great Letters. Elizabeth James and Carol Barkin. New York: Clarion Books, 1993.

A Story, A Story. African tale retold by Gail E. Haley. Boston: Atheneum, 1970.

Take Sky: More Rhymes of the Always Is and Never Was. David McCord. Boston: Little, Brown, 1962.

Teapot Switcheroo and Other Silly Word Games. Ruthven Tremain. New York: Greenwillow Books, 1979.

There Is No Rhyme for Silver. Eve Merriam. New York: Atheneum, 1962.

Tomfoolery. Alvin Schwartz, comp. New York: HarperCollins, 1994.

Tower of Babel. Adapted and Illustrated by Marilyn Hirsch. New York: Holiday House, 1981.

A Twister of Twists, A Tangler of Tongues. Alvin Schwartz, comp. Philadelphia: J. B. Lippincott, 1972.

Up Up and Away: A Book About Adverbs. Ruth Heller. New York: Grosset & Dunlop, 1991.

West from Home: Laura Ingalls Wilder, San Francisco, 1915. Laura Ingalls Wilder. Edited by Roger L. McBride. New York: Harper & Row, 1974.

The Whatamacallit Book. Bernice Cohn Hunt. New York: G. P. Putnam, 1976.

The Whim Wham Book. Duncan Emrich, comp. New York: Four Winds Press, 1975.

Whiskers and Rhymes. Arnold Lobel. New York: Greenwillow Books, 1985.

Why Do You Speak As You Do? A Guide to World Languages. Kay Cooper. New York: Walker, 1992.

Witcracks: Jokes and Jests from American Folklore. Alvin Schwartz, comp. Philadelphia: J. B. Lippincott, 1973.

The Wonderful Word Book: *Learn New Words and Love It*. Donald Wulffson. Middletown, CT: Xerox, 1978.

The Word Detectives. Heather Amory and Colin King. Usborne, n.d.

Words: A Book About the Origins of Everyday Words and Phrases. Jane Sarnoff and Reynolds Ruffin. New York: Charles Scribner's Sons, 1982.

Words, Words, Words. Mary O'Neill. New York: Doubleday, 1966.

You Can Speak Up in Class. Sara Gilbert. New York: Morrow Junior Books, 1991.

The Young Writer's Handbook: A Practical Guide for the Beginner Who Is Serious About Writing. Susan Tchudi and Stephen Tchudi. New York: Charles Scribner's Sons, 1984.

Seven

Easy Does It!

Their secret is out! For years, elementary library media specialists shared a wonderful secret with children. They have wanted to shout *it* to curriculum planners and educational researchers, as well as to teachers and parents of gifted children. Until recently, the philosophical climate was not right, but now *it* is in educational vogue!

What is the secret? *It* is a strategy for teaching thinking that is visual, aesthetic, literary, varied, and humorous. *It* is a program not susceptible to loss of memory brought on by power failure. *It* will never need debugging nor accuse the user of syntax error. *It* is a concise, poetic way of making the complex seem disarmingly simple. Its practitioners include authors and artists of prominence and genius. *It* affirms Bruner's spiral curriculum and, like the peddler in *Caps for Sale*, wears De Bono's many colored hats. Voltaire's words from his *Dictionnaire Philosophique* written in 1764 apply to *it*.

What is an idea? It is a picture painted in my brain. Are, therefore, all your thoughts pictures? Truly: because the most abstract ideas are just the sequences of all the objects I have seen. I have ideas only because I have pictures in my head (Voltaire 1956).

Fifth graders in a gifted writers workshop spent a long time deciphering the following definition, also applicable to *it*:

An information retrieval system, based on a 26 element matrix, which stores information in geometric array on thin membranes. Both sides of the membrane are used. The membranes are configured into a serially arranged design with either random or ordered digital access. The system is called ********* [BOOK] (Shapiro 1982)

87

THE EASY COLLECTION

BOOK is a low-cost alternative to the computer! The secret is that, despite its misnomer, the E for Easy is a powerful teaching tool with highly able learners. In this category, called easy, are picture story and information books of subtlety, outstanding language, artistic distinction, and sophisticated content. Included also are the "I Can Read" books, many of which are delightful and evocative, thanks to the late Dr. Seuss, whose *Cat in the Hat* led the way. Easy-reading nonfiction books are classified and shelved by Dewey decimal number in subject sequence.

Picture books are equally effective as a teaching strategy with gifted children in groupings of kindergarten through second, third/fourth, or fifth/sixth grades. What differs is the emphasis, the context, and the level at which the teacher expects the group to respond. In the early grades, where it is important to nurture giftedness, the easy books are a foundation upon which to build literary and subject area concepts. Easy-to-enjoy and easy-to-read books introduce cultural literacy at a primary level. These same easy books are difficult-to-emulate examples of higher-order thinking for intermediates. At each level, the books concretely introduce:

- story grammar: the elements of character, setting, plot and theme;

- literary forms or genres: fiction—realistic, humorous, science, mystery, adventure, fantasy; traditional literature—folk, fable, fairy tale; poetry and drama; anthologies and collections; biography; and literary devices: metaphor, et al;

- visual literacy: aesthetic awareness as a component of intellect and the nonverbal as conveyor of content;

- a more personal context for thinking than workbook exercises;

- library media information terms and skills: alphabetizing, contents, chapters, indices, sequels, and parts of a book;

- narrative and expository materials: fiction and FACTion;

- evaluative issues, such as personal reading tastes, censorship, stereotyping; and

- primary sources, including works in translation.

Before the easy collection can be used to reinforce these instructional goals with upper-grade students, the teacher or library media specialist must work with students to change the disdain toward picture books that many bright children and their parents profess. With protestations of "I read that book when I was a baby," children dismiss the picture storybook with a shrug and a sneer. Unfortunately, eager early readers have been encouraged to skip this part of a collection in favor of harder books. The omission is regrettable because the picture storybook is a concise way of presenting complex ideas in manageable bites within limited time frames. It is a *shorthand* system for intellectual exploration and expansion. What more enjoyable technique can a teacher employ to show the paths imagination can take; offer a rich sampling of the field of knowledge; develop criteria for choosing, discussing, and evaluating ideas and issues; or model and practice visual and verbal communication skills? With upper-grade students, the focus can widen to include a study of the creative process, the art of storytelling, and the picture book as a jumping-off point for thinking and verifying. Filmmakers in 1996 realized the potential of this book medium, translating *Jumanji* and *The Bravest Dog Ever, The True Story of Balto,* into feature films. Arthur the aardvark and his family have joined Ms. Frizzle and her class as stars of popular television series.

Authors

The list of authors and illustrators of narrative and expository picture books who are masters of the genre is long and varied:

Aliki, Jose Aruego, Byrd Baylor, Raymond Briggs, Eric Carle, Demi, Tomie dePaola, Gail Gibbons, Marilyn Hirsch, Tana Hoban, Stephen Kellogg, Robert Kraus, Anita and Arnold Lobel, James and Edward Marshall, Ann and Harlan Rockwell, Alice and Martin Provensen, Peter Spier, James Stevenson, and Chris Van Allsburg.

Venerable authors, such as Dr. Seuss, Margaret Wise Brown, Robert McCloskey, Maurice Sendak, and Charlotte Zolotow, are names that challenge first-grade shelf readers to alphabetize on the easy shelves. Ask them to name and count the holdings by each author. Which of their favorite authors is not on the list? As new writers continue to enter the exploding field of books for young children, they, too, will find a place on the easy shelves.

Narration Teaches

Walking through a 1990s megabookstore or a library sets a teacher's lesson planning juices to flowing. Indeed, publishers and the periodical *Book Links* make the connections for them. The examples that follow are the author's personal meanderings in the world of picture books turned into successful lessons. The selections do not separate into neat packages, each illustrating an objective or skill. Interrelating the parts better demonstrates the flexibility of the easy book idiom.

The first grade teacher asked the library media specialist to restate calendar concepts. *Little Sister and the Month Brothers,* Beatrice De Regniers' version of a Slavic folk tale, portraying the months as 12 seasonally dressed brothers, was chosen for the lesson. When the magic staff passed from Brother January to Brother February to Brother March, with each passing changing the season, Patrick blurted out indignantly, "That's not the way it really happens!" His comment triggered a discussion worthy of a high school essay question: How does the story's folkloric reason for the seasons conflict with the scientific explanation, or compare and contrast the science and mythology of the changing seasons? Other re-tellings of this "pourquoi" genre tale retain the Russian motif, but story style and illustrations are different.

"Point of view" is a difficult-to-explain element of the novelist's craft. When does the young listener to *Two Hundred Rabbits* realize the identity of the narrator? *Uncle Elephant* is another first person narrative. Its theme of loss and return, the story within a story, the gentle parody and humor, and the bittersweet ending are skillfully woven into this "I Can Read" first person chapter story.

Dream Wolf, originally titled *The Friendly Wolf,* was used in a human relations exercise to combat stereotyped thinking among first and second graders. Besides its value as a striking depiction of Plains Indian tribal life and an example of a Native American legend, the story was one of the few in which a wolf is a sympathetic character. In recent years, the wolf's real-life image has become more positive. The classes had previously met *Doctor DeSoto,* where a fox is the would-be villain. To the question, "What other stories have a fox as a main character?" many first and second graders named *The Three Pigs* and *Little Red Riding Hood.* When asked why they thought this identification of the fox and the wolf occurred, the gist of the answers was that both animals had bushy tails, long faces, and a bad image, so the distinction was blurred. Does their response indicate something about stereotyping? When asked why stories were being used for sensitivity training, the answer was, "So we'll learn to be kind." On another occasion, the same class wanted to know why *The Village of Round and Square Houses* separated the boys and the girls.

The Mystery of Sara Beth by Polly Putnam tells an original story with clues given logically as the plot unfolds. Hints along the way help the reader hypothesize about the solution. Audiences of first and second graders do not solve the mystery completely until the story ends. The revelation of an impoverished family's attempt to cope is one that evokes sympathetic discussion. The children rate the book highly as Dennis commented, "Probably because a librarian wrote it, and she should know what children like." Poverty, homelessness, hunger, and riots are heavy themes for a picture storybook, yet Eve Bunting and other gifted writers show daily life in *Yard Sale, Shelter Folks,* and *Smoky Night.* They write about a father and daughter living in an airport, a child helping in a soup kitchen, a boy remembering his grandfather at the Vietnam Wall, or *Rose Blanche* observing people behind barbed wire outside her German town. In the genre of the realistic picture book, the skill of the author and illustrator make the difference between an artistic or didactic portrayal of a societal problem.

The *Ernest and Celestine* books by Gabrielle Vincent are imports from Belgium, translated from French. Mouse and Bear, a delightful pair, enjoy gentle adventures in a European countryside setting. The four stories in the series afford an introduction to the concept of stories in translation with settings in foreign places. Babar began in French, Pippi was Swedish, and Tikki Tiki Tembo was Chinese.

Whole class story times that include several different genres in easy book format become occasions for thinking. Similar opportunities exist for making abstract concepts more tangible, hence more understandable, to younger children. Thinking comes easily!

The passage of time is an abstraction developmentally beyond the ken of primary age children. Yet, some picture storybooks that express the years between generations so "image-it-ively" that they do communicate some sense of time. *The Sky Was Blue* moves back in time from a contemporary child asking questions of her mother to her mother asking questions of her mother to her mother asking questions of her mother, depicting changes in style of life between four generations, while highlighting those things that remain constant. *Miss Rumphius* by Barbara Cooney is a memoir of a quiet heroine's life, spanning three generations, as she brings her love for learning and life into the lives of people in each period. Cooney combines beautiful settings, a universal theme, and a vivid character. Other picture book illustrators re-create a particular historical period with equal appeal. Neighborhood development encroached upon *The Little House,* Virginia Burton's classic. "That's just like Olney," gasped the first graders who watched daily as the bulldozers changed their village. Younger readers still may not fully comprehend times past, but illustrations do much to clarify for them differences between times and places of long ago and the recent past.

Dakota Dugout describes pioneer life in a sod hut similar to that inhabited by Laura Ingalls's family. *Fish Fry* and *When I Was Young in the Mountains* are two vignettes of life in early twentieth century regional America; one is set in east Texas, the other in the Appalachian Mountains of West Virginia. In her easily read autobiography, *Best Wishes,* Cynthia Rylant illustrates with photographs how her life was written into her books: the real *Henry and Mudge, The Relatives Came,* and her grandmother's house. She tells how libraries and book stores were unavailable, so she read mostly comic books. She goes on to describe her daily routine as a writer. *My Great-Aunt Arizona* grew up to teach in the same region. The pictures from *Long Ago* show authentic details of life in colonial times, even though the characters that are framed on each sampler page are small animals. Robert McCloskey's classics set in Maine are contemporary realistic fiction. So are Lucille Clifton's, Vera B. Williams's, and Ezra Keats's stories of urban life. What contrasts they afford!

Robert Kraus chose more exotic locales for his illustrators, Jose Aruego and Ariane Dewey, to bring to life. In *Leo the Late Bloomer,* Leo takes his time at blooming late in the jungle; in *Milton the Early Riser,* Milton arises early each day in high mountain panda country; while in *Herman the Helper,* Herman lends his helping tentacles to friends of the deep. Then, in *Three Friends,* they all meet to trade adventures in the three settings.

Anno's Journey through northern Europe, Italy, Britain, and the United States do more than paint authentic settings. They are optical tricks called *trompe l'oeils.* John Goodall pictures life in Edwardian England and, in half-pages, village and castle life. Aliki celebrates *A Medieval Feast* as painstakingly as she details *Mummies Made in Egypt.* For upper graders, there is many a "research" assignment in these and similar books! Peter Spier chronicles

London Bridge's falling down with the same ink wash detail he uses to transport the reader to market or out with the fox on a chilly night or down the Dutch canal with Hendrika, the floating cow. Marilyn Hirsch is fanciful with her facts as *Hannibal and His Thirty Seven Elephants,* all wearing giant earmuffs to fend off the cold, cross the Alps to get to Rome in 318 BC. This is not far from fact as the National Museum in Rome displays an engraving of Persian soldiers on elephants delivering supplies. Kandi was *America's First Elephant*, brought from Bengal "in perfect health. The first ever seen in America, a very great curiosity." The account of her tour of the United States was reported in the *New York Argus* on April 18, 1796. In Philadelphia, she and George Washington met. Historical fact introduced as historical fiction is a teaching strategy that works.

Less dependent on spectacular artwork are the "I Can Read History" books. They, too, are examples of their authors' skill at capturing events from the past in simple language without losing the relevance of the events to the times. *The Drinking Gourd, Long Way to a New Land*, and *Wagon Wheels* each tell a story of one family's journey through a moment in history between 1858 and 1878. Peter Spier flies *The Star-Spangled Banner* during the bombardment of Fort McHenry. Barbara Mitchell's *Cornstalks and Cannonballs* tells about a little-known naval operation off the shores of Lewes, Delaware. *Abigail's Drum* saved the town of Scituate from the British. *Washington City Is Burning* offers an eyewitness account of the burning of the White House by the British, narrated by Virginia of Madison, a young slave to President Madison's wife, Miss Dolley. Four kinds of writing, four different perspectives, at three different levels, with one common thread: All are about the War of 1812. Any of these books can inspire a lifelong love of historical fiction as a genre or may pique curiosity about one particular period or event. Even in the easy format, the past reaches out to the reader. After reading a selection of easy books set in different time periods, fourth graders defined the years for each story, lining themselves up chronologically to create a relevant time line of events in American history or world history.

The drawings for *The Bell Ringer and the Pirate* illustrate daily life in the California Mission of San Juan Capistrano. The book is based on an incident in 1818 when the Indians and padres of the compound were threatened by invading pirates. The story may lead to more books about a sure-fire topic—*pirates.*

In the realm of fantasy, it is a short trip into the nebulous world between reality and illusion masterfully drawn by two stylists as different as Mitsumaso Anno and Chris Van Allsburg. From *Jumanji,* the game played on a life-sized board, it is easy to imagine *The Shrinking of Treehorn* to fit on a small game board. These stories imply a lot about adults in the lives of children. Take a few steps ahead to the modern-day fables of Treehorn's and Pulcifer's creator, Florence Parry Heide, or to the thirtieth anniversary edition of *Frederick's Fables*, then go back to Jack Kent's interpretations of Aesop's fables. *Andy and the Lion* tells the same Aesop story in modern dress as Grabianski's *Androcles.* Move on to Arnold Lobel's original *Fables*. From there, it is only a few steps to a comparison of Lobel's dual role as author/illustrator with his author-only role in books lavishly illustrated by his wife Anita. From the Lobels, one can go next to the work of another award-winning husband-wife team, Alice and Martin Provensen, and their Newbery illustrations in *A Visit to William Blake's Inn* and their Caldecott collaboration, *The Glorious Flight*.

Grandparents loom large in most children's lives and in children's books as well. Grandfathers created by James Stevenson and James Flora are great tellers of tall tales. Flora's grandfather character appears in *Grandpa's Ghost Stories* and *Grandpa's Farm*. Stevenson's character loves to regale his grandchildren Louie and Mary Ann with stories about *That Terrible Halloween Night*, or *What's Under My Bed?* especially when they tell him *We Can't Sleep*. First and second graders appreciate the flashback technique with its change to first person narration and laugh at the anachronism of Grandpa as a mustached little boy.

Grandmothers rate too. Some are unconventional and live on islands, as in *My Island Grandmother,* or fly, like *Abuela*. Some are the traditional Nonas and Nanas, or Bubbes with babushkas. Some are youthful and hip as in *The Grandma Mix-Up*, while the grandmothers of Lucille Clifton and Vera B. Williams are the family pillars. Grandparents appear as characters in other picture storybooks, many bittersweet or poignant, concerned with themes of aging, illness, death, and special intergenerational relationships. Carla Stevens tells one such tale about *Anna, Grandpa, and the Big Storm* that was the New York blizzard of 1888.

It is an easy trip from tall-tale-telling grandfathers and modern grandmothers to examples of humorous writing, such as parody, slapstick, irony, and satire. The characters in these stories may be real children, like Judith Viorst's three sons, Alexander, Anthony, and Nicholas, or they may be animals talking and behaving like people, as in the clever writing of James Marshall, either alone or in collaboration with Edward Marshall or Harry Allard. Young listeners respond to the loving insight with which these authors capture human foibles, differentiating between the slapstick of *The Stupids Have a Ball* and the gentle humor of *Fox in Love, Troll Country,* or *Three by the Sea*. "Boy, those teachers and principals sure have funny names" is the reaction to such literary educators as Mr. Paige, Miss Toggle, Mr. Stickler, Mr. Spurgle. "Why are the Cut-Ups always boys?" and "Why do the adults not listen to the kids?" are some astute Think Trixes asked by the first graders whose teacher went to Higher Order Thinking School.

The easy shelves are also the home of those picture books that are two stories high. *Rain Makes Applesauce* and *Thirteen* provide patterns for choral speaking and creative writing. Other books, such as *Graham Oakley's Magical Changes*, *Zoo City*, and *Look Again* have unique page patterns and perspectives.

Easy Exposition

Narration, alone, does not exhaust the easy medium. Each year new examples of simple yet ingenious expository writing are published. Children can spend a vicarious *Three Days on a River in a Red Canoe* by opening the marbleized cover of a standard composition book. Vera B. Williams has noted and sketched in journal form a first person fantasy adventure manual for a camping trip. She also sent postcards on *Stringbean's Trip to the Shining Sea.* Sue Alexander has assembled *Witch, Goblin, and Ghost's Book of Things to Do* for her young readers. Another *Little Witch's Book of Yoga* enables readers *To Be a Frog, a Bird, a Tree. Humbug Witch* uses codes to create a *Humbug Potion.* Students learn about rebuses, mystery games, putting together a play, magic tricks, and secret code writing, all activities cited in curriculum guides as higher order thinking. Has anyone ever explained quicksand more definitively than Jungle Boy and Jungle Girl in Tomie dePaola's *The Quicksand Book*? Or about clouds, popcorn, or the manufacture of cloaks in his other books? Compare Charlie's cloak-making cottage industry in *Charlie Needs a Cloak* with Pelle's in *Pelle's New Suit* or the weaving of *Goat in the Rug*. Cat lovers get a complete course in the care and enjoyment of felines when *The Kids' Cat Book* is combined with the poems in *My Cat Has Eyes of Sapphire Blue* and the wordless *Cat's Eyes;* the unit culminating in *The Birth of Sunset's Kittens.* These books will be lost to an audience most capable of appreciating their artistry unless a teacher sets the stage for their use. From Charlie to sheep cloning—that would be an interesting trip!

The versatility of dePaola, Aruego, and Kent take the young inquirer from the easy narrative to the 500 shelves. *Bill and Pete* are companions in adventures along the Nile. The crocodile and plover have a mutually dependent and profitable relationship. Some children may also recognize that a crocodile and plover were also friends of *Leo the Late Bloomer*. These unusual friendships are, of course, symbiotic. Jose Aruego defines the same term *Symbiosis* with equal graphic originality, but in more scientific language. *Strange Partners* subdivides the symbiotic process into commensalism, mutualism, and parasitism. Analysis of the root words, *sym, bio,* and *sis,* can carry a group into a different area for discussion and development. Aruego and Dewey use the game, *We Hide, You Seek* to give humorous but accurate representation to the biological concepts of adaptation, animal habitation, and camouflage. The end papers themselves are a unit on East Africa, sampling habitats in bush, desert, swamp, plains, river, and forest life. Add a field trip to the zoo to complete the experience! Other animals live in woods and fields, yards and gardens, ponds and streams, and along the seashore. Some animals from these habitats make good pets. *The Seven Sleepers* inform children about animal groups and *Where They Go in Winter* when animals hibernate and migrate.

The Caterpillar and the Polliwog is a reference point for a scientific discussion of metamorphosis. The story also allows for the treatment of such heavy themes as the quest for the meaning of life or one's appropriate feelings of self-worth versus pride. A natural time for this story is in the early fall, when children can have the real scientific experience of searching for milkweed pods, collecting larvae, then nurturing, observing, and recording as a caterpillar spins its chrysalis and emerges to wend its autumn way to Mexico. Or perhaps the time for the story is in the spring, when eggs transform from polliwogs to frogs.

Series

Series books for the youngest set introduce geography, science, family remembrances, language, and biography. They show how to "Count Your Way" in many languages, with "Passports To" countries around the world. To "Take a Trip" often requires a sense of humor with books of jokes of all kinds that "Make Me Laugh." Joan Hanson's word books illustrate the nuances of syntax. *Winter Days in the Big Woods*, *The Dance at Grandpa's*, *County Fair*, and *Going to Town* are title of books about "My First Little House," episodes in Laura Ingalls Wilder's life adapted for beginning readers. Primary grade students read about the daily life of Native Americans in the Tundra Books on dwellings: *Mounds of Earth and Shell, Houses of Bark*; *of Hide and Earth*; *of Wood*; *of Adobe*; *of Snow, Skin and Bones*. The National Geographic Society has Books for World Explorers. Ecology and nature are the subjects of Owl/Firefly "Question and Answer" books and Schoolhouse Press's "Endangered Species of America for First Readers."

David Adler's "Picture Life of" books introduce the genre of biography. The "Meet the Author" collection, published by Richard C. Owens acquaints young readers with autobiography by skillfully combining first person accounts of authors' lives with their writing experiences. These photographic essays bring prominent visitors Verna Aardema, Eve Bunting, Lois Ehlert, Jean Fritz, Paul Goble, Ruth Heller, Lee Bennett Hopkins, James Howe, Karla Kuskin, Patricia Polacco, Laurence Pringle, Jane Yolen, and others into the schoolhouse to give life to the writing process.

SNUGGLE AND READ: CONNECTIONS

Literature as a jumping-off point is a major premise of CUES. Gifted children, whether in a whole class or a small differentiated group, enjoy this kind of mental maneuvering. The Belmont "Snuggle and Read Coloring Book," adapted from a publisher's promotion, became a weekly worksheet for reinforcing beginning library media concepts with first graders. A drawing, a scene, or a sentence from an attractive picture storybook was reproduced in combination with some questions about spine label, title, author, illustrator, or a comparison to another easy book. The Snuggle and Reads, accumulated in personal folders, summarized the first-grade media scope and sequence in a contagious way, as children began to recommend titles to be added. They became adept at similar linkages between subject, theme, characters, authors and disciplines.

Animal Fact/Animal Fable is an all-in-one-book example of this springboarding technique. Over the years, groups of younger kids have named this approach, "Fiction and FACTion." It develops when an attractive easier-to-read trade book about a current curriculum or trendy topic is acquired for the library media center. The topic connects well with other materials treating the same or related subjects in a contrasting genre or informational book, so the library media specialist or teacher contiguously share the ideas. The lesson follows any feasible path that emerges. *Margaret, Frank and Andy: Three Writers*, a collective biography by Cynthia Rylant, connects the lives of Margaret Wise Brown, E. B. White, and L. Frank Baum. Add to this the information that Dr. Seuss, as a child, lived near the library and the zoo, and so he learned about books and animals. When he grew up, *Oh the Places He Went*, as he became an artist in advertising, until he decided he could write better children's stories than the Dick and Jane series. Today, mothers-to-be read his books aloud to ensure that their babies will love stories. Any web search engine with the name Seuss will get the reader to Seussville.

Alistair Griddle was a busy boy who had no time for nonsense. A sensible boy, a boy of science who understood gravity *and* plant growth, he lived the quiet life of an ordinary school boy. A most unusual boy, he was botanist, collector of specimens, astronomer, space traveler, rescuer of those in distress, whether human, animal, or alien. No one else was quite like him in the universe. "What about those Alistair clones in space?" ask the listeners. He worries about library books not being on time and keeping his room neat. "Our parents do that for us." First graders understand the subtle humor as they predict what is coming. They laugh knowingly at the discrepancy between the final word that all's well and the foreboding final picture.

When *Alistair's Time Machine* went further back than the day before yesterday for which it was set, he encountered knights at a round table, danced at a royal ball in a French palace, sailed on a pirate ship, and braved lions in a Roman arena. He enlightened a cave era campsite by giving the cavemen matches. After he sent the marauding mammoth into time, he sat for his portrait on a cave wall. Still, he lost the Twickadilly science fair competition because the judges would not believe his adventures and he could not prove them. Could he? *Patrick's Dinosaurs* were imagined, but the facts about them, their attributes, comparisons, and ratios are interwoven into the story. Alistair and Patrick introduce time travel, time lines, chronologies, and eras to compare with *Life Story,* Virginia Burton's picture time line of the earth's geological history.

Miss Murphy's second graders said they would go back in time to "before the earth was created . . . before America was discovered . . . before electronics . . . when mommy and daddy, my grandmother, were little . . . the saber-toothed tiger and dinosaurs . . . when I was born, a baby."

The versatile Alistair had extraterrestrial connections. Aliens were in his bedroom, in his classroom, and on his spaceship. Megan wondered whether these aliens would trick-or-treat with Space Case on Halloween, or maybe even travel home on the same spaceship. Third graders said they would go ahead in time to "Saturn and Mars . . . when I'm an adult . . . the times ahead, when I get into trouble to avoid them."

Archibald Frisby "read a lot and saw things in ways that others did not." Archibald was an identified gifted lad. Science experiments were his specialty. "This story has rhyming words, just like Alistair," interrupted Janet.

He took things apart, dissected flowers, and read algebra at recess. When his mother sent him to camp to forget science, he tested soup, observed stars, built kites, analyzed caves, recycled, collected old bones, applied physics to baseball, and returned home a changed boy. What if Alistair and Archibald, so well behaved, were in the same class with cut-ups like Spud and Spike and Beverly Cleary's Otis Spofford or on a field trip in the Magic School Bus driven by Ms. Frizzle with *Crinkleroot* as their nature guide?

The books are not shelved together, but Mrs. Reynolds paired *James and the Giant Peach* with *Bugs* for second-grade research. First, she read Roald Dahl's story, with its great descriptions of Aunt Sponge and Aunt Spiker and the terrains over which the peachship flew. Flying on the giant peach was compared to Van Allsburg's travel tales. The attributes and human vanities of the bugs were noted. Then came the special assignment for a group of bug researchers. With the library media specialist, the students were to gather facts about grasshoppers, spiders, ladybugs, centipedes, earthworms, silkworms, and glowworms. From the glossary and story sequence of *Bugs*, by Nancy Winslow Parker, they found which of James's bugs were named. Quite a few, they discovered, as they began taking notes about the insects common to each book. "A good lesson, Mrs. L. We learned a lot."

Primates for Primaries

Other paths pursued are topical. *Ethan's Favorite Teacher* is a short narrative about Ethan who contemplated unanswerable questions during schooltime; he was too busy daydreaming to learn his arithmetic facts. At his favorite place, the nearby zoo, Ethan is invited to watch two orangutans who have learned to play tic-tac-toe. Sadie, the unbeatable orangutan, becomes his opponent. For the first time, Ethan is challenged to work systematically at mastering math and logic skills. The story touches several responsive chords among gifted listeners. The question is always asked, "Is that true?" It is, in the sense that primates have been studied for many years, while researchers probe the extent of their intelligence. *KoKo's Kitten* reflects any child's feelings about the loss of a pet. Another investigation into primate behavior and communication is reported photographically in *The Story of Nim: The Chimp Who Learned Language. Jane Goodall: Living Chimp Style* is an easy-to-read biography that branches out to other areas for further exploration. In it, a now-famous young woman, accepted as a serious researcher without academic credentials, lives with and studies an endangered species for years. Goodall's research has been the subject of *National Geographic* articles, books, and television specials. Her studies may help prove or disprove theories about human and animal behavior and origins. These slim books about primates have the potential to open up a lifetime of study!

A primary teacher who opens these doors nurtures students' quests for knowledge. When a teacher of intermediate-age children adopts these valid but unorthodox sources, the resulting research and report products will be very different from the usual "encyclopedia and five other sources" report. Of course, this presupposes that a prior acquaintance and guided practice with standard reference and research techniques have provided the base from which to expand. Picasso and abstractionists knew anatomy and realism before they became Cubists. Teachers of gifted children must help students acquire a knowledge base while encouraging them to soar divergently. Imaginative direct instruction is a logical first step.

Young students travel by time machine, flying carpet, and magic school bus. Aboard the "good ship easybook" they used to cruise through the card catalog and the Dewey decimal classification system in pursuit of a topic of interest. They traveled by author and title to subject headings, tracings, and analytics to number classification and the triumph of shelf location. In the 1990s, the card catalog is no longer a tool for gaining access to information; it was replaced, first by microfiche, then computer printed catalogs, and now computer databases. A few descriptors typed into the computer produces reams of data without ever touching a printed page or card. Library of Congress classification shares the verso page of each published book with the Dewey call number. Fiction and FACTion software is available for CD ROMification. Access to information channels continues to change rapidly. It has come a long way from the Maryland farm roads of *Clara and the Bookwagon,* when girls could not go to school or learn to read. Today, *A New True Book of the Internet* allows novices of any age to travel the electronic highway with the easy collection as guide.

Children should be made familiar with facts from which generalizations may be made long before their minds are ready to receive the generalizations themselves. (Inscribed on the wall of the Alexander Graham Bell Museum, Baddeck, Nova Scotia)

REFERENCES

Shapiro, Irv. 1982. Bytes. *The Washington Post,* 15 November.

Voltaire. 1956. Philosophical Dictionary: Ideas. *Candide and Other Writings.* New York: Random House.

BIBLIOGRAPHY

Abigail's Drum. John A. Minohan. New York: Pippin Press, 1995.

Alistair and the Alien Invasion. Marilyn Sadler. New York: Simon & Schuster, 1994.

Alistair in Outer Space. Marilyn Sadler. New York: Simon & Schuster, 1984.

Alistair Underwater. Marilyn Sadler. New York: Simon & Schuster, 1988.

Alistair's Elephant. Marilyn Sadler. New York: Simon & Schuster, 1983.

Alistair's Time Machine. Marilyn Sadler. New York: Simon & Schuster, 1986.

America's First Elephant. Robert McClung. New York: Morrow Junior Books, 1991.

Andy and the Lion. James Daughty. New York: Viking, 1938.

Animal Fact / Animal Fable. Seymour Simon. New York: Crown, 1979.

Anna, Grandpa, and the Big Storm. Carla Stevens. New York: Clarion Books, 1982.

Anno's Journey. Mitsumaso Anno. New York: Philomel, 1978.

Archibald Frisby. Michael Chesworth. New York: Farrar, Straus & Giroux, 1994.

Be a Frog, a Bird, a Tree. Rachel Carr. New York: Doubleday, 1973.

The Bell Ringer and the Pirate. Elinor Coerr. New York: Harper & Row, 1983.

Bill and Pete. Tomie dePaola. New York: G. P. Putnam's Sons, 1978.

Birth of Sunset's Kittens. Carla Stevens. New York: Young Scott Books, 1969.

The Bravest Dog Ever: The True Story of Balto. Natalie Standiford. New York: Random House, 1989.

Bugs. Nancy Winslow Parker. New York: Greenwillow Books, 1987.

Caps for Sale. Esphyr Slobodkina. New York: HarperCollins, 1947.

Cat in the Hat. Dr. Seuss. New York: Random House, 1957.

The Caterpillar and the Polliwog. Jack Kent. Englewood Cliffs, NJ: Prentice-Hall, 1982.

Cat's Eyes. Anthony Taber. New York: Dutton Children's Books, 1978.

Charlie Needs a Cloak. Tomie dePaola. Englewood Cliffs, NJ: Prentice-Hall, 1973.

Clara and the Bookwagon. Nancy Smiler Levinson. New York: HarperCollins, 1987.

Cornstalks and Cannonballs. Barbara Mitchell. Minneapolis, MN: Carolrhoda Books, 1980.

Could Be Worse. James Stevenson. New York: Greenwillow Books, 1977.

The Cow Who Fell in the Canal. Phyllis Krasilovsky. New York: Doubleday, 1972.

Crinkleroot's 100 Animals Every Child Should Know. Jim Arnofsky. New York: Simon & Schuster.

Dakota Dugout. Ann Turner. New York: Macmillan, 1985.

Doctor DeSoto. William Steig. New York: Farrar, Straus & Giroux, 1982. (Africa)

Dream Wolf. Paul and Dorothy Goble. Scarsdale, NY: Bradbury Press, 1974.

The Drinking Gourd. F. N. Monjo. New York: Harper & Row, 1970.

An Edwardian Christmas. John S. Goodall. New York: Atheneum, 1977.

An Edwardian Holiday. John S. Goodall. New York: Atheneum, 1978.

An Edwardian Summer. John S. Goodall. New York: Atheneum, 1976.

Ernest and Celestine. Gabrielle Vincent. New York: Greenwillow Books, 1982.

Ethan's Favorite Teacher. Hila Colman. New York: Crown, 1975.

Fables. Arnold Lobel. New York: Harper & Row, 1980.

Fables You Shouldn't Pay Any Attention To. Florence Parry Heide. Philadelphia: J. B. Lippincott, 1978.

Fish Fry. Susan Saunders. New York: Viking, 1982.

Fox and His Friends. Edward Marshall. New York: Dial Press, 1982.

Fox in Love. Edward Marshall. New York: Dial Press, 1988.

The Fox Went out on a Chilly Night; An Old Song. Peter Spier, illustrator. New York: Doubleday, 1961.

Frederick's Fables. Leo Lionni. New York: Alfred A. Knopf, 1997.

The Glorious Flight: Across the Channel with Louis Bleriot, July 25, 1909. Alice Provensen and Martin Provensen, New York: Viking Press, 1983.

Goat in the Rug. Charles Blood. New York: Simon & Schuster, 1990.

Graham Oakley's Magical Changes. Graham Oakley. New York: Atheneum, 1980.

The Grandma Mix-Up. Emily McCully. New York: Harper & Row, 1988.

Grandpa's Farm: Four Tall Tales. James Flora. New York: Harcourt Brace, 1965.

Grandpa's Ghost Stories. James Flora. New York: Atheneum, 1980.

Grandpa's Great Big City Tour: An Alphabet Book. James Stevenson. New York: Greenwillow Books, 1983.

The Great Big Especially Beautiful Easter Egg. James Stevenson. New York: Greenwillow Books, 1983.

Hannibal and His Thirty Seven Elephants. Marilyn Hirsch. New York: Holiday House, 1977.

Henry and Mudge. Cynthia Rylant. New York: Bradbury/MacMillan, 1987.

Herman the Helper. Robert Kraus. New York: Windmill/Dutton, 1972.

Humbug Potion. Lorna Balian. Nashville, TN: Abingdon, 1984.

Humbug Witch. Lorna Balian. New York: Abingdon, 1965.

Internet: A New True Book. Lora Koehler. Chicago: Childrens Press, 1995.

It's So Nice to Have a Wolf Around the House. Harry Allard. New York: Doubleday, 1977.

Jack Kent's Fables of Aesop. Jack Kent. New York: Parents Magazine Press, 1974.

James and the Giant Peach. Roald Dahl. New York: Alfred A. Knopf, 1989.

Jane Goodall: Living Chimp Style. Mary Virginia Fox. Minneapolis, MN: Dillon, 1981.

Jumanji. Chris Van Allsburg. Boston: Houghton Mifflin, 1981.

The Kids' Cat Book. Tomie dePaola. New York: Holiday House, 1979.

Leo the Late Bloomer. Robert Kraus. New York: Windmill Books, 1971.

The Little House. Virginia Lee Burton. New York: Houghton Mifflin, 1978.

Little Sister and the Month Brothers. Beatrice De Regniers. Boston: Houghton Mifflin, 1976.

Little Witch's Book of Yoga. Linda Glovach. Prentice-Hall, 1979.

London Bridge Is Falling Down. Peter Spier. New York: Doubleday, 1973.

Long Ago. Cyndy Szekeres. New York: McGraw-Hill, 1971.

Long Way to a New Land. Joan Sandin. New York: Harper & Row, 1981.

Look Again. Tana Hoban. New York: Macmillan, 1971.

Margaret, Frank and Andy: Three Writers. Cynthia Rylant. New York: Harcourt Brace, 1996.

A Medieval Feast. Aliki. New York: Thomas Y. Crowell, 1983.

Milton the Early Riser. Robert Kraus. New York: Windmill Books, 1974.

Miss Nelson Is Back. Harry Allard. Boston: Houghton Mifflin, 1982. Also *Miss Nelson Is Missing*. 1977.

Miss Rumphius. Barbara Cooney. New York: Viking, 1982.

Mummies Made in Egypt. Aliki. New York: Thomas Y. Crowell, 1979.

My Cat Has Eyes of Sapphire Blue. Aileen Fisher. New York: Thomas Y. Crowell, 1973.

My Great-Aunt Arizona. Gloria Houston. New York: HarperCollins, 1992.

My Island Grandmother. Amy Schwartz. New York: Morrow, 1993.

The Mystery of Sara Beth. Polly Putnam. Chicago: Follett, 1981.

Oh the Places He Went: A Story About Dr. Seuss. Margaret Weidt. Minneapolis, MN: Carolrhoda Books, 1994.

On Market Street. Arnold Lobel. New York: Greenwillow Books, 1981.

Patrick's Dinosaurs. Carol Carrick. New York: Clarion, 1983.

Pelle's New Suit. Elsa Beskow. New York: Harper & Row, 1929.

The Quicksand Book. Tomie dePaola. New York: Holiday House, 1977.

Rain Makes Applesauce. Julian Scheer and Marvin Bilick. New York: Holiday House, 1964.

The Relatives Came. Cynthia Rylant. New York: Bradbury Press, 1985.

Rose Blanche. Robert Innocenti and Christopher Gallo. New York: Steward, Tabori and Chang, 1990.

The Seven Sleepers. Phyllis S. Busch. New York: Macmillan, 1985.

Shelter Folks. Virginia Kroll. Grand Rapids, MI: William Eerdmans, 1995.

The Shrinking of Treehorn. Florence Parry Heide. New York: Holiday House, 1971.

The Sky Was Blue. Charlotte Zolotow. New York: Harper & Row, 1963.

Smoky Night. Eve Bunting. New York: Harcourt Brace, 1995.

The Star-Spangled Banner. Peter Spier. New York: Doubleday, 1973.

The Story of Nim: The Chimp Who Learned Language. Anna Michael. New York: Alfred A. Knopf, 1980.

Strange Partners: The Story of Symbiosis. Annabel Dean. Minneapolis, MN: Lerner, 1976.

Stringbean's Trip to the Shining Sea. Vera B. Williams. New York: Greenwillow Books, 1988.

The Stupids Have a Ball. Harry Allard. Boston: Houghton Mifflin, 1978.

Symbiosis: A Book of Unusual Friendships. Jose Aruego. New York: Charles Scribner's Sons, 1970.

That Terrible Halloween Night. James Stevenson. New York: Greenwillow Books, 1980.

Thirteen. Remy Charlip and Jerry Joyner. New York: Parent's Magazine Press, 1975.

Three by the Sea. Edward Marshall. New York: Dial Press, 1981.

Three Days on a River in a Red Canoe. Vera B. Williams. New York: Greenwillow Books, 1981.

Three Friends. Robert Kraus. New York: Windmill/Dutton, 1975.

Treehorn's Treasure. Florence Parry Heide. New York: Holiday House,1981.

Treehorn's Wish. Florence Parry Heide. New York: Holiday House, 1984.

Troll Country. Edward Marshall. New York: Dial Press, 1980.

Two Hundred Rabbits. Lonzo Anderson and Adrienne Ames. New York: Viking, 1968.

Uncle Elephant. Arnold Lobel. New York: Harper & Row, 1978.

The Village of Round and Square Houses. Ann Grifalconi. New York: Little, Brown, 1986.

A Visit to William Blake's Inn: *Poems for Innocent and Experienced Travellers.* Nancy Willard. New York: Harcourt Brace Jovanovich, 1982.

Wagon Wheels. Barbara Brenner. New York: Harper & Row, 1978.

Washington City Is Burning. Harriette Gillem Robinet. New York: Jean Karl/Atheneum, 1997.

We Can't Sleep. James Stevenson. New York: Greenwillow Books, 1982.

We Hide, You Seek. Jose Aruego and Ariane Dewey. New York: Greenwillow Books, 1979.

What's Under My Bed? James Stevenson. New York: Greenwillow Books, 1984.

When I Was Young in the Mountains. Cynthia Rylant. New York: E. P. Dutton, 1982.

Witch, Goblin and Ghost's Book of Things to Do. Sue Alexander. New York: Pantheon Books, 1982.

Yard Sale. James Stevenson. New York: Greenwillow Books, 1996.

Zoo City. Steven Lewis. New York: Greenwillow Books, 1976.

Eight

Information? Please! But Help Wanted

PATHS BEYOND THE LESSON

Harriet the Spy has a friend named Janie who is a bedroom chemist. The distraught parents of both girls, in an effort to make their daughters more like everyone else's daughters, are planning to send them to dancing lessons. Janie relays this alarming news to Harriet with the lament that no one sent Pasteur, Madame Curie, or Einstein to dancing class.

Fifteen fourth graders were reading this chapter from *Harriet the Spy* as part of a curriculum unit pegged for gifted fourth graders. The students perfunctorily performed the higher-level activities built into the unit. The teacher acted on a hunch. She asked why Janie chose those particular three names. One student thought he recognized Einstein's name from science, but no one in the group understood Janie's allusion to the three scientific pioneers. None of them was curious enough to pursue the reference; but then, neither was the curriculum writer. Was this dialogue retained in the 1996 screenplay of the novel?

The teacher, a library media specialist, commented that knowing about these people might be more important than anything else in the book. She asked three students to find out how Pasteur, Curie, and Einstein affected their daily lives. After referring to the card catalog and encyclopedias, the students were able to recap facts about each person, but none of them could relate these facts to the teacher's question. After the topic was analyzed a bit further, Sandy commented sheepishly, "We're better at divergent thinking."

The time was ripe for abandoning Harriet for more profitable pursuits—for the teacher to impart the knowledge that the children lacked. She did not, because she felt locked into a timetable for the unit as written, but she resolved to digress the next time. By seizing the right moment, she could have led this

103

group toward an adventure familiar to voracious young readers of a generation past when they discovered the 1926 classic *Microbe Hunters*. Paul De Kruif's fast-paced account of the travail and excitement of scientific breakthroughs by Leeuwenhoek, Spallanzani, Pasteur, Koch, and others inspired many a bright child to explore the lives of famous scientists.

While De Kruif's book may be passé, contemporary books communicate the same sense of being on the threshold of great knowledge. The Science Discovery Series books published by Coward, McCann, and Geoghegan also tell about great moments of discovery, sometimes accidental, but more often after years of painstaking searching, failure, and trying again. They recount such occasions as

- the unearthing of Stone Age paintings in the caves at Altimira;

- Spallanzani's work with microbes;

- Faraday's experiments with coils, magnets, and rings;

- Dr. Beaumont's studies of the digestive system;

- the universe of Nicholas Copernicus;

- Darwin's voyages to the enchanted isles;

- Charles Willson Peale's museum and mammoth;

- Marie Curie's world of rays;

- Mary Ann Anning's finding the creature Icthysaurus; and

- the founding of modern chemistry by Lavoisiere who later died on the guillotine.

Good lessons come from diversions like these that encompass biography, science and the scientific method, the research process, the history of ideas, and the use of reference tools and primary resources. The vertical file contained a book review about great science discoveries illustrated with a drawing of an autographed baseball. Among the names inscribed were M. Curie, A. Einstein, L. Pasteur (Harris 1983). What other names can students add and justify? Imagine all this serendipitous learning from a starting point in *Harriet the Spy*.

Also in the picture archives was an advertisement from the *New Yorker* showing nine small portraits with the caption: "Of all the world's great thinkers, which is the greatest?" (See figure 8.1.) None of the faces are identified in the text, but, among the should-be recognizable faces are Plato, Leonardo da Vinci, William Shakespeare, Sir Isaac Newton, Thomas Jefferson, Charles Darwin, Madame Marie Curie, Albert Einstein, and a computer chip (*The New Yorker* 1983). As an update, will Bill Gates's picture be in addition to or a replacement of the chip? A 1996 advertisement for Chase Bank is headlined *Everyone Has Dreams, A Few Have Strategies* and shows Cleopatra, Queen of Egypt; Alexander the Great, Greek Conqueror; Tokugaw Hidetada, Second Shogun of Japan; and Napoleon, Emperor of Europe. In another *New York Times* spread about Internet searching, Waldo info-seeks the Web. How many connections between times, places, people, and ideas are implicit in these advertisements? What questions can be asked? What a wealth of media exploration can be extracted from a clipping file! What skills can be developed? What debates about the nature of greatness initiated? These pursuits can happen only if students have associations for some of the people shown. How much is lost to our gifted children if, in the efforts not to dwell on dull facts and rote learning, curriculum planners continue to downplay the role of the same background knowledge that advertising copywriters seem to value?

Fig. 8.1. Some of the world's greatest thinkers. (Reproduced with permission from Allied Signal Inc.)

A composite photograph of the late Carl Sagan, seated next to an enlarged Rosetta Stone against a backdrop of the Sphinx and a Great Pyramid (*Mainliner Magazine* 1979), was part of a display of Egyptian artifacts and archeology in the library media center. Fifth grade participants in a gifted writers' workshop were asked to write a descriptive sentence about the scene. They had some setting for their thinking: they recognized that Egypt was involved, and a museum replica of the Rosetta Stone was in the display. They did not recognize Dr. Sagan as a prominent scientist-writer, host of the television series *Cosmos*. Their responses included:

A man has just found an artifact in Egypt which could be very useful to archeologists. . . . Egyptian artwork is excellent, especially carving. . . . The guy sitting down has just found a piece of evidence leading to the Sphinx. . . . I think the Sphinx represents a grave that has been lost for a long time and this guy found it. . . . The picture is a man related to the man the sphinx was modeled after.

After the lesson, the Rosetta Stone replica was propped on a table for passersby to examine. Ralph, another fifth grader known to teachers for his curiosity and thirst for knowledge, noticed the different styles of inscriptions, asked questions, then looked for answers. Later, he returned to the center with Jeremy, who had been in the writer's workshop. Together, the boys worked on deciphering the messages, after which they set up an eye-catching display, including the replica, a descriptive caption, a challenge to find out more, and copies of *Time Traveller Book of Pharaohs and Pyramids* and *Pyramid*. The talk of the school for many days was their discovery of the key to Egyptian hieroglyphics. Archeology was in! The fifth-grade teacher capitalized on the enthusiasm by starting her unit on historical fiction earlier than planned.

On another occasion the kindergarten class tiptoed through the library media center on marshmallow feet en route to art class. Eric's T-shirt caught the library media assistant's eye. On the front of the shirt was written, "Dewey had a point." On the back were the names of selected subjects with their Dewey decimal numbers. Eric was invited later to talk about his shirt. The library media specialist copied the numbers on the shirt to use as a starting point for a lesson on the classification of materials. Her planning focused on the levels at which such a lesson might be applicable—for the unusually gifted five first-grade researchers; for *all* the third graders with differentiation for the top group; or as a design-a-Dewey T-shirt project for grades four and five.

SCOPE AND SEQUENCE
FOR FINDING OUT

The anecdotes about Janie's names, the men of science advertisement, the Rosetta Stone, and Eric's T-shirt illustrate two strands of the CUES pattern—involving students searching for the knowledge that resides within the library media center, then helping them make this knowledge their own. In a book that equates literature with curriculum, why not refer to these strands with Ben Franklin's words *useful* and *ornamental*! The useful side enables students to become more proficient in the process of finding out about any subject through mastery of the necessary tools; the ornamental side encourages them to value literary paths to learning. The curriculum demands of different instructional levels may emphasize one strand over another, but an integrated approach toward learning to know and knowing to learn works best. At the introductory stage with young gifted children, kindergarten through second grade, where identification is based largely on empirical data and the approach is nurturing, a CUES progression might include units as follows. The unit names were suggested by students, quite aptly. Those in quotes are original; those in italics are book titles. An overall strategy for imparting library and information skills emerges out of these course names.

Kindergarten	*Just Open a Book*
First grade, overlapping	*What Do You Do with a Kangaroo?*
First and second grades	*How Can I Find Out?*
Second and third grades	"Fiction and FACTion"

In grades three through six, when cognitive test performance and personal attributes ratings tend to be the main screening factors, a CUES progression may look like this:

Third and fourth grades	"1, 2, 3s of the ABCs"
	"Art Sings Many Languages"
	"Readers, Writers, and Storytellers"
Fourth and fifth grades	"Miscellany Matters"
	"Where in the World?"
	"References Required"
Fifth and sixth grades	"Literary Capers"
	"Information? Please!"

Just Open a Book assesses a child's previous involvement with books enabling the teacher to plan for acceleration for early readers and enrichment for all. *What Do You Do with a Kangaroo?* demonstrates how things can be arranged, while *How Can I Find Out?* capitalizes on curiosity and the browsing habit. The goal for these primary grades lessons is to convey a feeling that the library media center is an all-knowing place and that each child possesses the key to unlocking the door.

In the intermediate grades, the "1, 2, 3s of the ABCs" highlight the connectedness of the search process; "Information? Please!" and "Where in the World?" focus on the location and arrangement of information and the world. "Miscellany Matters" and "References Required" familiarize students with hard and soft databases. "Art Sings Many Languages" opens young minds to visual and aesthetic literacy, while "Literary Capers" invites students to synthesize their skills with their interests to embark on knowledge pursuits of their own.

WHAT'S THE POINT?

Primarily Fun

When a kindergarten class first visits the library media center, either for a class lesson or for individual book selection, the library media specialist develops their literary know-how in three ways:

1. by assessing their previous experiences with literature, i.e., through Mother Goose rhymes, counting and alphabet books, and authors like Keats, Sendak, and Seuss;

2. by helping them make their first book choices on their own, books that some can read and all enjoy;

3. by introducing stories and materials to instill the idea that books can teach anything.

Just Open a Book

Simple books about libraries as all-important and all-knowing places include titles like *Just Open a Book, Calico Cat Meets Bookworm, Blue Bug Goes to the Library, Beatrice Doesn't Want To, How My Library Grew by Dinah,* and *I Took My Frog to the Library.* The heroines of *Too Many Books* and *The Library* collected books until they overflowed their houses. They solved the problem by donating their collections to their town libraries. These stories are more than entertaining picture books. They offer diagnosis and extension of the young listener's visual and cultural awareness. They are doors to the library through literature written in poetic or divergent language, cleverly illustrated . . . and the list is always growing. "The Family Circus" cartoon strip showing "poor Billy all alone in his room" makes a wonderful preassessment test. "He's not alone!" shout the children as they look at Billy reading on his bed, imagining all of his literary friends around him. Young audiences love to name them, either as a specific character (e.g., Captain Hook), a book title (*Peter Pan*), or a book genre (pirate stories). In a similar episode, ghostly characters from books on the shelves shout to Billy as he walks through the "silent" stacks of the library.

Some stories test the literary IQs of young children. *"Snow White and the Seven Bears"*—"Oh no," groan the listeners. *Each Peach Pear Plum: An I-Spy Story* and *The Boy Who Would Not Say His Name* similarly rely upon knowledge of nursery tale characters: the first, an I-Spy hidden picture presentation, the other portraying a hero who role-plays storybook people. The breadth of response enables the teacher to judge the literary sophistication of the class as a group and as individual students. Differentiation follows accordingly.

What Can You Do . . .

With a kangaroo or a garden or a mitten or a crictor? Students' knowledge of basic order can be gauged and stretched via books. When *Morris* (the Moose) *Goes to School,* in one full day he learns his ABCs, the addition of simple numbers, and easy words to read and spell. He enjoys lunch, outdoor recess, art, music, and dramatic play. The narrator of *What Do You Do with a Kangaroo?* has a problem with rambunctious animals invading her daily life. In her tale, she encounters seven contentious mammals who make exorbitant demands of her. At first she fights them, but her efforts are unsuccessful, so she joins them. Once the story has been read, the random sequence in which she meets a kangaroo, an opossum, a raccoon, a moose, a llama, a camel, and a tiger can be more systematically rearranged. Children suggest arranging the list by size, alphabetic order, or attributes (e.g., nocturnal versus diurnal habitat). When the list is transformed from story sequence to alphabetical order, some children immediately commented on all of the double vowels and consonants. A few children may be ready to look up animals in a source like Kathleen Daly's *A Child's Book of Animals*. To introduce botanical order, the flowers and names in *Alison's Zinnia* are an alphabetical chain linking girl-verb-flower. Leonard Fisher's *Alphabet Art* and *Number Art* impart history as they connect two kinds of order. *Tomorrow's Alphabet* and *Q Is for Duck* are tricky, skipping around the alphabet according to a sequence of order the reader must discern. What animals go to the library, into *The Mitten*, live on Kapiti Plain, want to learn *The Name of the Tree?* What fruits and vegetables are planted in *The Garden for a Groundhog* or *Linnea's Windowsill Garden* or Lois Ehlert's edible collage picture books? How can all of these plants and animals be rearranged?

How to Find Out

Mary Bongiorno's *How Can I Find Out?* is a guided start toward independent learning. It is a simple prototype for the reference and research process that includes observation, questioning, use of primary sources, interviewing, looking up information in traditional references, then reporting. A three-step unit for first and second graders parallels Timmy's experiences.

1. Set out curiosity objects (e.g., shells, feathers, snake skins, wasp nests, rocks, fossils, and bones) for examination, discussions, and hypothesizing. The objects are then named and grouped in an order most logical for confirmation.

2. Read several books to the group as examples of classification, data retrieval, and data organization. *David's Pockets* shows how miscellany can be logically organized, and *Benny's Animals* sets up the classification of animals by genus and by Dewey. *Olly's Polliwogs* presents a concept—metamorphosis—that can be extended to other processes and stages, like camouflage, which is treated in *Snowy and Woody*, or basic economics in *More Potatoes!*

3. Let children develop their own lists of "I-want-to-find-out" topics, concepts, or processes. With Timmy's search as precedent, they follow through in the media center.

Upper Starts

Jason, early in his third-grade year, put the last link in the chain between the card catalog, the Dewey decimal number, and finding his book on the shelf. His eyes lit up as he exclaimed, "I just learned the 1, 2, 3s of the ABCs." He had figured out how to *Find It* inside his school library.

Jason's description is a terse summary of the information game. To satisfy the need or wish to find out, children have to master the system for arranging information and the index to the system. Successful access depends on a cross-reference between the two. Children do not permanently learn to alphabetize or numerically arrange items. While the skill is constant, the application changes each time a child goes to the card, microfiche, or intelligent catalog. Time is wasted on the Internet when keywords are spelled incorrectly. Is an alphabetic search conducted word by word or letter by letter? The electronic search is intolerant of input errors. Chances to explore and experiment with the relationship between the alphabetic order of a holdings catalog, the Dewey call number, and shelf location system, then between these and topic words and school subjects, may occur as early as first grade for an interested child when the activities are concrete. Class adventures probably should wait until third grade, especially if the intelligent catalog is the access. Teaching Dewey and "card catalog" are still academically relevant, as are the many skill books and props for so doing. The ideas expressed in this chapter provide occasions for students to manipulate and manage the Dewey decimal system and the catalog, so they may better understand how the cadre of knowledge common to us all is organized.

The 1, 2, 3s . . .

Classical mythology and folklore abound with stories of *Gods and Goddesses of Olympus* and the mortal others who don and doff marvelous garments or gadgets that transport them to far-off places or bestow upon them magical powers. Eric's Dewey decimal T-shirt is a similar device, enabling its wearer to shelf-hop around the world of the library media center, fortifying information gathering and retrieval skills along the way. The numbers and subjects chosen for inclusion on Eric's T-shirt reflect someone's priorities—perhaps those of a designer or a cataloger. The choices are worth a group discussion and rank ordering. Why were the particular categories chosen? How much do the students know about each one? Which topics and numbers would each of them include were they shirt designers?

Eric's T-Shirt

The numbers listed on Eric's T-shirt were:

001.64	Computers
133.52	Zodiac Signs
202.13	Mythology
333.33	Real Estate
495.1	Chinese
567.91	Dinosaurs
629.41	Space Flight
641.5	Cookbooks
780.92	Musicians
796.357	Baseball
822.33	Shakespeare
929.1	Genealogy

Such a list becomes a device for introducing the Dewey decimal system's 10 divisions and their main subdivisions. The subject areas are defined in words relevant to the specific age group. Students list topics of personal interest to which they assign simple call numbers, then they draw pictures of each topic. Each student posts 10 headings with assigned Dewey decimal numbers, one each on one side of a 3-by-5-inch catalog card, with a sketch or cut-out illustration for the category on the reverse. The cards can be used as a Concentration-like game, for numerical arranging, subject words, learning the Dewey decimal classifications, or finding books on the shelves. Dewey Dramas, like charades, can be enacted. Individual players or teams choose a subject from a Dewey decimal system category for the other players to guess, responding not with the word, but with the Dewey decimal number. Dewey Decimal Wheels are mechanical devices. Students can design other products to mass market the Dewey decimal system; not only T-shirts, but posters, placemats, and paper goods.

In the ninth abridged edition of the Dewey decimal classification (Lake Placid Educational Foundation 1965), the listing included:

001	Knowledge
.5	Communication (communication, theories, and cybernetics)

The 1979 listing (Lake Placid Educational Foundation 1979) expanded to include:

001.535	Artificial Intelligence (use of computers and related machines for the solution of problems)

001.6   Data Processing
             .61 Systems analysis
             .62 Nonmechanical
             .63 Automatic
             .64 Electronic
                  .640-4 Minicomputers
                  . -42-44 analog and digital
                  .642   Computer programs and programming
                       -3 program, flow chart, and flow charting
                       -4 program, language, and coding
                       -5 software and its usages
                  .644   Input, storage, and output
                           (equipment use and operation)
                  .644-04 Network systems
                           (on-line, time sharing, real-line, and
                            multiple access)
                  .644-2   Input and storage
                           (punched cards, paper and magnetic tape,
                           optical scanner, audio input, core, disk, data
                           cell, drum, and magnetic tape storage)
                  .644-3   Output

The twentieth edition of the Dewey decimal classification, the 1989 listing (third summary), included:

000	Generalities
001	Knowledge
002	The Book
003	Systems
004	Data Processing, Computer Science
005	Computer Programming, Programs, Data
006	Special Computer Methods
007	blank
008	blank
009	blank

Subject Headings for Children, 025.49, (Winkel 1994) lists: computer animation (006.6 & 741.5); computer art (006.6 & 760.02); computer assisted instruction (371.3); computer crimes and prevention (364.1); computer engineering and engineers (621.39); computer games (794.8); computer games–fiction; computer graphics, including software and vocational guidance (006.6); computer industry (004); computer input-output equipment (004.7); computer literacy 004; computer music (788.7); computer networks (004.6); computer programmers (005.1); computer programs/software (005.3); computer science (004); computer sound processing (006.5); computer storage devices (004.5); computers (004); computers and the handicapped (362.4); computers–biography (004.092); computers–

cartoons and comics (004.0207); computers–dictionaries (004/.03); computers–history (004/.09); and computers–vocational guidance (004/.023). Materials on the Internet and the World Wide Web are shelved as 004.67.

Discussing the Dewey decimal system with advanced thinkers should trigger some philosophizing and debate about the technology explosion and megatrends. The library media specialist sets the stage by explaining that 000 to 099 represents the area of Generalities. Until recently, 031s, encyclopedias, and their ilk have been top dog in this section. The 001.6 for computers was a Johnny-come-lately to the area of Knowledge 001. Should this interloper 001.6 head the list of numbers on Eric's T-shirt? The explosion of materials published about computers and computing makes this classification the fastest growing shelf list section of most collections. The old category 001.6 no longer handles it all. Where is there room in the system for expansion? Where will cyberspace go? What about the World Wide Web and the Internet? What will fill blank spots in 007, 008, and 009? What further changes will be reflected by the year 2000?

. . . And the ABCs, with a Possible D

Arranging and Building a Card Catalog—or Dis-carding One

The contents of libraries are organized by authors, book titles and classification/categories. This has not changed, but the way to search has. Is the better database the old-line paper and wood or the new online system? In this era of the electronic library, is the card catalog a dinosaur? Both nostalgia and controversy exist about its destiny as Nicholson Baker chronicles its steady demise in a *New Yorker* article, entitled "Discards" (Baker 1994).

For the current generation of school library media center users, the card catalog is becoming a quaint artifact. A brief recap of its history is interesting. In 1791, after the French Revolution, when libraries of aristocrats and monasteries were confiscated, the new government needed to inventory their acquisitions. Every book in a seized library was given a number to be written down on a playing card together with author, title, library location, and brief description. These cards, strung together and alphabetized by author, were sent on to Paris. In England in 1848, the Keeper of Printed Books for the British Museum entrusted each title to a slip of paper to be moved around alphabetically as needed. By the 1860s, library holdings were recorded on cards stored in cabinets with many drawers, accessible not to the public, but to library staff.

It was every librarian's nightmare—that some child would trip the latches and pull the rods spilling millions of cards all over and out of order. Worse than that happened in the euphemistic process known as "retrospective conversion." Cards from the great libraries have been trashed, sent aloft tied to balloons, sold as souvenirs, transformed into conceptual art, used for scrap paper, or surreptitiously hidden by whistle-blowing librarians. Children could have fun brainstorming ways of recycling the cards and the knowledge they contain. While most professionals agree that change was needed to handle the information overload, many of them would have liked the less destructive way of freezing the card catalog, as a user-friendly piece of the past, then changing to new ways of storing and retrieving information.

In 1996, *The Inside-Outside Book of Libraries* transports the reader from the great libraries of history to *Clara's Bookwagon,* from small town libraries to the Library of Congress, with illustrations of their architectural spaces and their contents.

ORGANIZING THE SEARCHER

The Velveteen Catalog

Nicholson Baker likens the card catalog to the Velveteen Rabbit, shabby, beloved, and becoming alive. One of the user's pleasures was watching the catalog grow. The card catalog is disappearing from most school library media centers, but resident Gail Gibbons can help re-create a card catalog from the whole library of FACTion books she has written. The 1997 *Children's Books in Print* devotes two pages of small print to the list of Gail Gibbons books, more than 70 titles from beacons to zoos. For a hands-on simulation of how a collection spreads to fill the shelves, pack all of the Gibbons books in a box to be unpacked before an audience of second or third graders. As each book emerges from the box, children read the title. Does it tell the topic? Who is the author? "G-a-i-l G-i-b-b-o-n-s," they begin to chant gleefully. Ask how all of these books can be arranged for best access. By color or size, some say; "the author's the same for all the books," others say, "so it's alphabetically by title." Ask how the books may be arranged by subject. A–Z? No, by number, a few will say. Distribute the books so the children can form a living line alphabetically by title. What happens to the line-up when they re-arrange the books in numerical order? Have them put their books on the correct shelves. Which order is better? Point out the cataloging, classification, and copyright information, as well as the summary, on the verso page. Mix in books by another prolific author of simple visual books, such as Aliki. Of her 40 titles in the 1997 *Children's Books in Print,* some will be shelved as easy fiction, biography, ancient and European history, the sciences, folklore, and social sciences. Together, Aliki and Gibbons will show *How a Book Is Made,* help students *Check It Out,* and even provide the *Lights, Camera, Action* to transform a book to film. If new books still come with sets of printed cards in the book pockets, children can see the number of cards needed to add just one book to the card catalog. If an author writes mostly easy stories, where are the titles shelved?

Another tangible asset of the card catalog was that it was **there,** a distinctive piece of library furniture, firmly ensconced. Like the troll lurking under the bridge for billy goats three to cross into his territory, the library media specialist waited to catch timid searchers at the start of their card catalog adventures. According to Baker, fourth, sixth, and eighth graders were 65 percent successful with a card catalog search, while no fourth grader was successful with an online search (Baker 1994).

Topicana

Children are astounded to see the thickness of an official compilation of topics in the card catalog. Such a compendium may be adapted from an authority on subject classification, such as Sears, or an alphabetical list of headings for a vertical/picture file. The Hirsch Core Knowledge series expands on the same 23 topics in each volume. Just as Gibbons's books were used to introduce the card catalog, the library media specialist as teacher of a gifted group shares other topical books by well-known matters-of-fact authors. The instructional goal is to open the realms of knowledge to exploration, starting from students' personal vocabularies of information topics. An early acquaintance with some of these topics as books in the media center is background knowledge leading to better understanding of the basic subjects in a school curriculum—science, social studies, and language arts.

Topics by the 000s

A School of Names for the 500s

The face of the librarian in the children's room of the New Rochelle Public Library lit up when the visiting school library media specialist asked for some titles by M. B. Goffstein. "May I ask how you know about Goffstein? Are you a librarian too?" They agreed that all of Goffstein's books were simple, yet sophisticated gems, too little known to children and unused by teachers. *School of Names* explores the earth in poetic prose that links knowing the name of an object to holding its spirit, a belief from ancient traditions. The narrator wants to be able to name the contents of the sky, the oceans, the lands and all the living things. The book, a 508, subdivides science. When a third-grade group heard the list of names in the school, they picked up on the terms that related to their study of biomes—geography!—their astronomy unit was included as well. Second graders knew the names that fit in with their study of animals—zoology!—as well as names for plants and weather. Fifth graders recognized their geology terms, especially those that coincided with *The Magic School Bus*'s trip inside the earth. This unusual link between us, our natural world, and the subject names on the shelves is a unit unto itself. Jean George wrote about the different ecologies of animal life in her Thirteen Moons series. Opening *Anno's Mysterious Multiplying Jar*, asking *How Much Is a Million?*, and imagining what could be done *If You Made a Million* make the complexities of numbers tangible to young mathematicians.

970 Is a History of US

It is hard to resist a history book series when the title page of each volume is framed with the words

In these books you will find explorers, farmers, cowboys, heroes, villains, inventors, presidents, poets, pirates, artists, slaves, teachers, revolutionaries, priests, musicians, girls and boys, men and women, who all became Americans (Hakim 1995).

The author, Joy Hakim, wrote *A History of US* "especially for children and for families and all ages to enjoy together." The popular 10-volume series, completed in 1995, was in the writing process for seven years and took five years to find its publisher, Oxford University Press. The text, together with the layout of graphics, photos, original documents and illustrations, is to be savored and dwelt upon. Much more than textbooks, the series is an outstanding example of how to keep kids interested and excited in learning by connecting history and children's literature. The fifth-grade teacher found out about the book series when she read that her library media specialist had recommended them to the book review editor of the Sunday paper, who then praised them in a special column. After a feature story about Joy Hakim in the Sunday MiniPage, students came to the library media center to locate the books. They were surprised to find that the books were not side by side on the shelves. All were 973s except for *The First Americans* (970.1). Books 2 through 10 were separated by Dewey decimal points. The suggestion was that the set should be kept together, like an encyclopedia set. The Hakim series is a chronology of American history. In shorter volumes emphasizing photographic archives, Crestwood House time lines offer more recent American history through the decades of the 1900s.

World History

Joy Hakim's next series will be on world history, which is also the subject of Peter Bedrick Books' Inside Story series—*Egyptian Pyramid, A Greek Temple, A Roman Fort, A Roman Villa, Medieval Castle, Cathedral, Shakespeare's Theater, 16th Century Mosque, Frontier Fort,* and *World War II Submarine.* Primary grade children can "Journey Through History" from *Prehistory to Egypt,* through *The Greek and Roman Eras, The Middle Ages,* and *The Renaissance* to *Modern Times* and *The Contemporary Age.* The six brightly illustrated and easy-to-understand volumes of this series published by Barron are translated from the Spanish for young American readers. *There Once Was a Time* explores societies, governments, customs, inventions, and other topics of world history revealed as *Archeologists Dig for Clues.*

Countries and *Culturgrams*

In the years before children chased around the United States and the world to find Waldo or Carmen Sandiego, in books, software, or on public television, geography was included nondescriptly as the boring part of social studies. The five-themes-of-geography approach has a flow that current trade books reinforce. The words, themselves, have vitality as the student considers location, place, relationships, movement, and regions; beyond mere latitude and longitude, land forms, populations, and statistical facts.

The 917s are the books on United States Geography, in orderly state-by-state arrangement. Second-grade Readers Three—Arthur, Adam and Matthew—wanted to "research" our 50 states using easy series books about familiar states. They thought their initials looked like a radio station's call letters so they re-named themselves BAAM. When Leah joined them, the readers four became BLAAM. From their log of Friday the 13th (March 1987):

> We read the book *Being an American Can Be Fun* by Munro Leaf. There is a list of the fifty states in alphabetical order. We named some we knew. We used a beginning atlas to find the states on a map. We read *whole* books about states. We shared what we found out. Kansas and Arkansas are spelled the same but said differently. U*N*C*L*E S*A*M is a symbol for America. No reports today.

At their next meeting, the task was to connect the Eiffel Tower, the Statue of Liberty, and the Empire State Building—factually and imaginatively. They decided that all were tall, famous buildings for sightseers. The Eiffel Tower is in France, which gave us the Statue of Liberty, which is in New York, as is the Empire State Building.

Fifth graders exploring geography on the shelves deciphered the logic of the code for arranging state books by region and country books within Dewey decimal points for continents. The topic Countries of the World is effective in demonstrating statistical comparison. Series about states or countries range from the easy-to-read to the *Culturgrams* leaflets developed at Brigham Young University. Each series has a consistent pattern for *Geography from A–Z* that teaches students *How to Be Naturally Geographic*.

Frameworks

Mary's chart was alongside a photograph of the Library of Congress catalog room displayed atop the wooden cabinets in the school library media center. It read, "There are two card catalogs. The one in our school uses Dewey numbers. The world's largest card catalog in the Library of Congress uses letters." Years later, after a home search of America Online revealed the secrets of library codes and keywords, Jim adapted it to fit into a computer graphic of an automated card catalog:

Category Score: Dewey 10; LC 38		
[The]	[Automated]	[Library]
[Numbers]	[Two Systems]	[Letters]
[Dewey]	[Subject]	[LC]

!000!	General Works	! A !
!100!	Philosophy	! B !
!200!	Religion	! C !
!300!	Social Sciences	! H !
!400!	Language	! P !
!500!	Pure Science	! Q !
!600!	Applied Science	! T !
!700!	Arts & Recreation	! N !
!800!	Literature	!PN !
!900!	History	!DEF!
!920!	Biography	! CT!
!020!	Libraries	! Z!

Fig. 8.2.

In their advancing searches for information, young people will progress from cataloging by Dewey to cataloging by LC, from numbers to letters, linking the 1, 2, 3s and the ABCs. Along the way, how do teachers help them to absorb and integrate information from old and new sources? To teach them *How to Be School Smart*, introduce books like *How to Write a Great School Report*, which summarize steps for collecting information, and *How to Write Your Best Book Report*. Teach students how to jot down brief topical notes on index cards that can later be shuffled, interfiled, and rearranged by keywords. Teach them old-fashioned outlining. Continue to use ditto sheets, familiar to all. Or teach students to use and create data retrieval sheets specifically designed for the assignment at hand. These blank charts or matrices coordinate what the student wants to know about a subject with the facts collected from different sources to show *How to Write a Term Paper*.

All of these suggestions are graphic organizers, frameworks to interrelate and cross reference the variables of the topic being explored. The T-shirt has become a ubiquitous Graphic Organizer, most recently appearing on the cover of a Sunday *New York Times Magazine* issue devoted to "Women of Our Times."

Databases from the first *Appleworks* to the more sophisticated software of the 1990s are also graphic organizers that allow students to customize their searches, whatever resources they use. The software built into most personal computers today has all of the basic tools for writing, printing, graphics, spreadsheets, databases, and Internet access. Today's search helpers have names like Archie, Yahoo, Gopher, Lynx, and Sailor, but the giant "database" that is the library media center still connects the search with the searcher. When asked, "How will you report all that you have learned to the rest of your class?" BLAAM member Arthur responded, "Try to remember it and shorten it." Centuries earlier, similar advice was anonymously given:

> Whatever you have to say, my friend, condense as much as ever you can, and say it in the readiest way. Whether you write on rural affairs or particular things in town, just a word of friendly advice—Boil it down. (Anonymous)

REFERENCES

Baker, Nicholson. 1994. Discards. *The New Yorker*, 4 April.

Hakim, Joy. 1995. *A History of US*. Ten Volumes. New York: Oxford University Press.

Harris, Sidney. 1983. *Science '83* 4 (September): 100.

Lake Placid Educational Foundation. 1965. *Dewey Decimal Classification and Relative Index Devised by Melville Dewey*. 9th abridged ed. Albany, NY: Forest Press.

Lake Placid Educational Foundation. 1979. *Dewey Decimal Classification and Relative Index Devised by Melville Dewey*. 19th ed., Vol. 2, edited by Benjamin A. Custer. Albany, NY: Forest Press.

Mainliner Magazine. 1979. Photo. (July): 173.

The New Yorker. 1983. Advertisement. 17 October.

Winkel, Lois, ed. 1994. *Subject Headings for Children*. Albany, NY: Forest Press. Also OCLC (On Line Computer Library Center).

BIBLIOGRAPHY

Alison's Zinnia. Anita Lobel. New York: Greenwillow Books, 1990.

Alphabet Art: Thirteen ABCs from Around the World. Leonard Fisher. New York: Four Winds Press, 1985.

Anno's Mysterious Multiplying Jar. Anno. New York: Putnam, 1983.

Archeologists Dig for Clues. Kate Duke. New York: HarperCollins, 1997.

Beatrice Doesn't Want To. Laura J. Numeroff. New York: Franklin Watts, 1981.

Benny's Animals. Millicent Selsam. New York: Harper & Row, 1966.

Blue Bug Goes to the Library. Virginia Poulet. Chicago: Childrens Press, 1979.

The Book of Where, or How to Be Naturally Geographic. Neill Bell. New York: Little Brown, 1982.

The Boy Who Would Not Say His Name. Elizabeth Vreeken. Chicago: Follett, 1959.

Calendar Art: Thirteen Days, Weeks, Months, and Years from Around the World. Leonard Fisher. New York: Macmillan, 1987.

Calico Cat Meets Bookworm. Donald Charles. Chicago: Childrens Press, 1978.

Check It Out. Gail Gibbons. New York: Harcourt Brace, 1985.

The Chemist Who Lost His Head: The Story of Antoine Lavoisier. Vivian Grey. New York: Coward, McCann & Geoghegan, 1982.

A Child's Book of Animals. Kathleen Daly. New York: Doubleday, 1975.

Coils, Magnets and Rings: Michael Faraday's World. Nancy Veglahn. New York: Coward, McCann & Geoghegan, 1976.

Culturgrams. David M. Kennedy. Provo, Utah: Brigham Young University, Center for International Studies, 1996.

Dance of the Planets: The Universe of Nicholaus Copernicus. Nancy Veglahn. New York: Coward, McCann & Geogehegan, 1979.

Darwin and the Enchanted Isles. Irwin Shapiro. New York: Coward, McCann & Geogehan, 1977.

David's Pockets. Ellin Goins. Austin, TX: Steck Vaughan, 1972.

Doctor Beaumont and the Man with the Hole in His Stomach. Sam Epstein and Beryl Epstein. New York: Coward, McCann & Geoghegan, 1978.

Each Peach Pear Plum: An I-Spy Story. Janet Ahlberg. New York: Viking, 1979.

Find It: The Inside Story at Your Library. Claire McInerny. Lerner, 1989.

The Garden for a Groundhog. Lorna Balian. Eden Prairie, MN: Humbug Books, 1994.

Geography from A—Z: A Picture Glossary. Jack Knowlton. New York: HarperCollins, 1988.

Gods and Goddesses of Olympus. Aliki. New York: HarperCollins, 1994.

Harriet the Spy. Louise Fitzhugh. New York: HarperCollins, 1964.

How a Book Is Made. Aliki. New York: Crowell, 1986.

How Can I Find Out? Mary Bongiorno and Mabel Gee. Chicago: Childrens Press, 1963.

How Much Is a Million? David Schwartz. New York: Lothrop, Lee & Shepard, 1985.

How My Library Grew by Dinah. Martha Alexander. New York: H W. Wilson, 1983.

How to Be School Smart. Elizabeth James and Carol Barkin. New York: Lothrop, Lee and Shepard, 1988.

How to Write a Great School Report. Elizabeth James and Carol Barkin. New York: William Morrow, 1993.

How to Write a Term Paper. Elizabeth James and Carol Barkin. New York: Lothrop, Lee and Shepard, 1980.

How to Write Your Best Book Report. Elizabeth James and Carol Barkin. New York: Lothrop, Lee and Shepard, 1986.

I Took My Frog to the Library. Eric A. Kimmel. New York: Viking, 1990.

If You Made a Million. David Schwartz. New York: Lothrop, Lee & Shepard, 1989.

The Inside-Outside Book of Libraries. Roxie Munroe. New York: Dutton Children's Books, 1996.

Inside Story Series. New York: Peter Bedrick Books, 1995.

Journey Through History. New York: Barron's Educational Series, 1988. Children's Press Choice.

Just Open a Book. P. K. Hallman. Chicago: Childrens Press, 1983.

The Library. Sarah Stewart. New York: Farrar, Straus & Giroux, 1995.

Lights! Camera! Action! Gail Gibbons. New York: Thomas Y. Crowell, 1985.

Linnea's Windowsill Garden. Christina Bjork. New York: Farrar, Straus & Girard, 1988.

Maria's Cave. William H. Hooks. New York: Coward, McCann & Geoghegan, 1977.

Mary's Monster. Ruth Van Ness Blair. New York: Coward, McCann & Geoghegan, 1975.

Microbe Hunters. Paul De Kruif. New York: Harcourt Brace & World, 1926, 1953.

Mister Peales' Mammoth. Sam Epstein and Beryl Epstein. New York: Coward, McCann & Geoghegan, 1977.

The Mitten: An Old Ukranian Folktale. Alvin Tresselt Yaroslava. New York: Lothrop, Lee & Shepard, 1964.

More Potatoes! Millicent Selsam. New York: Harper & Row, 1972.

Morris Goes to School. B. Wiseman. New York: HarperCollins, 1970.

The Mysterious Rays: Marie Curie's World. Nancy Veglahn. New York: Coward, McCann & Geoghegan, 1977.

The Name of the Tree: A Bantu Folktale. Retold by Celia B. Lotteridge. New York: Simon & Schuster Children's Books, 1990.

Number Art: Thirteen 123s from Around the World. Leonard Fisher. New York: Four Winds Press, 1984.

Olly's Polliwogs. Anne Rockwell. New York: Doubleday, 1970.

Pyramid. David Macauley. Boston: Houghton Mifflin, 1975.

Q Is for Duck: An Alphabet Guessing Game. Mary Elting and Michael Folsom. New York: Macmillan, 1980.

A Roman Fort. Fiona Macdonald and Gerald Wood. New York: Peter Bedrick Books, 1993.

A Roman Villa. Jacqueline Morley and John James. New York: Peter Bedrick Books, 1992.

School of Names. M. B. Goffstein. New York: Harper & Row, 1986.

Secret in a Sealed Bottle: Lazzaro Spallanzani's Work with Microbes. Sam Epstein and Beryl Epstein. New York: Coward, McCann & Geoghegan, 1979.

Shakespeare's Theater. Jacqueline Morley. Inside Story Series. New York: P. Bedrick Books, 1994.

Snowy and Woody. Roger Duvoisin. New York: Alfred A. Knopf, 1979.

There Once Was a Time. Piero Ventura. New York: Putnam, 1986.

Thirteen Moons. Series by Jean George. New York: HarperCollins.

Time Traveller Book of Pharaohs and Pyramids. Tony Allan. Tulsa, OK: Usborne/Hays Books, 1977.

Timelines. New York: Crestwood House, 1989.

Tomorrow's Alphabet. George Shannon. New York: Greenwillow Books, 1996.

Too Many Books. Carolyn Feller Bauer. New York: Frederick Warne, 1984.

What Do You Do with a Kangaroo? Mercer Mayer. New York: Four Winds Press, 1973.

"Women of Our Times." *New York Times Magazine.* November 24, 1996.

Nine

Curious? Read!

DO YOU HAVE A BOOK ABOUT . . .?

Curt, a second grader, was one of the first children doing independent study that the newly trained library media specialist met. He had an insatiable thirst for escalator books, a subject about which there is limited source material for second graders. It became a challenge for the library media specialist to satisfy his request differently than an encyclopedia or dictionary could, while moving him along the search spectrum.

Luckily, the library media specialist found the question "What is an escalator?" asked and answered on Page 146 of Mary Elting's *Still More Answers*. Years later, she was to think of Curt again as she read the contents of *Joe Kaufman's What Makes It Go? What Makes It Work? What Makes It Fly? What Makes It Float?* On page 47, opposite an article on elevators, was a diagram and explanation about escalators. At long last she was prepared with a compare-and-contrast challenge should another escalator buff come along! To this day, she continues on the alert for definitive information about escalators, recently discovering in *Incredible Cross Sections*, under the topic *subways*, that a step on the average escalator moves 10,000 miles and the longest escalator is in the London Underground. Other books about *The Way Things Work* are plentiful now, colorful and three dimensional, often as part of 600s series.

Over the years, similar experiences with other gifted children on single-minded searches widened her interpretation of their requests for assistance. In their dogged search for more books on a particular topic, they appear to have firm footing on a small piece of the knowledge gameboard; they seem ready to go further on their own but really need guidance in stepping beyond the familiar to related or new areas. They are fledglings whom we expect to fly too soon. We assume that they acquire library media skills instinctively because they are smart. We insist that research for reporting must involve multiple sources without teaching them about all of the information retrievable from one good source. They need stimulating practice experiences in information gathering. Just as Pippi Longstocking introduced Tommy and Annika to the wonderful pastime of thing-finding, so should the library media specialist acquaint children with feats of fact finding and, as the Usborne series suggests, *Collecting Things,* from cabbages and kings to fossils, miniatures, stamps, shells, cards, and miniatures. The library media center provides the milieu to display students' facts and artifacts. Raps about the rain forest from the World Wildlife Fund, and simple poems from *Weekly Reader* that teach first graders about the "Continents of the World" show that mnemonic fun need not be rote learning. It nurtures curiosity as the cornerstone for building research and reporting readiness.

Second grader Brett read the caption on a picture of the Washington Monument in the library media center. "You know, two Washington Monuments equal one Eiffel Tower." He had discovered the Tower height when he was assembling a model and computed the connection between the buildings. "I like this kind of math," he commented. Just the right moment to produce David Macaulay's books on *Cathedral, Pyramid,* and *Underground.*

REFERENCES REQUIRED

Caleb's mother, a library volunteer, confided her concern that her third-grade son read only reference books for pleasure. It was reassuring for her to see that information books become more readable each year, in quality and range of subject matter, as individual titles or as series. These books contain some of the best expository writing and visual representation. Part of the information exploration process is the comparison and evaluation of different treatments of the same subject and the overall appeal of the different publications. The term *reference book* covers encyclopedias, dictionaries, atlases, almanacs, and special references. How Caleb and other youthful reference buffs today would relish the *Student Reference Library,* a CD-ROM with all of the research tools in one bundle!

Dictionaries

The range of dictionaries today extends beyond the introductory easy picture version to giant unabridged-housed-on-its-special-table variety. Lexicography has transformed into CD-ROM and gone online. It is built into computer programs with spell checks, grammar checks, and thesauri. The *Lincoln Writing Dictionary* and *Webster's Student Thesaurus* may be more young user friendly than the unabridged and Roget, but if the habit of looking up the word in the (print) dictionary is a hard one to instill, how will the looking up information electronically habit fare any better? In a reversal of the usual pattern, *The Illustrated Reverse Dictionary: Find the Word on the Tip of Your Tongue* invites the reader to look up the meaning to find the word. The jacket states that it is contains more information than a thesaurus, with opposites, charts, illustrations, and history. The Merriam-Webster Online website address is @www.Webster Dictionary. References continue to be added to this site.

Encyclopedias

Lois, the comic strip mother, asks her preteen son, "How could you finish a 10-page report in 15 minutes?" When the relaxing researcher responds, "With a CD-ROM encyclopedia and a word processor!" her comment is "Modern technology has given a new meaning to the term 'plagiarism'."

Encyclopedias were circles of knowledge since their introduction, in the sixth century for the topical arrangement, and the seventeenth for the alphabetical. Today, are encyclopedias the first step or the last resort in researching a topic and reporting on it? The compact writing style of most encyclopedia articles makes it difficult for children to internalize the information and summarize it in their own language, hence there has been the impetus to copy. To prevent this, teachers would often ban the use of encyclopedias, thus eliminating a quick source of information that also models outline form and other organizational tasks. The advent of CD-ROMs and online sources makes the computer print-out, complete with copyright information on each page, an exciting part of the procedure. When laborious hand copying becomes unnecessary, more attention may be paid to how the information ties together.

Students become familiar with encyclopedias just for fun through exploratory lessons. Create tasks applicable to gifted students of all age groups, regardless of the readability level of the particular encyclopedia. Some skills that are developed may be quite advanced, others less so, yet practice with all of them will enhance the quality of students' later reference work. As they pursue topics of their own choosing, students become familiar with the encyclopedia. The R2R4R (reference-to-research-for-reporting) group of third graders summarized these specific and general skills they gleaned from encyclopedia practice, most of them above the grade level scope and sequence:

1. Alphabetic order introduction and practice
   - location of guide words and choosing correct volume
   - differentiation between two kinds of alphabetic order—letter by letter and word by word

2. Bibliographic practice with
   - article titles, headings, and subheadings
   - entry words and cross-references
   - title, volume, and page citation

3. Format and style analysis
   - index
   - editions, revisions, updating, and omissions
   - static versus changing information
   - organization form for articles (e.g., outline, related articles)
   - graphics, maps, captions, tables, illustrations, and charts
   - accompanying study guides and teachers' exercises
   - comparability and evaluation of treatment of subject—between articles, encyclopedias, and editions

4. Number and arrangement of volumes
   - one-volume encyclopedias
   - multivolume sets: alphabetic or topical arrangement

Single volume encyclopedias range from *My First Golden Encyclopedia* (o.p.) for beginning researchers to the *Random House Encyclopedia* and the *Columbia Concise Encyclopedia* for adults. Two current one-volume encyclopedias for the very youngest are both entitled *My First Encyclopedia*, one by Troll (1991), another by Dorling-Kindersley (1993). For the next level of encyclopedia novices are the *Kingfisher Children's Encyclopedia* (1992), *Random House Children's* (1993), and Usborne's Children's Picture World Series. *Barron's Junior Fact Finder* (1989) is topical. The new *Oxford Family Encyclopedia* calls itself the ultimate single-volume reference for home, school, and office. The two adult desktop volumes are meant to be handy rather than scholarly, putting quick information at one's fingertips to encourage the look-it-up habit. The revised *Random House Encyclopedia*, printed as *The Joy of Knowledge* in some countries, tries to convey just that feeling to its readers. Its dual organization into Colorpedia and Alphapedia sections gives the young reader experience with topical and alphabetic arrangements. The overall contents of the Colorpedia section consist of "The Universe," "The Earth," and "Life on Earth." The section contents are "Man, History and Culture"; "Man and Science"; and "Man and Machines." Each section has a comprehensive time chart. The Alphapedia consists of brief entries indexed to the Colorpedia. The cross-references are called "connections." The colorpedic content has attractive and exciting illustrations and graphics. The *New York Public Library Student's Desk Reference* is arranged into 24 sections that cover similar topical territory. It bills itself as "The ultimate guide with answers to common questions on homework, hobbies, and more." It is also available online.

Multivolume resources enable younger children to experience encyclopedias. The 16 volumes of *Compton's Precyclopedia* (1988) are meant more for browsing by good readers than for straightforward information gathering by beginning researchers. A particular subject (e.g. animals or babies) will contain several articles in various forms, such as a story about an animal, a poem, miscellany, or an evocative illustration. The set is an example of eclectic coverage of a topic in contrast with the more typical comprehensive factual treatment. Young readers need to understand the distinction. Contents, index, activities for each alphabetic volume, and the teacher's guide afford many opportunities for practice with encyclopedic information. Other multivolume and topical encyclopedias written for the 7-to-11 age group are the *Oxford Children's Encyclopedia* (1991) in seven volumes and the *Young Children's Encyclopaedia Britannica* (1988), a younger version of *Children's Britannica* (1993). Some of these have limited coverage, but they give practice and success to researchers-in-training.

Does any print encyclopedia compare well with an electronic multimedia counterpart? Probably not . . . at first. The interactivity and graphic action of the CD ROM or online encyclopedias that are built into home computer systems is tough competition. Microsoft's *Encarta 98, Compton's Interactive,* and *Grolier's* are now joined by IBM's *World Book* (for Kids to Adults) and the imperial *Britannica CD 98*. All of these offer quick-find, research helpers, network interfaces, and other features that lessen the need for alphabetic access. The *Infopedia* is a CD ROM database that combines encyclopedia, atlas, thesaurus, almanac, English language dictionary, compact book of quotations, and a biographical dictionary. With a limited budget for the acquisition of reference materials, the library media specialist's quandary is to decide whether to invest for onshelf or online.

Almanacs

Mrs. Roper, a fifth-grade teacher with a large top reading group, arranged for the group to be responsible for the daily school announcements, only to discover that, verbal as they were, they sounded terrible over the public address system. She devised a program to improve their speaking and script writing skills. She asked the speech teacher to coach them in public speaking techniques. The students composed short pieces, then delivered them, first on audiotape, then on videotape. They used check sheets to rate themselves on content, performance, and improvement. Then the library media specialist worked further with them to enliven the presentations of the calendar material chosen from *School Library Media Activities Monthly*'s list of daily events.

Instruction on almanacs, whether in print or on disk, follows the pattern previously outlined for fact gathering. Students wrote a brief description of an almanac based on what they already knew, revising it after they examined almanac samples. Their definitions were compared with that in *Webster's Third Unabridged Dictionary*. Then students located contents and index, data on states and countries, statistical lists—highest mountains, baseball stats, and anything else they wanted to put in quiz form for each other. Two final products were created: a weekly miscellany show in a television magazine format for the whole school and a shell computer quiz program based on *3-2-1 Contact*'s monthly "Factoids" feature.

Special Reference Books

Subject or special reference books are a valuable resource for surveying a field of knowledge. Until recently, most of these specialized tools were difficult to understand and apply, even for gifted readers. Now, however, publishers are producing exciting materials covering most of the subjects that arouse gifted students' interest. Such newer books do not replace standard references, such as *Roget's Thesaurus* or *Webster's Biographical* and *Geographical Dictionaries* or *Bartlett's Familiar Quotations*. Rather, the newer books encourage an understanding of reference tools at an earlier age. A sampling of survey books in the various subject areas contains:

Benet's Readers' Encyclopedia

Encyclopedia of Science (D-K)

The Everyman Anthology of Poetry for Children

Golden Book of the Mysterious

Golden Book of Quotations: From the Penguin Dictionary of Quotations

Great Pets: An Extraordinary Guide to Usual and Unusual Family Pets

National Geographic Book of Mammals

National Geographic Picture Atlas of Our Fifty States

National Geographic Picture Atlas of Our Universe

National Geographic Picture Atlas of Our World

Newcomb's Wildflower Guide

Oxford Treasury of Children's Poems

The Rand McNally Atlas of World Wildlife

Webster's Student Thesaurus

World History (D-K Pocketful of Knowledge Book)

National Geographic's *Book of Mammals* was among the first books to be transformed into a CD-ROM. How wonderful to watch first and second graders' faces as the animals moved or roared; what statistics were there for the gathering and printing! CD-ROMs are increasingly higher tech, but the novelty remains.

Henry Holt Reference Books announced new directions in children's reference with two series published in 1996: W5 for the ages 11 to adult, and Your World Explained for ages 8 to 12. The W5 Series explores "history with an attitude," telling about important people in their venues, such as *Caesar and Rome, Alexander and His Times, Ramses II and Egypt, Michelangelo and His Times, Montezuma and the Aztecs, Victoria and Her Times, The Beatles and the Sixties*, as well as *Lucy* (the Happy Hominid) *and Her Times*. Holt's

Your World Explained Series offers beginner's guides to the world of dinosaurs, the universe, the earth, and religions of the world. No longer do interested learners have to search afar for the great connections. The connections are right at home in the collection!

SERIES BOOKS

British (e.g., Warwick Press, Gloucester, MacDonald Ltd., and Usborne) and other European publishers were pioneers in the production of highly visual, easier-to-read information books covering the spectrum of classified knowledge. Who would have predicted the 1990s explosion of these kinds of books that fill the shelves at Barnes and Noble or Borders bookstores? Young history, science, or technology buffs now have access to many books from which to refresh their memories or extend their knowledge.

A selective list of well-reviewed series and their publishers is just a beginning. Among those suitable for primary grade students:

Carolrhoda Start to Finish Books

Eyewitness Series D-K, introduced as Dorling-Kindersley Grosset and Dunlap *Poke and Learn*

Lerner First Fact Books

Lerner Natural Science Books

MacDonald First Fact Library, now Raintree

MacDonald's Peoples of the Past

The New True Books

Rourke's *Original People*

Scholastic's *First Discovery* Books

Usborne-Hayes Time Traveller Books

Usborne World History Programme

Warwick First Look at Nature

Not to be forgotten are handbooks and field guides including those by Roger Tory Peterson, still around after 60 years, and the Golden Guides of Science, Nature, and Field. Groups of first and second graders decided that the 50 titles in the MacDonald First Fact Library Set could be arranged by size or color, alphabetically, or by larger topic, like books about animals. These options were expanded to include numerical arrangements—leading to their discovery of the Dewey decimal system! In early 1997, a task force of the Library of Congress charged with resolving the problem of lack of shelf space recommended that books no longer be arranged by subject, but by size!

The Start to Finish series follows a process from raw material to manufactured product. This series fits well with similar expository books, like dePaola's whimsies about cloaks, clouds and popcorn. The Lerner First Fact book on famous planes includes the one in which Monsieur Bleriot flew across the English Channel, the same subject that the Provensen's chose for their 1983 Caldecott winner, a topic also cited in *The D-K Visual Timeline of the 20th Century*. In the *New York Times* Book Review (November 10, 1996) D-K advertises its books: SKIES THIGHS SPIES SIZE THAIS FLIES, then WISE. Years after enjoying *Peoples of the Past* and the Usborne's Children's Picture World Series, students will feel that they are renewing old friendships when they get to William Langer's monumental *Encyclopedia of World History* in college survey courses.

MISCELLANY MATTERS

A jumping-off point for stimulating interaction between student and library media center is a student's own quest or questions, about Curt's escalators or "*Do Animals Dream?*" A next stepping-stone is the pursuit of the trivial. Once in disfavor as an academic goal for the gifted, this has changed over the years, sparked by the game of *Trivial Pursuit* and its clones. Children's appetites for the trivial have always been high, judging by the demand for all the Guinness record books or the *Believe-It-or-Not* paperbacks. *The Biggest, Smallest, Fastest, Tallest* I-Can-Read satisfies first grade requests for Guinness. When Guinness nine-ounce paper cups and *Believe-It-or-Not* wrapping paper were supermarket shelf items, bright students were asked to find an educational use for each. The cups were turned into a mobile and the wrapping sheets were dry mounted onto a three-paneled learning center. While these particular miscellanies appeal to 7- to 11-year-olds' sense of the gross, the same curiosity can be channeled to materials of a higher order of taste. Books about inventions can lead to the quest for what the inventors of Jello, microwave popcorn, FM radio, fortified milk, and lasers had in common. The answer: none of them profited financially from their inventions. Inventions as a topics leads to books such as *Mothers and Daughters of Invention* or *The Kid Who Invented Popsicles and Other Surprising Stories about Inventions*. *Accidents May Happen* tells about *Mistakes That Worked*. Some *Amazing Firsts* were remarkable preventions; some inventive *What Ifs* changed the world, and some famous foolishnesses flopped, or did they? Books of old wives tales and superstitions such as *A January Fog Will Freeze a Hog* and *Cross Your Fingers, Spit in Your Hat* invite hypothesizing about literary and scientific What-Ifs and I-Used-to-Think's.

TO BEE OR NOT TO BEE

Many are the ways to showcase excellence in the performing arts, media production, and academic accomplishment. A 1996 statement of Montgomery County (Maryland)'s policy on gifted education mandates participation in academic competitions. Thinking and knowledge competitions are as diverse as "Olympics of the Mind" and "It's Academic." Old fashioned spelling and geography bees start in classrooms before they go to schoolwide, local, and national venues. Tapes of the old "Quiz Kids" and "Information Please" shows exist. Final Frontiers, the creation of a science resource teacher, sponsored by the National Institute of Standards and local businesses, awards prizes to "Best Engineers" for intriguingly titled projects utilizing everyday materials.

The Chess in the Schools program has gone national, and now 300 schools and more than 20,000 students participate. The 1997 Super National Scholastic Chess Championships in Tennessee attracted 4,300 entrants, ages four through 18, from 45 states. Fourth and fifth graders are taught bridge in a New York City program that may expand as more adults volunteer to teach. Last year's tournament winners were fourth graders who bid and made a six no-trump contract. An Annual Technology Challenge for middle and high schools has sixth graders designing "Why Didn't I Think of That?" projects. Belmont fifth grade geography buffs developed a writing contest on American Iconography for the best illustrated stories that linked Mother Nature, Father Time, Uncle Sam, and Miss Liberty.

Games and Simulations

Chess and Bridge and other old-fashioned games of strategy can be played with the computer as opponent. But the games arena in which the computer excels is in its simulations. CD-ROMS allow children to create a *SimCity*, a *SimIsle,* or *SimEarth* with all the concomitant details and challenges—economic, political, and social. *Anno's Learning Games* are for "Math and Magic" and "Logic and Laughs." Set chess, bridge, and mental olympics amid the related 700 materials in a library media center and call it all child's play!

Cooperative Competitions

Cooperative formats for intellectual competitions, with the objective being to play rather than to win, are popular. *Teams, Games, and Tournaments* (TGT) is one such cooperative strategy (Johns Hopkins, n.d). TGT fits with any subject curriculum as a way to master needed factual knowledge with a human relations side to the technique to allow children of all abilities to enjoy and participate equally. The TGT pattern starts with the creation of questions about the topic to be learned (e.g., American History—Exploration and Discovery, the Colonial Period, the War of Independence). The teacher, or even better, students, write 25 questions with brief answers which are reproduced on Q & A sheets for each child to learn. Each question is recorded on an index card with its answer on the reverse. As many sets of Q & A cards are made as there will be tournament tables. The class is divided into teams of five or six persons. In the tournament, one member of each team competes at each table for a timed round of questions. The questions go around the table. A correct answer by the team member at the table gains points for the team. For the next rounds, team members move around to other tables, with only one member from a team at a table for each round. Members bring their scores to the team captain after each round. After a specified competition time or number of rounds, the highest scoring team is the winner.

TGT works with any grade or subject curriculum, as long as the participants can read the index cards. The questions are intended to be rote facts for memorization by the participants. The higher-order aspects of this competition are in developing the questions and the all-ability inclusion of children for each team, with smarter children helping their team members learn and perform, as well as the time, record-keeping, and statistical analysis skills involved. It is a no-fail technique, satisfying for teacher and students alike.

STEPPING-STONES

Stepping-stones to the acquisition of information or the honing of thinking should be placed where they will encourage further meanderings amid almanacs and atlases; calendars, compendiums, and chronologies; periodicals and potpourris; and questions, quips, and quotations. By themselves, the materials are eclectic, but grouped together they form a pattern for systematic information gathering. Here, at no cost, is a framework for fourth- and fifth-grade recreation with miscellany. Some stepping-stone work has paid off. A Rand McNally-sponsored Oldest World Wall Map (one still in active use) Search won $10,000 in maps, globes, and atlases for the Wisconsin elementary school which had been using the 1893 map as a teaching tool for learning how the world has changed. In Virginia, school children notified a publisher about outdated country names on maps reproduced in its nationally distributed study guide book.

Alphabet Antics

Alphabets can be alliterative as in *All About Arthur (An Absolutely Absurd Ape)*; or author-itative, as in alphabet books by Anno, Wildsmith, Sendak, or Rockwell. Alphabets can be actable, with Marcel Marceau's miming. They can be calligraphic, as in Leonard Fisher's *Alphabet Art: Thirteen ABC's from Around the World*; or categorical, as a *Farmer's Alphabet*, or *Easy As Pie* introductions to similes. Like their counting book counterpart, today's alphabet books are multicultural and multilingual.

Bibliographic Byplay

Bibliographies can be compiled according to: author; literary form—science fiction, historical fiction by era, or for beginning readers or devotees; theme—of survival or courage; topic—African American history; and academic subject— math or science. Another bibliography model may be a topic acrostic. An acrostic is a series of lines or words, the first letters of which, when put together, form a word or message. For instance, an acrostic for the genre "humor" has the searcher looking for humorous book titles for the letters H U M O R, i.e., from *Homer Price* to *Room 10*. Before long, students are designing their own acrostic bibliographies.

Calendars and Chronologies

Calendar variations follow the day, the week, the month and the year, citing significant quotes or events. Each book of a series entitled, *19—, The Year You Were Born,* is a daily almanac of that special year in a reader's life. Other chronologies encompass time lines and yearbooks. *The Timetables of History,* a horizontal linkage of people and events, and *Ribbons of Time*, world history year by year since 1492, are examples of this appealing presentation of history that is easy for students to emulate.

Differentiated Diversions

When students participate in differentiated diversions, they are traversing the territory of library and information skills in a personalized way—personal to the students, themselves, and to the particular library media center in which they search. The common focus is the reason for which the source material is used and how it is organized. As students work with miscellanies, they should learn to discern whether the organizing feature is alphabetical, chronological, numerical, calendar, or eclectic. They should be able to describe the material's content in terms of its function. Is it topical, thematic, or chronological data? Then they should be able to relate all of these factors to their search.

Billy brought a picture clipped from the local newspaper to school. It showed two Korean sisters, ages five and nine, proudly waving American flags at their naturalization ceremony. The caption mentioned that the girls could name the 50 states of their new country. Billy wondered why they could perform this memory task while he and most of his classmates could not. The library media specialist suggested to the teacher that the class might wish to "fool around with facts" about states and capitals. After gathering facts from atlases, almanacs, encyclopedias, state books, and state information offices, the students contributed to a permanent vertical file on states: a complete set of hand-drawn transparency maps, one for each state, showing vital statistics in picture symbols and an illustrated spiral-bound book about each region of the United States. In addition, Rob and Billy scripted and coordinated the class production of an animated film, wherein their hero, an Uncle Sam-like character, was walking across a map of the United States when it suddenly exploded into 50 pieces. As he put the scattered bits back together, each state's outline showed the bird, the flower, and the capital city. Seeking out the same data about their own state, a fourth grade annually holds its State Fair with displays for each county. More recent fifth- and sixth-grade groups quizzed each other on 100 sample questions and answers would-be citizens should know in order to reach *A Very Important Day* when they obtained citizenship.

Lists of Books and Books of Lists

Bibliographic research combined with logical thinking puts students to work with lists of books and books of lists. The activity title itself is a *turnabout*, a form of wordplay suitable for exploration. Books of lists are popular, following the pioneer publications, the original *Guinness Book of World Records* and *Famous First Facts*. While these books are requested by all children, the reading and appropriateness levels are not below third grade. Second generation issues are many, and some are "easy-to-reads" with child appeal. A few titles include:

The Elementary School Kids' Book of Lists from the Kids' Stuff People

The Kids' Book of Lists: Kids' Firsts

The Teachers' Book of Lists

The World by Sevens: A Kid's Book of Lists

After reading books similar to these, students can be challenged to draw up lists of their own. The model for their lists can come from a workbook, a periodical, or, better still, students' original ideas.

Children see lists of books long before they are fluent in using them. Many basals have lists of recommended books at the end of each section. Children's rooms of public libraries have prepared illustrated leaflets listing titles for "Zooming Off into Reading," for I-Can-Reads, for the 50 best preschool books and the like. Adeptness at using or preparing a bibliography comes after practice with all kinds of categorizing. An adult title, *The List of Books: A Library of over 3,000 Works* selects over 3,000 works in 50 categories of an imaginary library. This is another model to adapt as a bibliographic project with children.

The largest and most unwieldy of book lists was the card catalog itself, the index to the contents of a library media center. Its replacement, whether book catalog, microfiche or intelligent catalog lacks the same charm and information. The world's largest card catalog once dominated the main reading room of the Jefferson Building at the Library of Congress. In the building's recent restoration, the catalog has been replaced by an adjacent computer room.

Periodicals and Potpourris

Children rarely ask for instruction in using periodicals, but they benefit from guidance in "discovering" their value. The assortment of magazines available for elementary collections is large and fluctuating. Some long-time favorites have ceased publication to be replaced by newer titles. Those in which content is topical rather than timely retain their usefulness as instructional tools, for providing valid information and practice in indexing and for making collages. Several titles are especially recommended for teaching purposes.

Scienceland is a monthly written for primary grades with applications for students in higher grades. Each issue has a well-explored theme with audience appeal and curricular relevance. The publication offers interesting material, good expository writing, superior graphics, and features a vocabulary and glossary. *Dragonfly* is a magazine for young investigators. *Cobblestone*, a magazine of American history, is topical, graphic, and informative. A survey of annual issues indicates how information can be grouped and regrouped according to different access features: calendar order—a year of monthly issues; alphabetical order—an index; and chronological order—a time line of American history. These arrangements can be tied into the Dewey decimal classification system or a literary form, such as biography or historical fiction. The Cricket Magazine Group publishes four magazines to entertain infants to 14-year-olds. *Babybug, Ladybug, Spider,* and *Cricket* are examples of literary anthologies with age-appropriate selections culled from many sources. *Weekly Reader* celebrated 60 years of news for kids, from 1928 to 1988, with their "best of" collection. As elementary students use the acknowledgments to trace articles back to original or primary sources, they gain experiences directly transferable to later academic research.

The Cobblestone Publishing Company's 1997 Spring Catalog, showing the covers of all its magazines' past issues, cries out to be a lesson in indexing and topical searching. *Faces* is to cultural anthropology as *Odyssey* is to science as *Muses* is to museums and *Calliope* to world history. Cobblestone's *Teaching with Primary Sources* and other resource books give teachers the reproducible wherewithal to enliven the teaching of history, geography, science, and the classics. Candlewick Press produces *The History News* of amazing facts about *Explorers* and *Medicine* and news about life in ancient civilizations, such as *The Egyptian News, The Greek News*, and *The Roman News*. These all include items about facts and fads, perhaps to inspire student newscasts from the past.

Online-Offline is a fascinating index of themes and resources for students in grades K-8. On America Online, *Cyberkids*, a resource created for children's cybrarians, is available. *Horizon: The Learning Section*, is a weekly supplement to a daily newspaper, *The Washington Post*. It is a higher-level *Weekly Reader* type of resource. The choice of topics and the manner in which the material is presented make it an ideal tool for gifted classrooms—either by subscription or on the World Wide Web. *Time* magazine publishes a news weekly for kids, with a scavenger hunt quiz attached. Owl publishes *Cybersurfer, the Owl Internet Guide for Kids*. Curriculum connections abound through e-mail and on websites.

Potpourri books are general mixtures covering a wide range and flavor of topics. Sometimes these books have a strong thread tying the parts together, like *The Hodgepodge Book: An Almanac of American Folklore* or *The Spice of America* that tells of the (almost) state of Franklin and other American phenomena. Other books have more tenuous or contrived themes: conglomerations of facts, riddles, jokes, and calendar data. Accordingly, some books have more significance or literary merit than others, but they all serve the function of opening up the world of information gathering.

Questions and Quotations

The question and answer format has been around for a long time. In some content areas, such as science, new knowledge often makes old answers obsolete; but, for the most part, books in question format provide information on popular subjects, even as they show how facts can be accumulated, presented, and organized. For more than 30 years, Mary Elting has been writing answers to children's questions about history, technology, and themselves. Charles Schultz published five books of Charlie Brown's science Qs and As—books about how things work, all kinds of animals, the earth and space, and people. Ann McGovern's books give answers to what life would be like *If You Lived in Colonial Times* or with the mammoth hunters or sailed on the *Mayflower* or grew up with Abraham Lincoln who attended "blab school." Lerner and Four Winds have series books of Qs and As about robots, space travel, and other scientific frontiers. Even *Star Wars* is in the business of publishing questions for answering. *You Asked?* and OWL Books answers 20 years of questions.

"To learn is to change" and "education is a process that changes the learner" are two statements on the subject of learners. "To communicate, put your thoughts in order, give them a purpose, use them to persuade, instruct, to discover and entice" is also useful advice. These *bon mots* are gleaned from *The New York Times Book of Twentieth Century Quotations* via America On Line. Many collections of quotable quotes with instructional applications fill the shelves of the megabookstores. Quotations are discussion provokers and connectors between clever words, the people who said them, and the circumstances in which they were said. Proverbs and epigrams link biography and history. They are examples of sentence structure, verbal acuity, and pithy writing. Quotations may be alphabetically or chronologically arranged. They represent words children may or should know, written or spoken by significant people they may or should know. Words and people can be matched or mixed. Who said this? Who was this person? Younger children put *First Things First* when they choose their own useful sayings. Older students can find personal favorites in the *Golden Book of Quotations,* the *Home Book of Quotations*, the CD-ROM version of *Bartlett's,* or the fourth edition of *The Oxford Dictionary of Quotations* to arrange sayings as a calendar with a quote for each day throughout the year. The daily newspaper is a source of quotes of current newsworthiness. Going beyond the proverbial wisdom of Ben Franklin, 1,500 entries of aphorisms, idioms, and catch phrases are included in the newly published *Random House Dictionary of Popular Proverbs and Sayings. Too Many Cooks . . . and Other Proverbs* may be written out then cut apart like jigsaw sentences, for students to unscramble and discuss. Have students find notable quotes from quotable notables to combine with biographical information. They can even fool around with misquotes.

Serendipity Searches and Stone Soup

Two variations on the theme of miscellaneous matters depend on the teacher being attuned to seizing the right moment.

Serendipity Searches begin when, in pursuit of other information, students come across some hitherto unknown fact or facts that pique their curiosity. Is this true? is the typical reaction. The teacher should then seek verification from a standard reference source. In one such sequence, students were reading aloud bits and pieces from *You Can't Eat Peanuts in Church and Other Little Known Laws*, a book about strange laws still in effect. One item told of the prohibition against driving camels along Nevada's main highways. Coincidentally, at the same time, someone rummaging through the vertical file found an article entitled "Camel Power" in an old issue of *Highlights* magazine detailing the army's attempt to deploy camels in their desert operations after the Mexican War. The two items were enough to trigger a camel data verification hunt, unearthing the additional fact that it is against Arizona law to hunt camels. The ultimate camel confirmation came when that class visited the Arts and Industries building of the Smithsonian Institution. In an exhibit on military ordnance was a life-sized camel bedecked with saddle and small cannon ready for service in the Camel Corps.

Another case of the serendipitous development of a lesson series occurred after the reading of *Beautiful Junk: A Story of the Watts Towers*. The photographed story tells of a fictitious encounter between an angry boy who decries the squalor of the Watts ghetto in which he lives and an old man who has transformed it by building towering structures from junk heaps. The Watts Towers do exist, landmarks in Los Angeles, built by a mysterious eccentric, Simon Rodia. Tracking down the story proved to be an adventure, but beyond that, were opportunities to integrate ideas and materials about architecture, city ordinances, creativity, and pop art versus museum art. The Smithsonian Museum of American Art has on display a room-sized sculpture composed of tinfoil-wrapped junk. It had been found in an abandoned shed, where its creator, another recluse, had spent years working on his sculpture. A possible question for consideration is why the work was transferred to such a prestigious home. What about modern sculpture found in *A Child's Garden of Sculpture*? Other postscripts were added to the unit bibliography as the Watts Towers appeared on "The Grain in the Stone" episode of the television series of Jacob Bronowski's *The Ascent of Man*. Watts Towers later appeared on page one of *The Superman Book of Superhuman Achievements*.

Stone Soup is the art of making something from almost nothing. Publishers' seasonal catalogs and newspaper/magazine clippings are some of the scraps from which a soup is concocted. The "Clippers" were fifth graders who scoured catalogs for pictures and words that could be cut and pasted into collage vertical file materials. Their apple lessons sprouted from a picture file series of photographs of an apple in three stages: whole; with one bite out; and nibbled to a core. Where would a photo of apple slices fit? Some students remembered a kindergarten lesson about three apples, two cut to show vertical and horizontal cross sections and the third with a zig zag cut to open into what shape?

Students were asked to arrange the pictures sequentially with a story. Most obvious (to the teacher) was 1-2-3; what pedestrian thinking, compared to what the students did! Alex told about 3-1-2: "finished an apple, got another, began to eat." Megan's story went 2-1-3: "took one bite—didn't like, got another, finished it up." Davey's story was a reverse 3-2-1 about "a dog who had three apples. He tried one and, liking it, ate it to the core. He took a bite out of another. It was poisoned. He keeled over dead so the last apple was never eaten." Carrie suggested the apple could regenerate, like the rewind on a videorecorder.

They discussed apple aphorisms—"an apple a day" and "apples are . . . 'nature's toothbrush' and 'good for you' "; then the language of apples—delicious, juicy, red, rotted, brown; and then questions about apples—how many species, how long does it take to eat one, why call a computer Apple? Next the Clippers found apple data in the library media center . . . in fiction, folklore, legend, biography, nonfiction books on farming, seed catalogues in the vertical file, picture books, and nutritional cook books—the gamut of Dewey on the shelves. Then they were ready to compile an apple bibliography: *The Hungry Caterpillar*, *William Tell*, Aliki's *Johnny Appleseed, Snow White, A Is for Apple,* Gibbons' *The Season's of Arnold's Apple Tree*, and the role of the apple in the discovery of gravity by Sir Isaac Newton.

Wonderful Sevens of the World

The number seven is magic. A series of books about the Seven Wonders of the Ancient World, the Seven Modern Wonders, the Seven Natural Wonders, and the Seven Mysterious Wonders reconstructs these edifices in three dimensions. Recently, the American Society of Civil Engineers named the marvels built in the twentieth century that were the biggest engineering challenges or benefited humanity. They are the Channel Tunnel, Toronto's CN Tower, the Empire State Building, the Golden Gate Bridge, the Itaipu Dam in South America, the North Sea Protection Works, and the Panama Canal. A 1996 list of Endangered Monuments to Mankind, published by the World Monuments Fund, sadly lists more than seven *Wonders of the World*. One hundred sites in need of conservation are named, covering a gamut of time and place. Some on the list, like the Taj Mahal and Angkor Vat, are well known to be in need of preservation, while many of the other sites are not. Information and research potential is plentiful in archeology, geography, ecology, and history.

The activities described in this chapter are "QuickCapers" reflecting current catchwords and crazes of the popular culture. They are entertainments not to be given more attention than they merit, nor should their value be underestimated. They are linking tools that are concrete examples of the interrelatedness of learning. The library media rubric is a progression wherein students indicate their prior knowledge by briefly defining the source material, either orally or in writing. After this, the understandings of the group members are compared with an authoritative definition (e.g., from *Webster's Third Unabridged Dictionary)*. Students then practice locating facts using contents, index, and page browsing. The long-range goal is for students to be able to adapt miscellaneous information to their own purposes and present it in a format modeled after the sources. Many journeys thus begun on locating levels of thinking have been transformed by students themselves into clever middle-grade library media applications for the gifted, byways en route to a higher level of cultural literacy: a curriculum called "Literary Capers."

REFERENCES

Johns Hopkins Team Learning Project. n.d. *Teams, Games, and Tournaments.* Johns Hopkins Team Learning Project. Center for Social Organization of Schools.

BIBLIOGRAPHY

All About Arthur (An Absolutely Absurd Ape). Eric Carle. New York: Franklin Watts, 1974.

Alphabet Art: Thirteen ABC's from Around the World. Leonard Fisher. New York: Four Winds Press, 1978.

Animal Fact/Animal Fable. Seymour Simon. New York: Crown, 1979.

Anno's Alphabet: An Adventure in Imagination. Mitsumasa Anno. New York: Harper & Row, 1975.

Anno's Counting Book. Mitsumasa Anno. New York: Harper & Row, 1977.

Barron's Junior Fact Finder: An Illustrated Encyclopedia for Children. New York: Barron's, 1989.

Beautiful Junk: A Story of the Watts Towers. Jon Madian. Boston: Little, Brown, 1968.

Benet's Reader's Encyclopedia. 4th ed. Bruce Murphy, ed. New York: HarperCollins, 1976.

The Biggest, Smallest, Fastest, Tallest: Things You've Ever Heard Of. Robert Lopshire. New York: Thomas Y. Crowell, 1980.

Brian Wildsmith's ABC. Brian Wildsmith. New York: Franklin Watts, 1963.

Cathedral: The Story of Its Construction. David Macaulay. Boston: Houghton Mifflin, 1973.

Charlie Brown's Super Books of Questions and Answers. Charles M. Schultz. A series. New York: Random House, n.d.

Children's Brittanica. Chicago: Encyclopaedia Britannica, 1991.

A Child's Garden of Sculpture. Elinor Lander Horowitz. Washington, DC: Washingtonian Books, 1976.

Compton's Precyclopedia. Chicago: Encyclopaedia Brittanica, 1988.

The Concise Columbia Encyclopedia. New York: Columbia University Press, 1989. Also online.

Cross Your Fingers, Spit in Your Hat. Collected by Alvin Schwartz. Philadelphia: J. B. Lippincott, 1974.

Do Animals Dream? Joyce Pope. New York: Viking, 1986.

Do You Know?: More Than 100 Fascinating Things to Know. B. G. Ford. New York: Random House, 1979.

The D-K Visual Timeline of the Twentieth Century. New York: Dorling Kindersley, 1996.

Easy As Pie: A Guessing Game of Sayings. Marcia Folsom and Michael Folsom. New York: Clarion Books, 1985.

The Elementary School Kids' Book of Lists from the Kids' Stuff People. Sacramento, CA: Incentive, 1981.

Encyclopedia Brown's Third Record Book of Weird and Wonderful Facts. Donald J. Sobol. New York: William Morrow, 1985.

Farmer's Alphabet. Mary Azarian. Boston: Godine,1981.

First Things First: Useful Sayings. Betty Fraser. New York: HarperCollins, 1990.

The Goat in the Rug. Charles Blood. New York: Simon & Schuster, 1990.

Golden Book of the Mysterious. Jane Watson and Sal Chaneles. New York: Golden Press/Western, 1976.

Golden Book of Quotations: From the Penguin Dictionary of Quotations. J. M. Cohen and M. J. Cohen. New York: Golden Press, 1964.

Great Pets: An Extraordinary Guide to Usual and Unusual Family Pets. Sara Stein. New York: Workman, 1976.

Guinness Book of World Records. New York: Facts on File, annual.

The Hodgepodge Book: An Almanac of American Folklore. Duncan Emerich, comp. New York: Four Winds Press, 1972.

Horizon: The Learning Section. From the *Washington Post.* E-mail: horizon@washpost.com.

If You Lived in Colonial Times. Ann McGovern. New York: Four Winds Press, 1976.

The Illuminated Book of Days. Kay Lee and Marshall Lee. New York: G. P. Putnam's Sons, 1979.

The Illustrated Reverse Dictionary: Find the Word on the Tip of Your Tongue. Pleasantville, NY: Reader's Digest, 1990.

Incredible Cross Sections. Stephen Biesty. New York: Alfred A. Knopf, 1992.

A January Fog Will Freeze a Hog and Other Weather Folklore. Hubert Davis, ed./comp. New York: Crown, 1977.

Joe Kaufman's What Makes It Go? What Makes It Work? What Makes It Fly? What Makes It Float? Joe Kaufman. New York: Golden Press, 1971.

The Kids' Book of Lists: Kids' First. Margo McLoone-Basta and Alice Siegel. New York: Holt, Rinehart & Winston, 1980.

Kingfisher Children's Encyclopedia. John Paton. 4th ed. New York: Kingfisher, 1992.

Kingfisher Illustrated History of the World: 40,000 BC and Present. New York: Kingfisher, 1992.

The Last Cow on the White House Lawn and Other Little Known Facts About the Presidency. Barbara Seuling, New York: Doubleday, 1978.

Lincoln Writing Dictionary. Christopher Morris. New York: Harcourt Brace Jovanivich, 1989.

The List of Books: A Library of over 3,000 Works. Frederick Raphael and Kenneth McLeish. New York: Harmony Books, 1981.

Macmillan Illustrated Almanac for Kids. Ann Elwood, Carol Orsay, and Sidney Solomon. New York: Macmillan, 1981.

The Marcel Marceau Counting Book. George Mendoza. New York: Doubleday, 1971.

Mistakes That Worked. Charlotte Jones. New York: Doubleday, 1994.

Mothers and Daughters of Invention. Autumn Stanley. Lanham, MD: Scarecrow Press, 1993.

My First Encyclopedia. London; New York: Dorling-Kindersley, 1993.

My First Encyclopedia. Mahwah, NJ: Troll, 1992.

My First Golden Encyclopedia. Jane Werner Watson. New York: Golden Press, 1971.

National Geographic Book of Mammals. 2 vols. Also CD ROM. Washington, DC: National Geographic Society, 1978.

National Geographic Picture Atlas of Our Fifty States. Washington, DC: National Geographic Society, 1978.

National Geographic Picture Atlas of Our Universe. Roy A. Gallant. Washington, DC: National Geographic Society, 1980.

National Geographic Picture Atlas of Our World. Washington, DC: National Geographic Society, 1979.

The New Illustrated Encyclopedia of the World. William Langer, comp. New York: Abrams, 1975.

New York Public Library Students' Desk Reference. New York: Stonesong Press, 1993.

Newcombe's Wildflower Guide. Lawrence Newcomb. Boston: Little, Brown, 1977.

19— The Year You Were Born. New York: Tambourine Books, 1993.

Norman Rockwell's Americana ABC. George Mendoza. New York: Dell, 1975.

NYPL Student's Desk Reference. New York: Stonesong Press, 1993.

Oxford Children's Encyclopedia. London: Oxford University Press, 1991.

Oxford Family Encyclopedia. London: Oxford University Press, 1997.

Pyramid. David Macauley. Boston: Houghton Mifflin, 1975.

The Rand McNally Atlas of World Wildlife. Skokie, IL: Rand McNally, 1973.

Random House Children's Encyclopedia. New York: Random House, 1993.

Random House Dictionary of Popular Proverbs and Sayings. Gregory Titelman. New York: Random House, 1966.

Random House Encyclopedia. 3rd ed. New York: Random House, 1990.

SimCity 2000. Walnut Creek, CA: MAXIS. Also *SimIsle, SimPark, SimEarth, SimTower*.

The Spice of America. June Swanson. Minneapolis, MN: Carolrhoda, 1983.

Star Wars Question and Answer Book About Computers. Fred D'Ignazio. New York: Random House, 1983.

Still More Answers. Mary Elting. New York: Grosset & Dunlap, 1971.

Student Reference Library. Lewes, East Essex, UK: Mindscape. CD-ROM.

The Superman Book of Superhuman Achievements. Shep Steneman. New York: Random House, 1981.

The Teachers' Book of Lists. Sheila Madsen and Bette Gould. Santa Monica, CA: Goodyear, 1979.

365 Things to Know. Clifford Parker. New York: Western, 1969.

Too Many Cooks . . .: And Other Proverbs. New York: Green Tiger Press, 1992.

Underground. David Macauley. New York: Houghton Mifflin, 1976.

Usborne Book of Collecting Things. Kate Needham. London: Usborne House, 1995.

Usborne's Children's Picture World Series. London: Usborne House, n.d.

A Very Important Day. Maggie Herold. New York: Morrow Junior Books, 1996.

Webster's Student Thesaurus. Springfield, MA: G & C Merriam, 1978.

Weekly Reader: 60 Years of News for Kids, 1928-1988. New York: World Almanac, 1988.

What If? Fifty Discoveries That Changed the World. Dian Buchman and Seli Groves. New York: Scholastic, 1988.

Wonders of the World. Giovanni Caselli. Boston: D-K/ Houghton Mifflin, 1992.

The World by Sevens: A Kid's Book of Lists. Louis Phillips. New York: Franklin Watts, 1981.

You Asked: The Kids Q & A Book, rev. ed. New York: Grosset & Dunlop, 1988.

You Can't Eat Peanuts in Church and Other Little Known Laws. Barbara Seuling. New York: Doubleday, 1975.

Young Children's Encyclopaedia Britannica. Howard Goodkind, ed. 16 v. Chicago: Encyclopaedia Britannica, 1988.

Ten

Roots and Wings

Leonard Bernstein, the American composer and conductor, spoke as the honored guest on the occasion of the 350th anniversary of Boys' Latin School, his alma mater. His speech, delivered in Boston on November 21, 1984, was reported in the *New York Times*. He told of two important revelations. The first was about how he learned from his school:

> (It was) an initiation into the love of learning how to learn, that was revealed to me by my (BLS) masters as a matter of interdisciplinary cognition- that is, learning to know something by its relation to something else.

The second was about connections, connections between

> George Washington, Haydn, the French Revolution, Payne and the *Rights of Man*, the birth of Samuel F. B. Morse, the death of John Wesley, Mozart's death and the premier of his opera *The Magic Flute*, Wagner, Beethoven, Lincoln and the Civil War, the founding of the Ku Klux Klan and the laying of the trans-Atlantic cable.

> "Do you see?" he said in summation. "A known fact is like a dry dead thing. But when these connections are made, wham!" (Daniels 1984)

CULTURAL LITERACY REDUX . . . MULTICULTURAL LITERACY

Since 1636, a Latin School education has been synonymous with the idea of a classical education as the basis of cultural literacy. Cultural literacy as a goal of public education was put aside for many years until the publication of *Cultural Literacy,* when the phrase was reborn as the educational catchword of the next decade. Then came *A First Dictionary of Cultural Literacy: What Our Children Need to Know,* based upon the New York Public Library's *Reference Books for Children*. Following in 1991 was The Core Knowledge Book Series of resource books for grades one through six, the "stuff" of a good elementary education. Each book in the series presents topics according to subject/discipline, serially and spirally. Great resources of people and production—graphic and textual—are used in the series to introduce or refresh knowledge in the areas of language arts, geography and civilizations, the fine arts, and math and science. The original Hirsch lists were thought to be too Euro-centered to reflect today's students' world. The Core Knowledge series of books rectified this omission by including ideas from other cultures in each book.

Who Found America? is a challenging question asked in the title of Johanna Johnston's book written in 1973. The book was unique because of her usual free verse style and its inclusion of minorities as the first residents and finders of the new world. The word multicultural now embraces the four ethnic minority environments prominent in the United States, the African American, the Native American, the Asian American, and the Hispanic American, as well as the heritage from whence each came. The world of children's literature represented in the holdings of a school library media center should reflect all of these strands. The Tables of Contents of the Hirsch books and Simonton's *Graywolf Annual Five: Multicultural Literacy* become planning guides from which to develop bibliographies and lesson plans, as does *Sweet Words So Brave: The Story of African American Literature* (Curry and Brudie 1997). Cultural literacy in 1998 is multicultural literacy through the resources of the library media center. Expressed initially:

CL'98 = MCL via the LMC.

LITERARY CAPERS

The descriptor, "Literary Capers" was volunteered by Mike as the title the teacher should have chosen for the summer course. He was evaluating the course content and student participation while he helped her close out the classroom. He enjoyed the class, he told her, but the title, Story-ways, Story-wise, was a put-off. His advice was: "If you had just called it Literature or Reading Books, more of my friends would have signed up this year. Next year, be honest; tell them what it is—sort of literary capers—and the older kids like me will sign up; maybe even as first choice, over computers."

What did Mike mean by Literary Capers? He meant connections—between

current and past ideas;

curriculum disciplines;

fiction and nonfiction;

content, process, and product;

sources of information;

literary forms;

the popular and the academic;

familiar and emerging domains of knowledge; and

readers, writers, and storytellers.

Literary Capers nourish the roots and test the wings of elementary school children. They are bridges between the useful and the ornamental. They are conduits for merging children's own worthwhile ideas with the intellectual mainstream in a place where multicultural literacy is apart from doctrinal debates about prescribed curriculum content.

Literary Capers are the "Wham," a continuing, yet changing, series of explorations with gifted students. The library media center is the milieu through which to highlight well-expressed ideas, those that introduce or emanate from a basic subject, simultaneously enrich students' backgrounds and extend their databases. Specific lesson recipes are less important than the teacher's belief in his or her role as a builder of multicultural bridges. No text with teacher's guide exists, but the problem of what materials to use is minimal. A comfortable starting place is the teacher's own expertise and preferences. The best lesson development is often happenstance, independent of planning, as in the case of Harriet and the scientists in Chapter 8. While curriculum writers are not likely to predict the gaps in a student audience's background knowledge, the teacher who chances upon a gap should be ready to follow the new direction.

Because Literary Capers are informal lessons begun as book talks to supply or extend a gifted child's or group's experiences with familiar topics or themes, the technique often seems more spontaneous than planned. In reality, for any series of lessons, the library media specialist must consider its purpose, the level of difficulty, the materials of input, the time required, how to record what happens, and an expected output. The kind of children themselves is a factor affecting the planning and execution of the unit. Priscilla Vail categorizes the range of children who fall under the umbrella of the identified gifted: a range from bright child to gifted child to prodigy to genius (Vail 1979). This sets a range of working group size from fifteen to eight, to four, down to one in any class, grade, or school.

As Transition Curriculum

Literary Capers dovetail with a model proposed by Sandra Kaplan. In order for students to acquire an appreciation for any subject (e.g., literature), Kaplan proposes that a teacher must help them "know the subject as a separate entity, as foundation for other learnings in other disciplines, as it relates to another subject, and as an integral part of other learnings." Literary Capers fits Kaplan's definition of a transition curriculum as one "designed to aid the gifted learner in making the transition from being a participant in the general standard, or regular, curriculum to the differentiated curriculum. The Transition Curriculum serves as a passage, link, or bridge between two curricula that each demand different modes of learning, responding, and being" (Kaplan 1984). Transition curriculum describes much of the ad hoc programming developed to provide for the needs of gifted children at a local level. As such a curriculum for able students, Literary Capers

encourage or reinforce learning through trade books;

add to students' databases and widen their horizons;

stimulate the imaginative expression of ideas; and

guide students toward creating literary capers of their own.

As CUES Curriculum

The objectives of a CUES curriculum—whether daily or weekly—stipulate that students will choose books and other library materials to study, discuss, and evaluate. They will use different literary forms and library media formats to enrich their language proficiency and extend their fields of knowledge as they devise ways to share their interpretations.

Informed choice is a fundamental part of decision making and problem solving. Giving students some criteria by which they can choose and evaluate library media materials is a step in this direction. The Choose aspect of CUES concentrates on students as consumers and critics. It offers quick tricks for sizing up materials—the blurb, the flyleaf, reviews, appeal of format—to help children weigh literary merit, social significance, popularity, and personal taste. It confronts them with issues of judgment, censorship, and ethics. Children are open to having their repertoires extended, so it is worthwhile to spend class time learning how to choose books.

Some factors influencing reading choices are: exposure to an assortment of materials, an interesting topic, a contemporary setting, characters of the audience's age, paperback format, more action and less descriptive narration, illustrations, and some name recognition—through peer recommendation, television/film version, or story hour introduction. Many teachers who once dismissed the class visit to the library as time wasted just reading stories now clamor for read-aloud programs. The topic of current popular books is a good departure point for using lists to verify or extend a class's literary choices. Two *Booklist* reprints by Barbara Elleman and Betsy Hearn, entitled *Books for Every Child*: *Contemporary Fiction Classics* and *Books for Everychild: Picture Book Classics,* each select 50 books "that belong in the life of every child's growing years." Which books have been all-time favorites? How does the top 50 list change each year? *Literary Laurels: Kids Edition* is "A Reader's Guide to Award-Winning Children's Books." The selections in Scholastic's Children's Book of the Month Club roster are a combination of long time favorites and current classics. The New York Public Library's showing of the Books of the Century can be emulated in a school library media center.

In the Use part of CUES, the objective is to help students become familiar with the glossary and distinguishing features of different literary forms and media formats. Genre, or literary form, includes

- fiction and nonfiction;

- folklore and fairy tales;

- realism and fantasy;

- narrative and expository;

- adventure and mystery;

- humor as parody, satire, or slapstick;

- short story and anthology; and

- poetry, drama, and speeches.

Students also need to be aware of media formats: print—magazines, charts, posters, and pamphlets; and nonprint—filmstrips, films, realia, models, artifacts, video tapes, exhibits, software, and online.

The E element in CUES, Enjoy, is something that is not measurably taught—the intrinsic reward. Perhaps a better goal for the E to stand for is Enrichment or Extension of students' abilities to interpret ideas as they read, talk, write, think, and learn about anything or everything. Some able children naturally arrive at a balance between learning and knowledge, an equilibrium fostered by a childhood in which books were treasured. Visits to a public or school library were "open sesames" to a larger world of the reader's own making, a world to be shared at home and in school. But, alas, the prospect of finding out about our cultural, scientific, and literary heritage is not an automatic inspiration for all bright children. Usually someone, parent or teacher, has to set the stage. This realization alone justifies Literary Capers as an instructional program for gifted children in the elementary school.

The Share objective of CUES entails students producing information for sharing with others, be it something printed, performed, programmed, or projected.

CULTURAL LITERACY—
LITERARY CAPERS

In the first chapter of *The Green Book*, Father tells the children to pack a change of clothes, two personal items, and one book each as they prepare to evacuate the Earth in advance of a great disaster. When asked to jot down how they would follow these instructions, some members of Literary Capers classes opted to take an extra book instead of one personal item. In later chapters of Jill Paton Walsh's survival science fiction novel, the questions of trading books, other people's choices, and unworthy editions of classics arise. Another element for discussion is Patty's choice of a blank bound book. At first, her family expresses chagrin at her apparent waste of a limited resource, but when she produces her record of their new life on the planet Shine, the green book becomes an asset to the community, a latter-day commonplace book.

The Classics

Patty might have chosen a classic to take to Shine, one recommended by her parents and teachers. Is that what classics are—books fondly remembered by adults who think they should be read by children today? Are classics books that have stood the test of time, have literary merit, and deal with universal themes, values, and the human experience? Are classics those books that are the most popular or the best-sellers in the children's book departments? Can contemporary books be classics? Are classics the books that all of the kids are vying to check out? Are classics the books that would be placed in a sealed time capsule, taken to a desert island, or put in a backpack? The answer to all of these is yes, but the question is really one of personal choices based on all of the given reasons. A valuable resource is a vertical file labeled "Books and Reading." It should contain articles by authors, book reviewers, teachers, children, or anyone who treasures books and libraries in their lives. There young readers will find that Katherine Paterson's childhood favorites were *The Secret Garden* and *The Yearling* and that Beverly Cleary's third-grade favorites were Lucy Fitch Perkins twins series books, which are about to be revised for today's market. The old Dick and Jane reading primers are returning. Their dog will share the "Spot" light with his namesake, Eric Hill's adventurous Spot, as well as Margaret Wise Brown's sentient Muffin. And what could be more classic than the centennial Anniversary Edition of *Treasure Island* with the 1911 illustrations of N. C. Wyeth?

Classic status for current books is directly related to popularity and best-seller lists. Many questions of the Literary Quotient (LQ) in Chapter 5 reinforce this fact. After students have used the LQ as an ice breaker, it becomes a survey instrument for tabulating and a database for recording and collating reading habits and interests. A summary of responses over the years shows a curious mix in awareness about favorite authors, kinds of books, and range of interests. Where once the names Judy Blume and Beverly Cleary led the list of authors and a surprising number of older titles and authors appeared, the Choose Your Own Adventures and Sweet Valley High series appeared. Like Nancy Drew, the Hardy Boys, and other stable written series of the past, librarians considered these titles unsuitable for their collections. More favorably considered are the American Girls Collection of stories (and merchandise) about girls who lived in different eras. Under pressures of censorship and the teaching of "values," R. L. Stine's Goosebumps series revives the perennial quandary: Is any reading better than no reading?

Media Uses of Classics

Adapting classics for a younger audience is not new in the book world, but today's media adaptations are, on video tape, on film, and online. On public television, *Wishbone,* the Jack Russell terrier, jumps into each episode of adult and children's classic stories. When Michael in sixth grade chose to read *The Red Badge of Courage*, it was Wishbone that made the novel appeal to him. Fifth-grade Girl Scouts on a museum tour were unusually cogent about myths and legends and American history. When the docent praised this background knowledge, the answer was not "We learned it in school," but "We watch Wishbone." Not only does Wishbone tread the boards each day, he also travels the country performing for thousands of children. He sells products, of course, but he sells adventures with books, too. As do *Barney, Sesame Street, Mr. Rogers*, and others. Newbery award books like *Shiloh* become well-reviewed films. Marc Brown's aardvark Arthur and his sisters star in a public television series that will appear in 96 countries. What multicultural power! Click on the *Washington Post* Web icon to read first chapters of currently reviewed books. Chat rooms for kids encourage further reviewing and discussions. Dr. Seuss's zippy style was adapted into rhymes advertising Ford cars. At the American Library Association's meetings, the exhibits are outstanding multimedia.

Folklore Treasures to Explore

Collections galore of tales from around the world exist to compare and contrast—anthologies distinctive to the narrative and artistic styles of their author/illustrators. Judy Sierra is a newcomer to the anthology ranks with her *Nursery Tales Around the World. Eric Carle's Treasury of Classic Stories for Children* includes the author/illustrator's versions of works by Aesop, Hans Christian Andersen, and the Brothers Grimm. *The Best Children's Books in the World* promises a *Treasury of Illustrated Stories*. Which titles are there? *When the World Was Young* is a collection of creation and why tales from around the world. *The People Could Fly* offers stories in the African American idiom, both familiar and less known tales. The lilting speech and child/animal connection of the "Little Daughter" character and the girl in *The Gunniwulf* trace back to the days when slaves were storytellers to their owners' children. How are these little girls like *Little Red Riding Hood* in her French and German originals of the story?

Other comparisons can be made and problems solved. How do the different artists and story retellers, such as James Marshall. Nonny Hogrogian, Jack Kent, or Anne Rockwell, characterize the villainous wolf? What quests end with questions for the reader? Which of Anansi's sons did the most to save his life? How do their unique powers compare with those of *The Seven Chinese Brothers?* Were the brothers present at the building of the Great Wall of China as the story illustrations suggest? How did Anansi the Spider Man come to be Aunt Nancy, then Brur Rabbit? Did Nyame really give Anansi all of the stories for the world? "That's better than what Pandora gave us," say sixth graders. How *did* the world get its color? Its languages? Why doesn't the "Girl Who Used Her Wits" to help Lotus Blossom and Moon Flower satisfy their mother-in-law's demand to bring back fire wrapped in paper and wind wrapped in paper have a name? *The Cow-Tail Switch* and the chief's stool and Anansi's melon are magical things about which to "Talk." Children bravely *Whistle in the Graveyard* as they search for the various magical, mischievous, and often scary little people, the boggarts, piskies, tomtens, trolls, leprechauns, fairies, and elves.

The beauty of *Princess Furball*'s coat is an aesthetic experience, even without the suggestion of another Cinderella tale. Demi's books, like *The Empty Pot* and *The Artist and the Architect*, whether folktales retold or original stories, enchant on many levels beside the beauty of the illustrations. Pages from *The Mitten* framed by Jan Brett's borders differ from Yaraslava's version. Similar stories from multiethnic sources are interpreted by illustrators with the motifs of each culture. Fracturing classic folktales injects a little humor with characters like Miserella and the Stinky Cheese Man. *Sleeping Ugly*'s 300-year nap takes her through wars, plagues, new kings, and new discoveries.

Tricksters abound in all folklore. Whether in Aesop or in African, Caribbean, Native American, or Asian tales, the characters are wily, tricky, dishonest, and usually lose in the end. The Plains Indian coyote of the Utes and Shoshone is an *Old Bag of Bones,* chased by killer rocks and crazy birds, painted in words and pictures by Janet Stevens who also adapted and illustrated Anansi and Aesop. The Zuni Coyote's nose for trouble always finds it. Like Icarus, he wants to fly, and trusting the feathers given by crows, he fails. In Paul Goble's stories coyote becomes Iktomi of the buffalo skulls, the ducks, and the two-level conversations. In a Caldecott runner up, *Tops and Bottoms*, children laugh at how trickster Rabbit cons ever-gullible Bear, while they name and alphabetize and learn how edible crops grow—as roots, ground runners, or above ground.

Star myths from different cultures share the idea of escape to the sky to avoid earthly trouble. The Blackfoot *Lost Children* turn into the Pleides as *They Dance in the Sky*. The mythology of biography transforms real lives into extraordinary ones. Fifth graders named some legends: Elvis, King Arthur,

Johnny Appleseed, and honest George and honest Abe. Introduce the legend-makers, like Parson Weems, the not-too reliable primary source who perpetuated the story of Washington chopping down the cherry tree.

WHYS OF THE STORYWRITERS

The Moon and I is a memoir by Betsy Byars. In the chapter, "The Write Stuff," she rates elements of a story in importance: character, plot, and setting. Good scraps are as important to making a book as to a quilt. Parts of the scrapbooks of a life are the neat things she sees, hears, and does. She does not think about theme and mood. Plot comes first in genesis. "My formula for a good book: plot with possibilities; characters to make plot happen, believable setting, lots and lots of good scraps" (Byars 1991).

In *Astrid Lindgren: Storyteller to the World* by Johanna Hurwitz, one author writes about another as part of a series, Women of Our Times. Young Astrid was one of four children living on a farm in the early twentieth century, the inspiration for Noisy Village. There were no public libraries but books were always important, even to their smell. What did she read? *Snow White*, the first book she owned; *Robinson Crusoe, Tom Sawyer*, and *Huckleberry Finn*. She acted out her favorite, *Anne of Green Gables*. Astrid's real adventures were translated into her books. She depicts the loneliness of her child characters. Pippi was born as tales told to Lindgren's ill daughter, who gave Pippi her name. The stories were written down later when Lindgren was laid up with a sprained ankle. Pippi, written in Swedish, is one of the 12 most translated books. Although her name differs in every language, her pictures are always similar so clearly is she described, and she is always nine years old. American publishers thought Pippi would not succeed in the United States, so the book's translation into English was delayed until 1950. In 1997 Russian President Boris Yeltsin and his wife, at their request, lunched with Lindgren. Pippi, in Russian translation, was a favorite read-aloud for their two daughters. Lindgren was also an editor and translator whose job was to decide which American books Swedish children would enjoy. Among her choices were *Homer Price* and *Charlotte's Web*. She considered *Winnie the Pooh* the greatest children's book of all (Hurwitz 1991). What would Lindgren choose from recent children's literature?

Cynthia Rylant grew up in the rural Appalachian setting depicted in her stories about relatives. No libraries were available for her either. She read comic books. At a time when mentoring is an important motivational strategy, the stories famous authors tell of what they read as children and why they became writers are sources of inspiration. Not only have many children's authors written books about their experiences, but there are also feature articles in magazines such as "Meet Your Author: Lloyd Alexander" in *Cricket*, as well as publishers' pamphlets such as Atheneum's "How I Came to Be a Writer" by Phyllis Naylor. Authors are invited to the classroom for "Good Conversations" on videotape. Authors like Karen Cushman interact with readers online. Vignettes from writers, collected as an anthology for the vertical/picture file, are both bibliography and manuals for writing. Assign research assistants to search out Lindgren's, Rylant's, Byars's, and other authors' stories to fill a vertical file drawer or traveling box called AUTHOR.

ISSUES, ISSUES, ISSUES

It takes a few years before young lovers of Pooh, Piglet, and friends realize that A. A. Milne created a fantasy world of stories and poems inspired by the stuffed animals in his son's nursery. They like to find out that the 100 Aker Wood settings, map and all, are real places in the Ashdown Forest in East Sussex, England, near Cofford Farm where the Milnes lived. The Forest is a wildlife habitat, a park for local people, and in 1984, a place to which oil exploration and drilling rights were sold. Children are saddened to find out that the real Christopher Robin, who died in 1996, tried all of his adult life to hide his immortal self as the voice of reason in the world of Pooh.

In pursuit of Eeyore's lost tail, Winnie the Pooh sought Owl's advice. "Well," said Owl, "the customary procedure in such cases is as follows." Pooh being a Bear whose Very Little Brain is bothered by long words doesn't understand what Crustimoney Proseedcake means, so Owl explains that it is the thing to do, and the first thing to do to find Eeyore's tail is "First, issue a Reward! Then—" Pooh thinks Owl is sneezing even as he repeats the advice to "Issue a Reward."

Issues, Issues, Issues! The original Pooh and friends who reside in a glass display case at the New York Public Library were themselves subjects of a dispute, as many people demanded their return to Britain. What makes the realistic humor or the humorous realism of authors like Lois Lowry or Katherine Paterson or Judy Blume become issues? Their novels see the personal, social, and economic realities of the past and today. Ideas that seem mainstream now—mild profanity, separation as part of family life, antiracism, poverty, social malaise, feminism, peace, a holistic world view, the environment—are adversarial to people at either end of an ideological spectrum. Upholding the First Amendment is a fundamental cause for libraries. The American Library Association's list of books challenged or banned in the 1990s is motley, but one consistency is the inclusion of humorous stories or poems or brave new worlds that seem to undermine parental and societal authority. Often children themselves see the satire and laugh at the implicit joke in books about *The Stupids*. But principals and teachers struggling to end name-calling and lack of decorum see a different side of the story. The William and Mary units on the theme of change devote much thought to issues and controversies in contemporary children's literature. The large question of censorship and books being removed from library shelves is posed for discussion by children. The curriculum writers include sample letters to inform and obtain permission from parents for student participation in these activities.

Some old issues seem to have been resolved anew as outdated or emotionally charged classics have been changed. In 1996, two versions of Helen Bannerman's popular 1899 story, *Little Black Sambo*, were published. The story, set in British colonial India, was long ago withdrawn from the children's literature repertoire. It tells of a little boy, his fancy clothes, tigers, and pancakes. Julius Lester's new version, *Sam and the Tigers,* is told in an African American storytelling vernacular with a completely changed setting and talking animal characters depicted by illustrator Jerry Pinckney. It is dedicated to the Internet and Children's Literature. The other version reverts to the original title, *The Story of Little Babaji* (and his Mamaji and Papaji), with illustrations of village life in India. Will this old children's favorite be restored to "best sellerdom?" Reviewers differ on the artistic and literary merits of the two books, but the issue of racial stereotyping is very much alive.

The illustrations in *Harriet and the Promised Land* were stark and stylized, causing some discomfort for reviewers and would-be readers. Because the artist/writer is Jacob Lawrence, recognized as a great living African American painter, the book has just been reprinted. Current books, like artist/author Faith Ringgold's *Tar Beach,* were acclaimed, only later to be questioned for stereotyped art style.

Anastasia Krupnik's father used an expletive, the same word used by an adult Danish citizen referring to the Nazis in *Number the Stars. The Giver,* set in a futuristic and Utopian society free of bad words and bad deeds still stirred up a surprising range of responses. Lois Lowry, the author of these novels, responds to the many letters of praise or condemnation of her words or themes by telling the correspondent how carefully she chooses appropriate words for her characters to say, whatever their situation. Of the reactions to her theme, she writes that many adults find it scary when

> a world where adhering to rigid rules is the norm turned out to be very, very dangerous; and that people have to make their own choices. . . . I believe without a single shadow of a doubt that it is necessary for young people to learn to make choices. Learning to make the right choices is the only way they will survive in an increasingly frightening world. Pretending that there are no choices to be made—reading only books, for example, which are cheery and safe and nice—is a prescription of disaster for the young (Lowry 1997).

No less important than censorship is the issue of plagiarism. The concept of intellectual property and its ownership through copyright is a topic of debate as word processing, videotape, computer software, and online communication make the wide dissemination of all information easier and its attribution hazier. If authors and publishers disagree on what materials may be freely used; if educators reproduce print and nonprint materials without permission, what messages do young people receive about "copying"?

LITERARY SHARINGS

Literary connections were meant to be shared. Many ways are possible, but mirroring our electronic age, the most highly touted products are those that plug into electrical outlets—films, video tapes, databases, and computer programs. The slide/tape and filmstrip were among the first media productions to be part of the evolution from school library to library media center. An exceptional third-grade class wanted to tell their Iowa penpals about Washington, D.C. landmarks. In art class, they painted their impressions in delicate pen and ink washes. In the library media center, they collected facts and wrote simple descriptions of each place. Their slide/tape won an award at a local film festival; the collection of original paintings, mounted as a series of panels, was acclaimed at the annual student art show.

A bright fourth-grade class painted two murals of Maryland: one of the state's geography, the other of the state's history. With the addition of narrative, original music, and 35-mm SLR camera, their slide/tape reached a wider audience and became a resource in the school's Maryland archive. Although the filmstrip is obsolete, and less expensive camcorder productions are more likely projects than slide/tapes today, the preliminary class efforts remain the same.

Still satisfying to younger children are the old-fashioned ways of manipulating data through dioramas, bound books, charts, learning packets, models, and displays. Scriptographic pamphlets published by Channing Bete are examples of simple and graphic treatment of a nonfiction topic. Picture books use transparent overlays to add and subtract details to show "before" and "after" sequences. The advent of desktop publishing makes everybody's word-processed product look professional. Formats on which to model products are: a newspaper or periodical layout, cartoon and picture sequences, a penny or shadow puppet theatre, a published book, or a museum exhibit. Such products inexpensively use library media resources for the dual purpose of structuring the information search and framing the product.

Pictures, Cartoons, and Web Sites

"Minute Biographies" are based on a book long out of print. Figure 10.1 shows a sample layout for a minute biography that allows children to choose which events of their subject's life to highlight in words and drawings. It also sets up fields of information in a database file for later compilation into a group publication, that can be either printed or projected. Robby's minute biography of Matisse, fig. 10.2, began as research for a class slide/tape, not on Matisse's life, but on the class's creation of paper cut outs in Matisse's style.

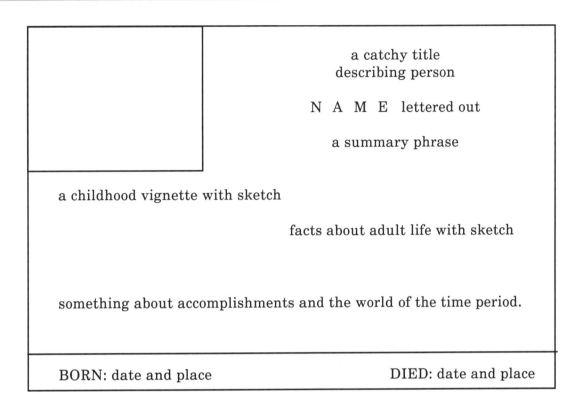

a catchy title
describing person

N   A   M   E   lettered out

a summary phrase

a childhood vignette with sketch

facts about adult life with sketch

something about accomplishments and the world of the time period.

BORN: date and place   DIED: date and place

Fig. 10.1. Sample Layout.

The Now series of books was intended for hi-lo reluctant reader use—a way of bringing classical literature to older children who might not be able to read the original books. But consider another application. Parallel to the retelling of the story in "graphic novel" (formerly called comic book) style, the series uses the author's own words for introductions and transitions, affording a good example of primary sources for younger able children. The daily and weekly cartoon, *The Family Circus*, is full of literary allusion: to books, ideas, and words in its "Oh-Pun Country" feature. An anthology of these cartoons gives opportunities for interpretation and imitation. The syndicated Sunday supplement *The Mini Page* is familiar to children all over the United States. Its popularity, the timeliness of the topics for each issue, and the functional layout make it an example for collecting and reporting data on one topic, for organizing miscellany, and for sampling how a tabloid newspaper looks. Many topics, like presidents, elections, holidays, or libraries, lend themselves for developing as time lines. *Weekly Reader*, the first of the school subscription newspapers available for each grade, celebrated its 50th anniversary with the publication of a retrospective anthology. *Flashbacks* appears in Sunday newspaper comic sections, recounting important moments in local history that confirm and enhance facts that children may already know. "Factoids" from *3-2-1 Contact* magazine present information interactively and interchangeably. Mix and match formats: Turn a minute biography into a minipage, a factoid into a highlight or a cartoon.

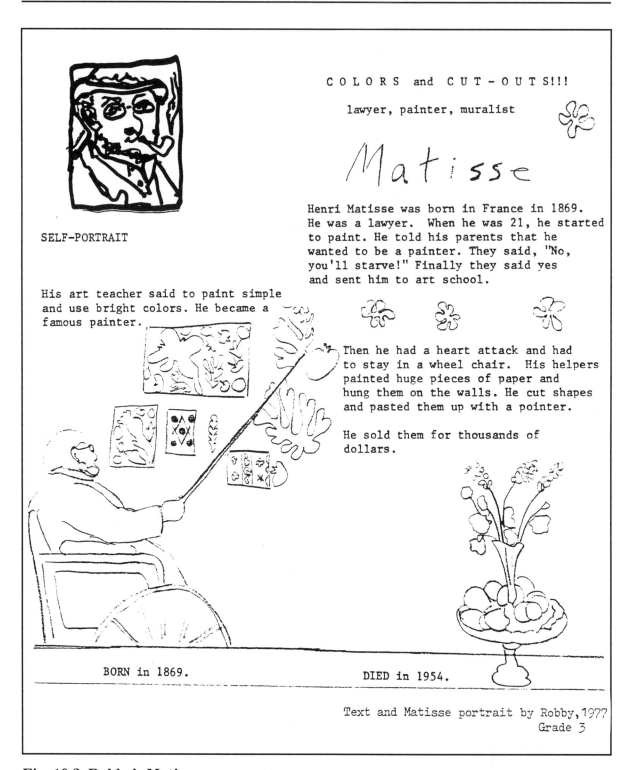

COLORS and CUT-OUTS!!!

lawyer, painter, muralist

Matisse

Henri Matisse was born in France in 1869.
He was a lawyer. When he was 21, he started
to paint. He told his parents that he
wanted to be a painter. They said, "No,
you'll starve!" Finally they said yes
and sent him to art school.

SELF-PORTRAIT

His art teacher said to paint simple
and use bright colors. He became a
famous painter.

Then he had a heart attack and had
to stay in a wheel chair. His helpers
painted huge pieces of paper and
hung them on the walls. He cut shapes
and pasted them up with a pointer.

He sold them for thousands of
dollars.

BORN in 1869.

DIED in 1954.

Text and Matisse portrait by Robby, 1977
Grade 3

Fig. 10.2. Robby's Matisse.

Houghton Mifflin is one of the first publishers to tie the Internet to print with its website on Cyberkids. On it, one can "ask the author," read other "kidsviews," browse the "author's bookshelf." For teachers, "classroom connections" to grade-level textbook themes are provided. Schools and classes also manage web pages to update and inform the world.

Penny Theatres, Collages, and Pop-Ups

The penny theatre evolved from a traditional English toy theatre to a cardboard carton stage to a portable wooden box miniature of a proscenium stage used in public library story hours for small groups of young children. It seems simple enough, but many fourth- through sixth-grade classes discovered that "it's one of the hardest projects we've ever worked on." The wooden box is about 24 inches wide, 15 inches deep and 17 inches high at the sides and back, with a slightly higher front proscenium. The sides are hinged and lie flat against the box for carrying. They are open when the theatre is in use to hide the people who are manipulating the characters and scenery. The top of the box is open, with notches along both sides to allow for suspending dowels draped with small colored lights and for slipping scenery backdrops in and out. Small scenery articles, like a rock or a tree, and the characters enter and exit from the sides. These are cutouts from the book that are pasted on reinforced cardboard attached to long wire rods (see fig. 10.3).

Fig. 10.3. Small Penny Theater Layout.

The tasks for the penny theatre planners and workers are many and complex. First, the story is chosen. Then the number of backdrop changes and character figure changes must be realistically plotted and created. Many questions must be answered: When the story is retold, what will be narrated and what will be dialogue? What kind of music will play? What sound effects will be added? What kind of speaking voices will the characters have? It is easier when sets and characters can be cut out from the picture book; more difficult when they have to be hand made. The timing of the performance, allowing for moving characters on and off stage and changing scenery, requires precision and planning. Once the medium is mastered as a device for bringing published stories before a small audience, some children go on to create their own adaptations of the penny theatre model. The same rod-moved characters and scenery can be projected from the table of an overhead projector for shadow silhouettes. Underneath them, the acetate rolls and the scenery changes in contrasting color.

Almost too simple to describe, learning collages are words and pictures culled from publishers' catalogs, magazines, and other inexpensive sources that are cut, pasted, and juxtaposed to develop a theme or topic. More illustrious are trophy panels, popular in the eighteenth century, that were assembled from objects representing the elements of a common theme, such as peace, love, arts, science, and music. Contemporary trophy panels become graphic organizers for relating children's attributes and interests to their stories, as they create three-dimensional personal, literary, or subject assemblages to hang, just as the ancient Greeks hung captured weapons from a tree.

Mechanical books were used for scientific instruction in the sixteenth century. The twentieth century pop-up is a fascinating three-dimensional book that synthesizes writing skill with artistic and mechanical ingenuity. The selections range from reproductions of antique books (depicting the nineteenth century circus, zoo, city park, children's theatre, or doll's house) to versions of Beatrix Potter classics to intricate creations, such as *Leonardo Da Vinci* and the best-selling *The Human Body*. After second graders Nicholas and Danny analyzed the simple movement devices used in Spot the Dog toddler stories, they went on to Leonardo for inspiration on how to paper engineer their next book report.

Curating an Exhibit

The library media center should be a showplace for the intellectual efforts of the school. With some direction, the students become curators for each special exhibit.

PREPARING AN EXHIBIT

(Background and directions for student)

An exhibit is a public showing of something for many people to see. A great example of an exhibit may be found in a museum. It has many exhibits about different topics that are shown in many different ways. A curator is a person who plans and stages an exhibit. Start on a small scale to turn a space in your school into a museum, a place dedicated to the Muses. Maybe exhibits, like the ones listed below at the Smithsonian Institute's museums, sound familiar.

Exhibit	Exhibit Technique
A hall of transportation	Uses models of transportation machines or a collection of real machines
An artist's work	Shows, for example, Matisse's paper cutouts with the story of how and why he made them
Clothing people wore	Displays of original dresses worn by our First Ladies, draped on life-sized dummies
Gems and minerals	Displays of specimens of rocks (called realia)
Dinosaur bones	Reconstruction of prehistoric animals' fossilized bones, which are wired together with man-made bones
Mummies	Arrangement of real objects, called artifacts, entombed with mummified persons
Early humans	Dioramas of life in the various epochs of humankind's history

Fig. 10.4. Exhibit Directions.

These examples illustrate that an exhibit combines many elements: dioramas, collections, realia, models, artifacts, photos, paintings, and floor plans. *Treasures to See: A Museum Picture Book* and *Visiting the Art Museum* are two helpful books for planning an exhibit. Below are steps to follow in the preparation of an exhibit:

1. Select a topic, such as clothing. Write a brief introduction including the directions for viewing the exhibit.

2. Think of an interesting way to show the information: samples of clothing, drawings, pictures or photographs of clothing, or dolls dressed in costume.

3. Arrange topics and subtopics in an order that best tells the story.

4. Write a brief description to accompany each picture or object. Everything in the exhibit should be labeled. The story could be taped as an Acousti-Guide to accompany the viewer. It could also be published as a family guide with questions and activities for all ages.

5. Set up the exhibit for people to enjoy. It can be on a bulletin board, a table, a display case, shelves, or a series of mat board panels hinged together.

By channeling student products into these modes, Literary Capers reflect the major repositories and transmitters of knowledge in our contemporary society: newspapers, schools, libraries, performances, museums, and the Internet.

THE ARTS SING MANY LANGUAGES

The word art originally referred to the *artes liberales*, or the seven branches of learning in the Middle Ages. These were grammar, rhetoric, and logic, the three-fold way to eloquence; and music, astronomy, arithmetic, and geometry, the four-fold way to knowledge. These seven disciplines later became the essence of a liberal arts curriculum. The word *ars* then came to refer to the skills and accomplishments of the Muses of poetry, painting, and music. In our CUES model, the library media center is the catalyst for forging connections between the arts and sciences in an elementary school. Art, music, and literature need to be considered as curriculum "basics." The science of art and the art of science converge with a National Science Foundation grant to teach chaos theory through movement. M. B. Goffstein posits that "an artist tries to make paint sing" and a Writer is "an observer and collector of images" who "cuts, prunes, and shapes" her words (Goffstein 1981). She is like a gardener whose seeds are ideas that grow into *Imaginary Gardens* of American poetry and art.

To the question "Do paintings have titles?" even first graders say "yes."
The question "Do paintings have authors?" gets a less certain response.
"What's the author of a painting in the museum called?" The children say, "the
illustrator," suggesting that the artistry in books may be their first meeting
with the fine arts. Tommy, who loved to draw, eagerly anticipated going to
school, sure that the long-awaited art lesson would begin immediately, until
he found out there was no art teacher for kindergarten. Throughout the grades,
he wanted to create, not copy, unfettered by rules of paint, paper, and class
plans. Tommy and his teachers compromised on his artistic efforts. He grew
up to be the prolific Tomie dePaola whose book, *The Art Lesson*, is now an
outstanding CD-ROM which tells the story in English or Spanish and allows
the reader to create art or interview the author.

Contemporary American artist Jasper Johns sees painting as a language.
Great works of art tell *The Whole Truths* about myths, allegories, fairy tales,
and history. The Meet the Masterpieces series teaches about ancient civilizations through their art. A time line of American social thought runs through
the Art of . . . series books by Shirley Glubok. Paintings and sculpture show a
progression through the eras: early American, Colonial days, the gilded age,
and modern times. The authoritative *History of Art for Young People* was
updated in 1992. Another way to survey art and music are the multimedia
book/kits, *The Art Pack*, and its companion, *The Music Pack. Murals—Cave,
Cathedral to Street* make impressive social studies projects. American landscapes
record the panorama of history and regional geography. They are the settings
for portraits of people and the plots of everyday life, spiced with Ruth Heller's
Color-Color-Color-Color, shapes that *Look Like Spilt Milk,* and the textures of
Lionni sketched in the quick lines of *Harold's Purple Crayon. Matthew's Dream*
of becoming a painter, expressed in torn paper collages, brings him to a
museum. Lois Ehlert shapes the animals on the *Color Farm* and in the *Color
Zoo.* The affinities between art, physics, and math show through *The Painter's
Eye* and *The Sculptor's Eye* and in the geometry of Picasso or Mondrian. Other
traditions of art history appear in children's book illustrations. Giuseppe
Arcimbaldi's sixteenthth century collage of "The Librarian" composed of fruits
and vegetables may have inspired Anita Lobel's concoctions *On Market Street.*
Peter Sis's illustrations allude to Breughel and Bosch. The D'Aulaires's worked
in abstract expressionism with artist Hans Hoffman. How is art analogous to
literature? Is abstract art analogous to abstract thinking?

The animals on newly discovered cave walls and the wooden animal
carvings by an isolated people of the Darien rain forest of Panama are
surprisingly modern and almost abstract. The *Noble Beasts* portrayed in
masterpieces of the National Gallery of Art lead to animal processions in folk
art and folklore through Kapiti Plain to learn *The Name of the Tree.* The folk
arts and crafts tell of varied cultures, even as they are frameworks and
metaphors for transmitting data about heritage. The Ashanti storehouse, it is
said, held 3,600 stories to be told from memory with audience participation.
The stories changed to reflect the people's new surroundings, as yams became
sweet potatoes and leopards became horses. *The Storyteller* dolls are valued
works of native American art and culture. Josefina's quilt was family history;

Ernest and Celestine had a patchwork quilt; and Sam Johnson's quilt earned a Blue Ribbon. *Tar Beach* had its beginnings in a quilt made by the author. American quilts, Storyteller dolls, Indian story bands, Ashanti appliquéd story cloths, and woven kente cloth are all devices used in story-weaving. The gathering and communication of information becomes more exciting when these art forms replace Venn diagrams as graphic organizers. *Art from Many Hands* encourages projects from many lands and products in many languages. *First Words, Premier Mots* and its sequel, *First Shapes,* present basic nouns in five languages—Spanish, French, German, Italian, and English—as a way of introducing children to the different art media and techniques from the collections of five world-famous museums. For a follow-up, third graders translated the same words into their own images using ethnic art techniques from Mexico, Japan, and Africa—the cultures they studied.

Report-on-an-artist is a frequent assignment bridging the media center and the art class. All of the standard reference sources exist for research, but in recent years, exciting materials have been published to enliven the learning and sharing. Series publishers make the reader an Eyewitness (D-K) to art or help them enjoy First Impressions (Abrams). Biographical sketches of *Great Painters* present profiles for background knowledge. Series such as Raboff's Art for Children, and the Metropolitan Museum's *What Makes a Monet a Monet?* (or a *Gauguin, Cassatt, Breughel, Degas, Raphael, Rembrandt, Van Gogh,* or *Leonardo*) introduce the artists. Some series even allow the reader to spend *A Weekend With . . .* them. *Looking at Paintings* helps children see self-portraits, seascapes, landscapes, children, families, and animals. Winslow Homer's seascapes *By Water's Edge* are settings for Robert McCloskey's Maine. Visit *The Princess and the Peacocks* in the room created by Whistler or the ballet studio with *Degas and the Little Dancer. The Princess and the Painter* meet in a story about Velasquez. Other easy fiction finds Van Gogh *Painting in the Wind* or at Cynthia Rylant's *Van Gogh Cafe.* Renoir's *Girl with a Watering Can* sprinkles color through a colorless garden of painting. Perhaps it is *Linnea in Monet's Garden* with *Camille and the Sunflowers.* Jane Yolen takes the reader to *Sacred Places* via poems and paintings of holy and magical places. The rock art petroglyphs of early Americans tell *Stories in Stone.* Johannes Vermeer's seventeenth century diagrams and model of the *camera obscura* were progenitors of modern photography. Douglas Florian's *A Painter* and Ed Emberly's guides explain how to become an artist. *Lil Sis and Uncle Willie* is an easy story based on the life and paintings of African American artist, William H. Johnson, told by his niece. *A Young Painter: The Life and Paintings of Wang Yani* is about a 14-year-old Chinese girl who had a one-person show at the Smithsonian, which was inspiring to student attendees.

The title of a New Zealand Ministry of Education guide to the writing process for primary and middle school teachers, *Dancing with the Pen,* suggests a crossover between the arts. When paintings by Jan Steen traveled from Amsterdam to the United States, the exhibit brochure was entitled *Jan Steen Painter and Storyteller.* "Color is like music. Are all your talents working in concert?" asks an advertisement in a February 1997 series in the *New York Times.* Within a picture frame is a composite grouping of recognizable musical subjects from many centuries of great art. The question may well be restated as, "Are all of your specialists working in concert?" Blending art, music, and movement with literature is a coordinated venture between teaching specialists that addresses multiple intelligences and classroom enrichment. Current studies suggest that music at an early age, especially piano playing, develops the brain, increasing ability for visual perception and improved reading scores—the Mozart effect. *Berlioz the Bear* with an illustrious musical name became the leader of an animal orchestra delayed en route to a village concert. *Stradivari's Singing Violin* was better known than he was, but the few facts that are known are told in a story. *The Philharmonic Gets Dressed* puts musical literacy right in the library media center.

Delightful to all, the *Artistic Trickery* of trompe l'oeil transports *Art Beyond Borders*, a new series by Lerner. Barry Polisar, an often zany modern minstrel, visits schools with songs for fun and learning. In a video series entitled *Barry's Scrapbook: A Window into Art,* he helps children look at museums, learn about the parts of art, create and sing about them. His setting for all this learning, satisfaction guaranteed is: IN THE LIBRARY, of course!

REFERENCES

Byars, Betsy. 1991. *The Moon and I.* New York: Julian Messner.

Daniels, Lee A. 1984. Homecoming for Leonard Bernstein. *New York Times* 22 November, sec. C.

Elleman, Barbara, and Betsy Hearn, comps. n.d. *Books for Everychild: Contemporary Fiction Classics.* Chicago: Booklist/ALA.

———. n.d. *Books for Everychild: Picture Book Classics.* Chicago: Booklist/ALA.

Goffstein, M. B. 1981. *A Writer.* New York: Harper & Row. Also *An Artist.* New York: Harper & Row.

Hurwitz, Johanna. 1991. *Astrid Lindgren: Storyteller to the World.* New York: Puffin Books.

Kaplan, Sandra. 1984. *Designing Appropriate Curriculum for Primary Gifted Children.* n.p.: Maryland State Department of Education.

Vail, Priscilla. 1979. *The World of the Gifted Child.* New York: Walker.

Resources for Planning Multicultural Units

Bishop, Rudine Sims, ed. 1994. *Kaleidoscope: A Multicultural Booklist for Grades K-8.* Urbana, IL: NCTE.

Curry, Barbara K., and James Michael Brudie. 1997. *Sweet Words So Brave: The Story of African American Literature.* Madison, WI: Zino Press Children's Books, 1996.

Day, Frances Ann. 1994. *Multicultural Voices in Contemporary Literature: A Resource for Teachers.* Portsmouth, NH: N. H. Heinemann.

Kruse, Ginny Moore, and Kathleen Horning, eds. 1991. *Multicultural Literature for Children and Young Adults,* 3rd ed. Madison: University of Wisconsin/Cooperative Children's Book Center.

Miller-Lachmann, Lyn. 1992. *Our Family, Our Friends, Our World: An Annotated Guide to Significant Multicultural Books for Children*. New Providence, NJ: R. R. Bowker.

Simonton, Rick, ed. 1988. *Graywolf Annual Five: Multicultural Literacy*. St. Paul, MN: Graywolf Press.

Smallwood, Betty Ansin. 1991. *The Literature Connection: Read-Aloud Guide for Multi-Cultural Classrooms*. Boston: Addison-Wesley.

BIBLIOGRAPHY

Art from Many Hands: Multicultural Art Projects. Jo M. Schuman. Worcester MN: Davis Publications, 1973.

The Art Pack. Ron Van Der Meer. New York: Alfred A. Knopf, 1995.

Artistic Trickery: The Tradition of Trompe L'Oeil Art. Michael Capek. Minneapolis, MN: Lerner, 1995.

Barry's Scrapbook: A Window into Art. Barry Polisar. ALA Video, n.d.

Berlioz the Bear. Jan Brett. New York: Putnam, 1991.

The Best Children's Books in the World: A Treasury of Illustrated Stories. Byron Preiss, ed. New York: Abrams, 1996.

The Best of the Mini Page. Betty Debnam. Kansas City, MO: Universal Press Syndicate, n.d.

By Water's Edge. Kay Barrie. Boston: Museum of Fine Arts, 1996.

Camille and the Sunflowers: A Story About Vincent Van Gogh. Laurence Anholt. Hauppauge, NY: Barron's, 1994.

Changing Ideas, Changing Perspectives: What Is the Role of Persuasion and Argument in Our Lives? Center for Gifted Education. Williamsburg, VA: College of William and Mary, 1994.

Color-Color-Color-Color. Ruth Heller. New York: Putnam, 1995.

Color Farm. Lois Ehlert. New York: J. B. Lippincott, 1990.

Color Zoo. Lois Ehlert. New York: J. B. Lippincott, 1989.

Degas and the Little Dancer: A Story About Edgar Degas. Laurence Anholt. Hauppauge, NY: Barron's Educational Series, 1995.

Eric Carle's Treasury of Classic Stories for Children by Aesop, Hans Christian Andersen, and the Brothers Grimm. Selected by Eric Carle. New York: Orchard Books, 1988.

A First Dictionary of Cultural Literacy: What Our Children Need to Know. E. D. Hirsch, ed. Boston: Houghton Mifflin, 1989.

First Words, Premier Mots. Ivan and Jane Chermayeff. New York: Abrams, 1990.

Flashbacks: A Cartoon History of Washington, D.C. Willow Street, PA: Red Rose Studio, n.d.

Great Painters. Piero Ventura. New York: Putnam, 1984.

The Green Book. Jill Paton Walsh. New York: Farrar, Straus & Giroux, 1982.

The Gunniwulf. Wilhelmina Harper, ed. New York: E. P. Dutton, 1967.

Harriet and the Promised Land. Jacob Lawrence. New York: Simon & Schuster, 1993.

History of Art for Young People. 4th ed. H. W. Janson. New York: Abrams, 1992.

The Human Body. Jonathan Miller and David Pelham. New York: Viking, 1983.

Iktomi and the Boulder. Retold and illustrated by Paul Goble. New York: Orchard, 1988.

Imaginary Gardens. Charles Sullivan, ed. New York: H. N. Abrams, 1989.

It Looks Like Spilt Milk. Charles G. Shaw. New York: HarperCollins, 1988.

Leonardo Da Vinci, the Artist, Inventor, Scientist in Three Dimensional Movable Pictures. Alice Provensen and Martin Provensen. New York: Viking, 1984.

Lil Sis and Uncle Willie: A Story Based on the Life and Paintings of William H. Johnson. Gwenn Everett. New York: Rizzoli, 1991.

Linnea in Monet's Garden. Cristina Bjork. Stockholm; New York: R & S Books, 1985.

Literary Laurels: Kids' Edition. New York: Hilliard, 1996.

The Lost Children: The Boys Who Were Neglected. Paul Goble. New York: Bradbury, 1993.

Matthew's Dream. Leo Lionni. New York: Alfred A. Knopf, 1991.

Murals—Cave, Cathedral to Street. Michael Capek. Minneapolis, MN: Lerner, 1997.

The Music Pack. Ron Van Der Meer. New York: Alfred A. Knopf, 1994.

The Name of the Tree: A Bantu Folktale. Celia Lottridge. New York: Margaret K. McElderry, 1989.

Noble Beasts: Animals in Art. Washington, DC: National Gallery of Art, 1994.

Old Bag of Bones: A Coyote Tale. Janet Stevens. New York: Holiday House, 1996.

On Market Street. Arnold Lobel and Anita Lobel. New York: Greenwillow Books, 1981.

The Painter's Eye: Learning to Look at Contemporary Art. Jan Greenberg. New York: Delacorte, 1991.

Painting the Wind: A Story of Vincent Van Gogh. Michelle Dionetti. New York: Little, Brown, 1996.

The People Could Fly: American Black Folktales. Virginia Hamilton. New York: Alfred A. Knopf, 1985.

The Philharmonic Gets Dressed. Karla Kuskin. New York: HarperCollins, 1982.

The Princess and the Painter. Jane Johnson. New York: Farrar, Straus & Giroux, 1994.

The Princess and the Peacocks or, The Story of the Room. Linda Merrill and Sarah Ridley. New York: Hyperion Books for Children, 1996.

Princess Furball. Charlotte Huck and Anita Lobel. New York: Greenwillow Books, 1989.

Sacred Places. Jane Yolen. New York: Harcourt Brace Jovanovich, 1996.

Sam and the Tigers: A New Telling of "Little Black Sambo." Julius Lester. New York: Dial, 1996.

The Sculptor's Eye. Jan Greenberg. New York: Delacorte, 1993.

Stories in Stone. Carolyn Arnold. New York: Clarion, 1996.

The Story of Little Babaji. Helen Bannerman. New York: HarperCollins, 1996.

The Storyteller. Joan Weisman. New York: Rizzoli, 1993.

Stradivari's Singing Violin. Catherine Deverell. Minneapolis, MN: Carolrhoda Books, 1992.

Tar Beach. Faith Ringgold. New York: Crown, 1991.

They Dance in the Sky. Jean Monroe and Ray Williamson. Boston: Houghton Mifflin. 1987.

Tops and Bottoms. Janet Stevens. San Diego: Harcourt Brace Jovanovich, 1995.

Treasures to See: A Museum Picture Book. Leonard Weisgard. New York: Harcourt Brace Jovanovich, 1956.

The Van Gogh Cafe. Cynthia Rylant. San Diego: Harcourt Brace Jovanovich, 1995.

Visiting the Art Museum. Laurene Krasny Brown and Marc Brown. New York: Dutton, 1986.

A Weekend With . . . Series. New York: Rizzoli, 1994.

What Makes a _____ ? Series. New York Metropolitan Museum of Art: Viking, 1994.

Who Found America? Johanna Johnston. Chicago: Children's Press, 1973.

The Whole Truths . . . and Other Myths: Retelling Ancient Tales. Washington, DC: National Gallery of Art, 1996.

A Young Painter: The Life and Paintings of Wang Yani. Zheng Zhunsun and Alice Low. New York: Scholastic, 1991.

Eleven

Some Roads to Wham

SEVEN LEAGUE BOOTS

Many years ago, a ten-year-old girl was rummaging around a rented beach cottage looking for something to read. One title beckoned to her from a shelf of dank smelling books. It was *Seven League Boots* by Richard Halliburton. Before long she became possessed of her own pair of seven league boots to stride across ages past to far away destinations of her own.

Halliburton was an adventurer who voyaged to see the wonders and mysteries of the ancient and modern worlds. In flamboyant style, he recounted and photographed his exploits. He swam the Hellespont, retraced Hannibal's elephant trek across the Alps, followed the route of the First Crusade and the sweep of the conquests of Alexander the Great, researched the fate of the Romanoff Grand Duchess Anastasia and her four sisters. In 1939, as he sailed from Hong Kong to San Francisco in his Chinese junk, he disappeared, lost in the Pacific during a typhoon. But stories persist that Halliburton, like Amelia Earheart, stumbled upon some pre-World War II secret military operation. The people and events he wrote about are reappearing in current books and media for children or adults.

Stories of people who disappear mysteriously while on daring voyages have long fascinated kids. So do stories about strange appearances, trips backward and forward in time, and journeys to real and imagined worlds. Today's adventure stories, fiction and FACTion, have the added dimensions of speed, space, and hi-tech to lengthen the "seven league" stride.

Journals and Journeys

Not all voyages have to end in disaster or disappearance to be interesting. John Goodall sent his *Victorians Abroad*, while author John Burningham rushed *Around the World in Eighty Days* in the footsteps of Phileas Fogg. Like author Jules Verne's hero, Burningham covered 44,000 miles and 24 countries in 80 days, sketching all the way. Miroslav Sasek's books merit sharing with the child or group about to depart on a field trip or family excursion to historic or interesting places. Compare Sasek's *This Is Historic Britain* with the modern English scenes in his *This Is London.* More recently, Roxie Munroe writes and draws The Inside-Outside Books . . . of London, Washington, Paris, and New York. Gulliver publishes Kid's Travel Guides to many cities. Students today keep journals for writing, science, and daily work/homework. Some record personal memoirs as literary sketchbooks with tradebooks as exemplars.

Rajat's family returned to India for a visit when he was in the second grade. He kept a journal. His sketches and narrative, drawn and written in ballpoint pen on lined notebook paper were outstanding (see fig. 11.1). With the help of the library media specialist, he turned the drawings into slides and taped the narrative. *My Trip to India* won second prize for primary grades in the local film festival. On the score sheet one of the judges commented: "Too bad you could not have brought a camera with you."

Anni's India Diary, published in 1992, was a fictional journal of a trip begun in Delhi. In an interesting coincidence, he describes many of the same modes of transportation as did Rajat. Fifteen years after Rajat, when Alex, a fourth grader, visited South America, he was equipped with laptop, cellular phone, and e-mail service—for sending back photographic images of textiles and landmarks via the Internet.

Sasparillo *The Armadillo from Amarillo* wants to find out where his Texas home stands in the larger scheme of things. He travels from his dugout through the bluebonnets to the Alamo, along ancient river beds through changing landscapes to cities, until he meets an eagle who flies him to a view from the sky to biomes and continents, then aboard a spaceship to the moon and beyond. Like Stringbean, Sasparillo sends hand-drawn postcards from everywhere to his cousin Brillo, a resident of the Philadelphia Zoo. In this rhyming book that is dedicated to Dr. Seuss, author-illustrator Lynne Cherry continues her creation of environmental literature for children. The publisher, Gulliver Green, focuses on aspects of ecology and the environment, donating part of the proceeds to tree planting projects. What an array of letter writing topics—poetry, letters, fantasy, animal life, geography, ecology, paintings, and social concern.

Fig. 11.1. Rajat's Journal.

Harold's Trip to the Sky was drawn with his purple crayon. Ben dozed off while studying for his geography test on great monuments of the world. Was *Ben's Dream* voyage a reality or merely another one of the Van Allsburg's superb illusions? Will students be able to identify Ben's monuments? Will they be able to name and sketch 10 of their own? What were the Seven Wonders of the Ancient World? the Modern World? or the Natural World? What are the endangered monuments of the present world?

Travel around the world, in fantasy and science fiction, echoes of the past or hints of the future—with *Twenty-One Balloons*, with the time warp trio on *The Not-So-Jolly Roger*, on *The Polar Express,* or in the driver's seat of *Henry 3*'s stationary X-15 car. Rhoda Blumberg takes her readers *Full Steam Ahead* in the race to build the transcontinental railroad. Her other books retrace the *Incredible Journey of Lewis and Clark* and the *Remarkable Voyages of Captain Cook.* Students may sail on Kon-Tiki and Ra with Thor Heyerdahl or accompany *Commodore Perry in the Land of the Shogun* or Darwin on *The Voyage of the Beagle.* Millicent Selsam edited Darwin's journals of the trip. History mysteries ask: *Did Marco Polo Go to China?* Did *Brendan the Navigator* precede Columbus to these shores? *The Tainos* were the Caribbean people who welcomed Columbus in an *Encounter.* Jean Fritz writes of the civilizations existing in *The World in 1492.*

Time travel is possible through *Metropolis: Ten Cities / Ten Centuries.* Objects *Lost and Found,* like *One Small Blue Bead,* around the *Home Place* or the arrowhead found inside the toy tea cup at *The House on Maple Street*, are artifacts that convey continuity and change, whether the setting is Stone Age Britain, the prehistoric southwest, an African American homestead or a 300-year-old house. *The Great Kapok Tree* and *Where the Forests Meet the Sea* recount the past and present and hint at a future for the Amazon rain forest. On a higher swing of the spiral, the world is seen as anthropology: the study of society, culture, and personality. Peter Spier's *People* represents the family of man in picture book panorama. Huck Scarry's *Our Earth*, first published as *La Nostra Terra,* transports young readers across millions of years and millions of miles in a sweeping look at civilization and its evolution. Hendrik Willem Van Loon's *Story of Mankind* was the first Newbery Award winner in 1922. Would it be considered today as either unbiased information or stylistic presentation? The collage of *A Child's History of America,* written and illustrated by "the children of America" in 1975 as a book of short pieces about times, people, and places in our country's history, is a model for a group to emulate.

Immigrants All

America the Melting Pot has been replaced by the idea that we are a pluralistic society of people from many traditions and heritages to be cherished and cultivated. Stories written about the different waves of people coming to America reflect the two interpretations. Certainly, historical perspective is necessary in helping children understand and evaluate materials. All kinds of people and their cultural journeys to the United States should be realistically depicted in any literature curriculum. Many well-illustrated, accurate accounts of the flow of immigration past and present are chronicled in *Leaving for America, Coming to America*, and then *Making a New Home in America. Where Did Your Family Come From?* is a family research project for many grades.

What *If Your Name Was Changed at Ellis Island? Sam Ellis's Island,* the "isle of tears," was the *Doorway to Freedom* through which many families passed. Renovated as a national historic monument and Immigration Museum, it sits in New York Harbor. In *Gooseberries to Oranges,* a young girl reminisces about her journey from a Russian village to the golden land, entering at Ellis Island sailing past the Statue of Liberty. School children from all over the country contributed to the restoration of the Statue of Liberty. The December 1982 and January 1983 issues of *Cobblestone* magazine were devoted to "Immigration" with drawings and photos from archives.

The language of Myron Levoy's collection of stories, *The Witch of Fourth Street,* is mellifluous, onomatopoetic, and simple. Each tale is a small gem about children living in New York tenements in the early 1900s when inner city poverty seemed more benign. Beginning with the title story, the reader meets the same children over again in "Vincent the Good," "Mrs. Dunn's Lovely, Lovely Farm," "The Fish Angel," "Andreas and the Magic Bells," and "Keplik, The Match Man." The stories are nostalgic and humorous until the final two. "Aaron's Gift" evokes memories of the cruelties from which many groups fled. At the same time, it foreshadows worse cruelties to come. The final story, "The Hannukah Santa Claus" is an enigma that never fails to leave young audiences wondering about what really happened to Samuel Moscowitz. This story coupled with Raymond Briggs's wordless *Snowman* stimulates great discussions of theme.

To Be a Slave and *The Slave Dancer* tell of *Many Thousands Gone,* African Americans forced into slavery. Arna Bontemps wrote of the uprising on the slave ship Amistad, as Jacob Lawrence painted it hauntingly. *All Times, All Peoples* gives a world history of slavery. *Now Let Me Fly* is an easy story of a slave family. In 1832 *A Place Called Freedom* was founded in Indiana by the newly freed Starman family as a refuge for former slaves. *All Us Come Across the Water* and *Black Is Brown Is Tan* are picture storybooks, each dealing with the theme of pride and self-identity.

The boat people who wonder *How Many Days to America?* endure a harrowing escape from their Caribbean home, arriving in America in time for a community Thanksgiving meal. Lest the story seem too stark to be true, Roberto, a kindergarten newcomer, when asked to make a picture for the word water (*agua*), drew a hand coming out of the sea. *A Jar of Dreams* is part of a fictional trilogy about a Japanese family's journey to America. Its author, Yoshika Uchida, continues her family story factually in *The Invisible Thread,* about the internment of Japanese American families during World War II. *How My Parents Learned to Eat* and *Grandfather's Journey* tell gentler tales about the small adjustments needed to bridge two cultures to a new life without losing memories of home, *The Land I Lost. How My Family Lives in America* is a book of photo essays of transported African American, Puerto Rican American, and Chinese American families. *Starting from Home* is the story of Milton Meltzer's personal journey as a writer of social conscience on issues such as slavery, the holocaust, and immigration.

The theme of moving around includes "flight-from" and migrant experience books. *Journey to Freedom* tells what happened *If You Traveled on the Underground Railroad, Deep Down Underground,* or in the sky. *Minty,* the person of conductor Harriet Tubman, speaks in many voices. *Sky* is *A True Story of Resistance During World War II. Judy's Journey* and *Roosevelt Grady* are classics about America's migrant workers, whose situation has not changed much since the books were written. Is there any relevance today to Lois Lenski's other regional stories or her poems about *The Life I Live*? Should or do children still read Marguerite De Angeli's stories of ethnic American children two generations ago?

Bards, Pilgrims, and Troubadours

Peregrinations with bards, pilgrims, and troubadours may be just the thing to capture the interests of a group of able fifth and sixth graders! For a *Child's Portrait of Shakespeare,* start with Don Freeman's story of Willoughby Waddle, the country goose in merrie Elizabethan England, who goes to London where he falls in with a promising young actor-playwright at the Globe Theatre. Did *Will's Quill* really start the *Bard of Avon* on his way to a personal Dewey number? Many fifth and sixth graders do *Shake Hands with Shakespeare* as they learn to *Speak the Speech.* When a summer class discussed their answers to the Literary Quotient Survey questions about treading the boards, acting in a play, or meeting the Bard *Under the Greenwood Tree,* Chris told the group that he had acted in many plays, the most memorable being his role as Julius Caesar. *Quotations from Shakespeare* gives general background about Will's life and times, play-by-play background, then act-by-act quotations. Other materials in the 822.3 sections are classic retellings of the plots for children—by Charles and Mary Lamb, Marchette Chute, and Edith Nesbit. Bernard Miles's *Favorite Tales from Shakespeare* summarize the plots in more contemporary language. Many ingredients connect: drama, famous quotations, the historical accuracy of the plots, and Shakespeare's own life—even to the ongoing question about who really wrote the plays.

Chaucer's pilgrims told stories to while away the hours as they journeyed to and from Canterbury, long before the Pilgrim fathers, the Separatists, stepped foot on Plymouth Rock. Share *Chanticleer and the Fox, Scornful Simkin*, or *Pinchpenny John* for a *Taste of Chaucer* as *Sumer Is Icumen In*. Of the many accounts of the Pilgrims on the Mayflower and in Plimoth Plantation, two with a slightly different flavor are Monjo's *The House on Stink Alley*, a firsthand account of the Pilgrims in Holland, and Phyllis McGinley's poetic description of their mirthless Yuletide told as an episode in *Mincepie and Mistletoe.* McGinley's illustrated vignettes tell about the holiday customs and celebrations of American colonials from Spanish, French, Dutch, and Native American traditions. *Molly's Pilgrim* celebrates Thanksgiving with flavors of the old life in Russia.

Fflewddur was the troubadour who accompanied Taran the Wanderer on his odyssey from pig boy to high king of Prydain. In *The Truthful Harp*, Lloyd Alexander introduces the inept King Fflewddur Fflam who yearns to be a bard, even though he flubbed the wisdom and musical aptitude parts of his bard exams. In vain, he strove to "have every morsel of learning on the tip of my tongue and every harp-tune at my fingers' end!" Ultimately, his virtue and goodwill won him the magical instrument. *The Man Who Loved Books,* the legendary Saint Columba, tells how the bards kept stories alive through the generations before they were set down in books. While Columba was in his self-imposed exile, the powerful bards demanded higher alms for their stories, only to be banished by the Kings of Ireland. Columba returned to mediate between the 1,200 bards and all of the local kings. Bardic ballads of old have given way to American folk ballads about Paul Bunyan and John Henry.

Arks, Towers, Castles, and Walls

Towers are for climbing as in skyscraper,
Eiffel, Rapunzel's, Babel, lookout and Sim;
For leaning, as in Pisa, for royal crowns in London.
Towers are made of silence, of strength, of ivory.
Castles are for moats, kings, chess, and haunting.
Castles are medieval and Macauley;
For building in the air, in Spain, in the sand.
Walls are for walking through time and place. . .
Wailing, Vietnam, Berlin, China.
Walls are to keep them out or keep us in.
Walls talk and we remember.
Arks are for embarking, two by two.
Escape and haven both.
Grand Constructions all to contemplate,
Replete with literary allusion.

What do you entitle a unit in which gifted students embark on an ark? Ark-eology, of course—the study of the ark as symbol, theme, and parable, appearing from Biblical times until the present. In traditional lore, art, and poetry, the ark is "well Noahn" as metaphor and analogy. Peter Spier's *Noah's Ark* is his own translation of an eighteenth-century Dutch poem. Noah is shown loading the ark, tending his flock of passengers lovingly, then efficiently managing their resettlement. *Why Noah Chose the Dove,* tells the reason that, of the 32 animals who boarded the Ark, the quiet dove was chosen to be the messenger of peace. Norma Farber's poem, *Where's Gomer?* shows the Noah family dressed by illustrator William Pene DuBois in early twentieth-century yachting outfits. Noah's favorite grandson, Gomer, misses the boat because he is playing. So do the unicorns in Shel Silverstein's poem. Noah and his family are worried about humankind's survival in a despoiled environment in two modern parables about this important theme, *Noah's Ark* and *Professor Noah's Spaceship. Aardvarks Disembark* alphabetically in Ann Jonas's version. The picture book by Marie Angel, *The Ark*, is a meticulously painted tableau, an unfolding of the animal processional, two by two, as in *One Wide River to Cross.* Benary-Isbert 's *The Ark* is realistic fiction about a family living in Germany during and after World War II. In *The Green Book*, the aging spaceship in which Patty's family leaves the earth is an all too possible ark for us today.

Fifth and sixth graders who listen to a little book by M. B. Goffstein, *My Noah's Ark,* will complain about how easy it is, until they are asked to explain the theme, a poignant one of old age, loneliness, and memory.

Study Haley's seasick animals, Spier's India ink-washed ones, and Wildsmith's loudly painted ones. Have students compare how different illustrators depict their arks' interiors, the animals, and the passengers to establish a prevailing mood. Animals can be arranged or compared. Different treatments in award-winning books by award-winning authors create imaginative variations on a theme of assorted arks!

EPICS, EPOCHS, AND ERAS

Historical fiction and historical chronology link together for another set of Literary Capers that connect the library media specialist's literary know-how with the classroom teacher's social studies agenda.

Epics

Epic poetry is as much a part of traditional literature as folklore, fairy tales, and fables. Television and computer superheroes have renewed the interest in the heroes of yore—Robin Hood, Don Quixote, King Arthur, and Sinbad. Faithful to the originals but in the idiom of today are retellings of the Babylonian Gilgamesh, circa 2000 BC; *The Children's Homer,* tales of Ulysses and Troy from the eighth century BC; the Anglo-Saxon eighth century *Beowulf;* and the 1140 Spanish epic *El Cid.* These books relate mythology to history, even as they strengthen students' notions of adaptations and translations. In 1230 AD, Snorri the Scandinavian historian narrated the saga of the last Viking warrior, *Harald the Ruthless.* The Viking Harald ruled from 1049 to 1066, when he invaded England. King Harold of England defeated the Norwegian forces and killed King Harald, only to be defeated by the Normans 19 days later at the battle of Hastings.

Epoch-ryphal and Era-tic Time Lines

To be memorable, a work of historical fiction requires a good story, interestingly told about an authentically depicted time and place. Within the limits of lesson time and students' developing time sense, it is practical to begin with a short story or easy historical narrative—even with fifth or sixth graders. Louis Untermyer's story "The Dog of Pompeii" affords a superb introduction to the genre. The story begins and ends with an archeological expedition's discoveries and questions. The many well-illustrated books and magazine articles showing the ruins and artifacts of Pompeii and Herculaneum enable the reader to reconstruct and verify Roman life before the eruption of Vesuvius. Students are especially impressed and curious when they see photos of the plaster castings of a real dog of Pompeii.

In another session on historical fiction, the group meets to build historical perspective. Who can name a story about a different time and place? World War II, World War I, pioneer days, the Middle Ages, the Revolution, Old World, New World, early man, and ancient Egypt. These are typically familiar times and places from the group's experiences. When these answers are written on strips of paper, arranged in time order as a lineup of students, or posted on a bulletin board, a rudimentary time line of history emerges. Eventually, the gaps will be filled in. The library media specialist offers a selection of novels for students to pinpoint the settings. Who wants to read a novel about a particular time period or event? Learning how to locate subject headings for periods of history is a complicated research skill. How does a card catalog indicate a time in history? How does the verso page tracing show the time period? These tools help students choose a novel of a particular period on which to report, emphasizing the authenticity of the setting.

Are real characters depicted, as is Paul Revere in *Johnny Tremain*? Choose a period from American history in which to set an original story. Or read stories that go along with events studied in American history. Little-known events are especially intriguing. *The Boston Coffee Party*? A Maryland Tea Party? "It's a mistake," laugh the children. "The author is confused about history." Yet the coffee story is based on a letter to her absent husband John, wherein Abigail Adams notes briefly that the women of Boston boycotted coffee. Each year in Chestertown, Maryland, there is an enactment of their tea dumping in 1774. When does a story about a real event become historical fiction? Is World War II now a historical setting? What about stories where characters reflect the stereotypes and settings of their times in language or actions that are no longer acceptable? Verify the flavor or life in a particular epoch by reading a picture history series such as the Hayes-Usborne Children's Picture History books.

Authors Monjo, Brenner, and Benchley specialize in easier-to-read historical fiction for second and third graders. Pompeii, the *Titanic,* and the discovery of King Tut's tomb appear in simple narratives. *Boy of the Painted Cave* is fiction set in Cro-Magnon times. *Zekmet, the Stone Carver* is the fictional creator of a model for the Sphinx at the behest of the Pharaoh Khafre. Upon reading such stories, the inevitable question is how does historical fiction reveal and relate people's lives to the events and locales of their times?

Sweep Across History

The world of author-illustrator Leonard Everett Fisher is boundless, crossing times and places. Fisher writes of mythological *Olympian Gods and Goddesses, Cyclops,* and the *Golden Fleece*; and of edifices: *The Alamo, Statue of Liberty, Ellis Island, The Great Wall of China, The Wailing Wall, The Tower of London,* and *The Pyramid of the Sun.* James Giblin approaches social history

From Hand to Mouth through stories of kitchenware and table manners; and of chairs and chimneys in *Let There Be Light. Where Will This Shoe Take You?* is a walk through history. Simultaneity is another device used to portray what is going on *All in a Day, Somewhere in the World Right Now.* On a tragic but real note, *When Plague Strikes* is about the battles against disease that were lost.

In earlier decades, Genevieve Foster explored people's lives horizontally across the spectrum of their historical times. Foster's books explore the worlds of George Washington, Abraham Lincoln, Andrew Jackson, Captain John Smith, Augustus Caesar, and Columbus. She reconstructs The Years of William Penn, the Pilgrims, Independence, the Flying Machine, and the Horseless Carriage. Her books celebrate *Birthdays of Freedom.* In a similar vein, *Michelangelo and His Times* and other titles in the recent 5W series evoke the life and times of eras past.

EXAMINED LIVES

Biography must have a prominent role in a literary curriculum for gifted students. All variations on biographical themes provide vicarious experiences with notable people. These should be as memorable and real as possible. Authors Huck, Norton, and Carr point out the problems and potential of the genre. (See Chapter 3 for more information about their books.)

Juvenile Biography

One problem with juvenile biography is the need to handle time appropriately for primary and intermediate age children. What seems like the recent past for the adult may seem very far away or unknown to the child. To bring events in the lives of the people who lived them home to children requires a good story made relevant to personal experience. Many books in the 92 section handle the time sense obstacle by watering down, glossing over subjects, or offering "see and read" or "childhood of" treatments. Barron's has published a series on Famous Children, including Bach, Handel, Haydn, and Mozart. The *Young Mozart* has many faces. He is the six-year-old *Wolferl*, then the boy Wolfgang Amadeus of *Letters to Horseface.* A 1982 first English edition of *Amadeus Mozart* was a translated picture book about the composer's childhood. *Eleanor* tells of the lonely childhood of the insecure and plain girl who became one of the most remembered women of America, First Lady Eleanor Roosevelt.

Another problem is that of communicating the complex ideas and events shaping the times in which biographical subjects lived. Yet another issue is how effectively an author weaves together these strands of times and ideas by a style balancing accuracy with narrative ease. Add the hurdle that children cite role models who rarely coincide with the names deemed worthy of study by teachers and authors. It is not easy to decide whose portraits, drawn by which authors, writing in what style for which children, will become the core of a biography study unit.

Some contemporary authors of juvenile biography, notably Jean Fritz, F. N. Monjo, Jane Yolen, and Aliki, write books of such high quality that the author, as much as the subject, becomes the reason for their selection as curriculum for the gifted. These writers have combined accurate research on significant, believably human subjects with sprightly individual writing style to give biography child appeal, a masterful achievement. The lives of *Queen Bess* of England and *Shaka, King of the Zulus* are richly drawn through the collaboration of Diane Stanley and Peter Vennema. Peter Sis's art for *Starry Messenger*, a story of Galileo, is a Caldecott spectacular. Leonard Fisher's noteworthy subjects include *Galileo, Gutenberg, Marie Curie*, and *Prince Henry the Navigator*. Add notable and Newbery books by authors like Syme, Eaton, and the D'Aulaires to widen the base upon which to build a unit by author/illustrator alone.

Autobiography

At some point in their middle grade years, children are expected to write about themselves—a personal reflection, a description of an actual incident, or how they see themselves in the present or the future. This, of course, is where autobiography begins. As part of the process, they come to the library media center to find autobiographies. A school library media specialist once was hard pressed to find an autobiography of a person recognizable by elementary school students and written especially for them. Helen Keller's *Story of My Life* and *The Autobiography of Ben Franklin* are long and adult, even when abridged. Now many author/artist/illustrators write about their lives in books that offer varied glimpses of a whole life or just a slice of it. Often, the young reader can identify with the creative urges and struggles of the authors. Not all of these author/artists are familiar to American children, but their well-drawn personal portraits instruct in the craft of writing.

Mary Bruce Sharon's *Scenes from Childhood* began as a book of reminiscences. Like Grandma Moses, Sharon began to paint after the age of 70. Her personal memories are accompanied by beautifully detailed paintings that depict family scenes as well as her meetings with famous people like John Roebling, Sitting Bull, Buffalo Bill, and Tom Thumb. Who do you know and where to find out more? are two good follow up questions about her portraits. *Drawn from New England: Tasha Tudor, A Portrait in Words and Pictures* is a photographic essay about the author's mother, but it also shows Bethany Tudor's own life within the family. Peter Pitseolak and William Kurelek are two well-known Canadian artists. Pitseolak was an Eskimo. Kurelek grew up in the prairie provinces of Alberta and Manitoba. He tells of these years in *A Prairie Boy's Summer* and *A Prairie Boy's Winter;* then chronicles his later years as a *Lumberjack*. A Cheyenne Indian, *Bear's Heart*, while imprisoned at Fort Marion, Florida, during the 1870s, drew scenes from his life in a school notebook. This was reproduced with accompanying text by Burton Supree. John Goodall recounts the years *Before the War: 1908 and 1939: An Autobiography in Pictures*. In the Addison-Wesley Self-Portrait series, Eric Blegvad, Margot Zemach, and Trina Schart Hyman, all gifted artist-writers, combine words and pictures to tell about themselves. James Stevenson has written six volumes of episodic memoirs starting with *Higher on the Door* and continuing on to *I Had a Lot of Wishes*.

Eloise Greenfield and her mother, Lessie Jones Little, collaborated on *Childtimes: A Three-Generation Memoir* about a grandmother, mother, and daughter. Jean Fritz wrote *Homesick: My Own Story* about her early years in China. Some of these autobiographies are merely sketches or vignettes. Others are full-length books spanning many years. All are "memoir-able."

A consummate storyteller, Isaac Bashevis Singer, recreates his life as a boy in his father's court in Poland between 1908 and 1918. He rewrote 14 stories from his adult memoirs into the children's autobiography, *A Day of Pleasure: Stories of a Boy Growing Up in Warsaw*. The photographs show a world never again to be—Jewish life in Poland before the Holocaust. The tragedy of this time is well remembered in children's literature, in novels by Lois Lowry and Jane Yolen, in memoirs by escapees and survivors, and voices from those who died, *Children in the Holocaust and World War II*.

While 92 is the number assigned to Biography, not all biographies are to be found shelved here. Kurelek's books are in the 917.1s or 6s; Peter Piseolak is found in the 970s. *Little Rascal* and other Sterling North autobiographical accounts of life with his pets are classified as 599. The sketchbook and journal kept by John James Audobon's assistant, Joseph Mason, tells of life *On the Frontier with Mr. Audobon*. Written by Barbara Brenner, it is based on authentic writings and invented conversations. Is it biography, autobiography, biographical fiction?

Laura Ingalls Wilder's Little House books are in fiction, while her diaries and letters are in 92. Some of Jean Fritz's books about Revolutionary Americans are called biographical fiction, others are fictionalized biography. What does the little record inserted in the back of *A Little Schubert* make Goffstein's book? Arnold Lobel's verse account of what happened *On the Day Peter Stuyvesant Sailed into Town* is an easy book. The cataloging of biographies by Dewey decimal number and subject headings reflect subtle distinctions in treatment that challenge some children who enjoy classifying. Features, like the use of dialogue, unauthenticated details, and invented characters may be discussed as determining factors.

Biographical horizons may be widened in other ways; when students consider the point of view from which the life is examined, evaluate many biographies about the same person, or define the biographer's personal style. Monjo frequently writes his stories of important lives from the perspective of a young person in the famous family, as a first person narrative in journal or epistolary form. Jean Fritz's titles are catchy questions. Robert Quackenbush adds the exclamation point in punctuating the titles of his humorous highlights of inventors' lives: *Oh, What an Awful Mess!* (Charles Goodyear); *Watt Got You Started, Mr. Fulton?* (James Watt and Robert Fulton); *What Has Wild Tom Done Now!!!* (Thomas Alva Edison).

How does the Ben Franklin of *What Is Papa Up to Now?* compare with *What's the Big Idea, Ben Franklin?* Or with *Poor Richard in France, The Picture Life of Ben Franklin*, the Ben drawn in Aliki's *The Many Lives of Ben Franklin,* the easy-to-read Ben, the American Heritage Franklin, or the Ben Franklin portrayed in the biography of one of his contemporaries? What characteristics of Franklin come out in his own writings, *The Whistle*, or *Poor Richard's Almanack? The Ben Franklin Book of Easy and Incredible Experiments* reveals him as scientific observer and innovator. *Ben's Book of Virtues* is his simple plan for success and happiness, adapted from his 1771 autobiography. He started with an outline of the 13 desirable virtues, keeping daily records on a grid page for each.

Collective Biography

Synthesizing individual lives with the larger framework of the history of an era or a profession is the function of collective biography. Books are written about musicians, artists, politicians, inventors, women, scientists, martyrs, winners, losers, presidents, doers, dreamers, and entrepreneurs, not to mention contemporary sports and entertainment idols.

In simple poetic language, Johanna Johnston writes of *A Special Bravery* shown by African Americans, beginning with those who accompanied the explorers to the New World. She also sings of *Women Themselves* and of *The Indians and the Strangers*. The Benets wrote *A Book of Americans* in patterned verse; these, too, are sketches of people who made America. M. B. Goffstein portrays *Lives of the Artists*, including Rembrandt, Guardi, Van Gogh, Bonnard, and Nevelson, each in barely 50 lines. Lightheartedly, in a series of four books filled with down-to-earth facts, Kathleen Krull reveals eccentricities in the *Lives of the Artists*, their masterpiece messes, and what the neighbors thought; then the musicians, their good times and bad times, and what the neighbors thought. Then she turns to the writers, their comedies and tragedies and what the neighbors thought; and, most recently, to *The Lives of the Athletes* with their spills and thrills. *My Fellow Americans: A Family Album* and *The Buck Stops Here* explore the tableaux of U.S. presidential history in the Provensens' distinctive style.

What to Do with a 92

The biography section of a typical library media center is large enough to accommodate the demand for the genre created by planners and teachers of the gifted. But students themselves are not automatically familiar with the treasures of this section, despite the outstanding writing and appeal of the subjects. A little intervention may be in order to transform the topic of biography into a broader Literary Caper.

1. Elicit student responses to the question What makes or who is a hero/heroine? Then collect names for possible groupings. Most likely, the list will mainly be names of contemporary media, rock, and sports superstars. It will also include other significant names—presidents, generals, explorers, a few women, and a few surprises. One or two children will name a personal hero, like an admired relative or family friend. Unless the library media collection has specialized in popular biography, there will be a disparity between the "biographies of excellence" cited by critics and reviewers and the names listed by students. The question is posed, "In 50 years, who is more likely to be remembered, Michael Jordan or Abraham Lincoln? Why?"

2. Present an easy historical fiction or biographical fiction selection about a main character who really lived. It could be Hannibal who crossed the Alps, the lead-headed King George who could not make the colonists behave, or Thomas Jefferson who enjoyed many happy times with his granddaughter Ellen. A composite historical fiction chronology from Ice Age to World War II for grades three through five evolves each year by rearranging eras familiar to each study group.

3. Survey other books relating to the person or the times. Then verify the facts in appropriate references, mainly general encyclopedias, biographical dictionaries, and books in the 92s. *Great People of the 20th Century* features the leaders, activists, pioneers, innovators, scientists, and newsmakers who were portrayed on *Time* magazine's covers. *The Oxford Children's Book of Famous People* and *Great Lives* are newer biographical surveys.

4. The group sees sample formats upon which to model biographical reports. These demonstrate how to transform factual data into a minute biography, a minipage, a name acrostic, a poem, or a chronology in Aliki's balloon cartoon style. Combine several subjects into a collective biography. Create a slide tape or a computer 92 fact quiz.

5. Encourage side trips into social history and historical fiction, in search of an unfamiliar life story.

Side Trips

The people who were *Crusaders for Freedom* fought for the same human and social rights that are still being fought for and which most middle-class children take for granted. Henry Steele Commager's conversational, fast-moving prose tells about those who led the struggles for the rights of children and women; the right to learn; the right of asylum; the right to a fair trial; and human rights. It is a veritable social studies curriculum as he introduces those who cared about our freedoms—of speech, of religion, from slavery—all through vignettes about those who worked for these causes. Jacob Lawrence's paintings illustrate the slave uprising led by *Toussaint L'Ouverture* in the 1791 fight for Haiti's freedom.

Three Cheers for Mother Jones stirred fifth graders' interest in child labor, protest and strikes, the Children's March of 1903, Theodore Roosevelt, and Mother Jones herself. The story, which is in I-Can-Read format, is narrated as if it were the journal of 10-year-old James, one of the marchers. They went on to read more books about the exploitation of children, like *Lyddie* in mills like *Slater's* and Macauley's. The theme of working conditions in the days of the Industrial Revolution continues to inspire juvenile authors. Ten-year-old Rebecca, the heroine of *The Bobbin Girl,* is based on an 1898 memoir by a mill worker who lived in a boarding house with other child laborers in the 1830s. Self-taught, she read *Gulliver's Travels*, attended Lyceum lectures where she heard Ralph Waldo Emerson. Avi's two volume *Beyond the Western Sea* takes its hero from the poverty of nineteenth century Ireland to the prejudice and poverty of nineteenth century Lowell, Massachusetts. *Charles Dickens: The Man Who Had Great Expectations* for better living and working conditions describes life in the grim London of *Oliver Twist. Kids at Work* tells of the continuing crusade against child labor in today's world.

Recent books about *Who Were the Founding Fathers?* and *The Ballot Box Battle* about Elizabeth Cady Stanton add color to the writing and amending of the Constitution. The right to vote, hard fought for and taken for granted in the United States, is new to the 100-year-old great-grandmother who votes for the first time on *The Day Gogo Went to Vote* in South Africa.

The Picture Life books, written by David Adler and illustrated by Alexandra Wallner, are a well-styled 92 section-in-miniature that is multicultural in scope. Beside the usuals for younger readers, Adler poses women and minorities in his literary portrait gallery. His subjects are Sitting Bull, Florence Nightingale, Sojourner Truth, Harriet Tubman, Simon Bolivar, Martin Luther King, Jesse Owens, Anne Frank, Rosa Parks, Eleanor Roosevelt, and Frederick Douglass. What are the threads for curating this gallery?

Decode Leonardo's journals. Look at the portrait of Juan de Pareja, Velaquez's slave and assistant, subject of a Newbery novel. Samuel F. B. Morse's story as inventor of the telegraph is told in *Quick, Annie, Give Me a Catchy Line!* He is less well known for being a diplomat and an artist. He became so discouraged when his 1822 painting of *The Old House of Representatives* was not bought for the U.S. Capitol that he turned to inventing. Another Morse masterpiece *Gallery at the Louvre* sold for one of the highest prices paid for a work of art at the time, more than Leonardo's codex (1980 sale), and more than the portrait of Juan de Pareja, raising the issue of how much more pictures and words are worth now, when the creators are long dead, than when they lived. Collective biography goes beyond book shelves onto the walls of a portrait gallery. The artist Christian Schussele painted two collective biographies; one entitled *Men of Progress* portrays important nineteenth century industrialists and inventors, the other shows *Washington Irving and His Literary Friends.* Whose portraits would students hang if they had the job of choosing for a national portrait gallery?

MAMMOTHS, MUSEUMS, AND RENAISSANCE MEN

Either 1977 was a good year for mammoths or it was just coincidence that the Epsteins wrote *Mister Peale's Mammoth* at about the same time Aliki wrote and illustrated *Wild and Woolly Mammoths.* In a Literary Capers sequence, once a series of topics seem to connect in a promising way (e.g., Charles Willson Peale, mammoths, and museums), the search begins for corroborating sources. In this case, the linkages were fleshed out with a *Smithsonian* article in April 1979 entitled "The Peale Family: A Lively Mixture of Art and Science." The article featured color reproductions of the paintings "The Artist in His Museum" and "Exhuming the Mastadon." The August/September 1979 issue of *The American Heritage* contained three articles about the Peale family and their ventures in the museum business. More newspaper articles and commentaries about Peale, his mammoth, and his museum appeared during 1982–83, when an exhibit entitled "Charles Willson Peale and His World" was mounted for travel to museums around the United States. In 1996–97 an exhibit about Peale and his family again traveled the country. The brief entries in standard biographical references like *The Readers' Encyclopedia* and *Webster's Biographical Dictionary* do not mention Peale's importance as a scientist, nor do the entries do him justice.

Mammoths were getting coverage during this period as well. The *Weekly Reader "Whiz"* of March 1, 1978, carried the headline "Frozen Mammoth Found" with a photograph and story about the discovery in Siberia of Dima, the baby mammoth. In 1982, local Maryland papers carried the story of a geology student who dug up the skeleton of a baby mammoth. *Owl* magazine of March 1982 contained an eight-page spread about "Woolly Monsters: The Real Facts About Mammoths." Altogether, the three sources—a fictionalized biography, a 569 Let's-Read-and-Find-Out Science book, and miscellaneous periodicals—afford the basis for an adventure branching in three directions. Mammoths still make good reading and visiting. In volume one of Hakim's history, there's a description of woolly mammoths and mastadons "with tusks like snowplows." A Smithsonian exhibit called Ice Age Mammals and the Emergence of Man allows a comparison between the skeletons of a nine-foot-tall mastadon from 2,000 years ago and its 14-foot-tall cousin, the mammoth, which vanished 10,000 years ago. The United States Post Office has published *Prehistoric Animals*, a stamp and book combination. The mastadon and the woolly mammoth are two of the four animals portrayed on postage stamps. Dima is preserved in St. Petersburg, while a plaster cast of her is displayed in a permafrost cave in Siberia.

In one direction, the life of Peale is the emphasis: American artist of the realistic school, painter of portraits, landscapes, and still lifes; scientific illustrator, father of 11 artists, children with inspiring names such as Raphaelle, Rembrandt, Rubens, Titian, Angelica, Linnaeus, and Benjamin Franklin; contemporary and friend of Jefferson, Washington, and Franklin; colleague of S. F. B. Morse; collector of specimens, and creator of the first natural history museum in the new United States.

A second direction takes the learner to the topic of museums: in fiction, as a setting for caper stories such as *From the Mixed-Up Files of Mrs. Basil E. Frankweiler*, *Funny Bananas*, or *Lost in the Museum* (a first-grade adventure); in fact, as a study of disciplines, careers, and collections that comprise a museum; and as a model for planning and creating a classroom exploratorium, collection, or personal museum.

A third direction ties many aspects together, under the theme of the Renaissance Man or the Enlightenment in the United States. While both of these are advanced concepts, the ideas involved are well illustrated by the lives of Peale and his compatriots, Jefferson, Franklin, and Morse. Jefferson's Declaration and buildings, Franklin's experiments and proverbial wisdom, and Morse's paintings and invention influence us still. Alexander Graham Bell was another such person, inventor, teacher, and thinker whose museum in Baddeck, Nova Scotia, challenges young minds with experiments. In another connection, a letter was written to *Dear Dr. Bell . . .* (from) *Your Friend, Helen Keller.*

Familiarity with people whose ideas and actions have made an impact on our society is a desirable goal. After hearing about Peale and tracing Ben Franklin's life through many books as part of his historical fiction project, Jeremy was given the writing task of stating briefly how Franklin and Peale were alike. His essay (fig. 11.2) was a cogent commentary about their versatility, their being contemporaries in an exciting era of American history, and their varied contributions. Gordon Parks is a contemporary Renaissance Man—an African-American, photographer, artist, composer, film-maker, and author—whose life and works inspire young people today.

The transformation from library media center into school museum is an exciting experience for all ages. Students are invited to become thing finders with a reading from *Pippi Longstocking*. Thing finding becomes collecting when criteria are set up. These are the organizational patterns within which found things must fit in order to be kept. What is collected has to be thoughtfully organized and attractively displayed as a minimuseum of artifacts, reproductions, realia, dioramas, replicas, models, mock-ups, or models similar to a museum of natural history, painting and sculpture, folk art, or technology and science. A student-made exploratorium may be oriented more toward discovery with touch and don't-touch items, browsing boxes, and shelf teasers.

Alicia replicated three of Bell's experiments:

1. A bottle of hot water is filled to the brim. When the water cools will the bottle still be full?

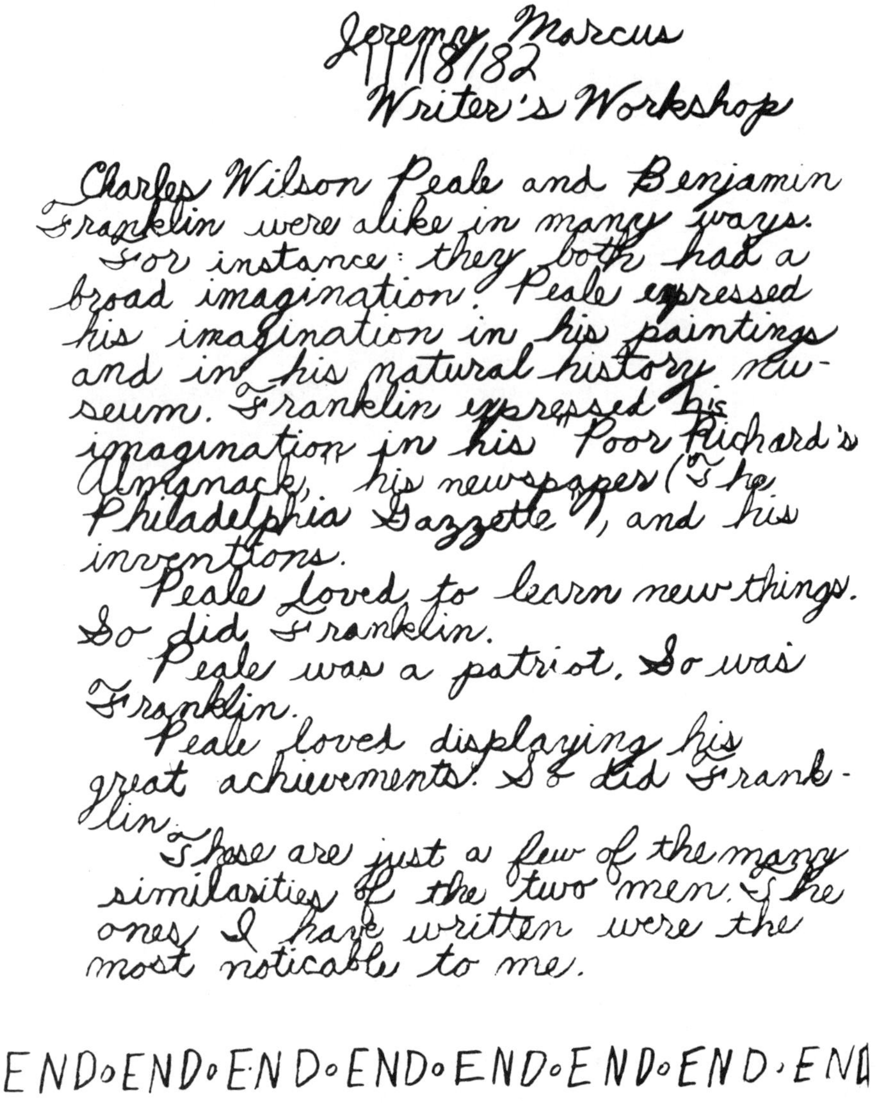

Jeremy Marcus
11/8/82
Writer's Workshop

Charles Wilson Peale and Benjamin Franklin were alike in many ways. For instance: they both had a broad imagination. Peale expressed his imagination in his paintings and in his natural history museum. Franklin expressed his imagination in his Poor Richard's Almanack, his newspaper (The Philadelphia Gazette), and his inventions.

Peale loved to learn new things. So did Franklin.

Peale was a patriot. So was Franklin.

Peale loved displaying his great achievements. So did Franklin.

These are just a few of the many similarities of the two men. The ones I have written were the most noticable to me.

END·END·END·END·END·END·END·END

Fig. 11.2. Jeremy's Essay.

2. A glass is filled with water then covered with paper. What will happen when the glass is turned over and the paper is removed?

3. Pins are stuck in the bottoms of two candles. What will happen when the candles are placed upright in water?

Through the creating, arranging, rearranging, and rotating of materials, students have direct experiences with primary sources, such as personal observations, interviews, oral histories, family documents, and memorabilia; with media product formats; and with research sources. Two variations on the museum theme have recently appeared: a Pollinarium greenhouse exhibit at the National Zoo and a national Newseum to document milestones in communication. Neither a minimuseum nor an exploratorium require a large investment. The capital assets are the enthusiasm, curiosity, and inventiveness of its young curators.

Another facet of the museum idea goes beyond the school via field trips to local or large city museums. If this is impossible, the museum can come to the school, literally, through docent visits or traveling exhibits, or vicariously, through the mail or via the Internet. The Picasso Electronic Field Trip via public television in May 1997 took classes on a live visit to the National Gallery's child-inspiring show of the young Picasso's art. Electronic reproduction of museum collections is fast growing, stimulating a debate about whether masterpieces on the screen will ever equal seeing the real thing. On a less grand scale, most museums have education and publication departments with ideas and materials to share. Visit museum websites like the San Francisco Museum at www.exploratorium.edu. Read trade books such as *Museum People*, *The Smithsonian Experience*, *Treasures of the Smithsonian*, and *Frozen Snakes and Dinosaur Bones* or magazines such as *Smithsonian* and *Natural History*. Cut and paste from old issues to construct a museum setting. Articles on museum teaching appeared in *National Geographic World* (June 1983), *Sesame Street* (December/January 1983–1984), and *Instructor* (September 1983).

Many museums have newsletters or brochures. *Art to Zoo*, published four times a year by the Smithsonian, is doubly valuable for its treatment of a theme and as an example of data retrieval design. Museums also have slide and film presentations to lend and slides, prints, replicas, and postcards to sell. Students have put these together in "museum boxes" to simulate the offerings of a particular museum. In the current book, *Lucy's Bones, Sacred Stones, and Einstein's Brain* even students far away from the originals can see the Rosetta Stone, the Book of Kells, the Hope Diamond, Babe Ruth's sixtieth home run hitting bat, and other curiosities of the Smithsonian collections. Museums are now going beyond being the destination of a two-hour field trip through "multiple visit programs," where the museum is an actual classroom for teaching academic subjects, like geometry through architecture or ancient Mexico through the symbols of Olmec artifacts. Wonderful as this sounds, the venture often occurs in school jurisdictions where art and music teachers have been eliminated.

Bill Gates, a leader of the communications revolution spoke at a Harvard University seminar in 1996, reflecting on the influence of hearing lectures on *The Iliad*, *The Odyssey*, and Hector and Achilles upon a young undergraduate. Still a young man, Gates may be the wealthiest person in the world. He is the person who bought Leonardo da Vinci's *Codex Leicester* in 1994, promising to share it with the world. The 72-page manuscript, compiled between 1506 and 1510, consists of 360 pen-and-ink diagrams, drawings, and sketches describing Leonardo's observations, theories, and speculations about geology and astronomy and his predictions of inventions to come. The left-handed Leonardo wrote the document backward from right to left using a mirror. The *Codex Leicester* is on a voyage to museums around the world. Displayed (interactively, of course), da Vinci's sixteenth-century ideas are transplanted to late twentieth-century scientific knowledge and technology.

Luckily, a chapter entitled Literary Capers need never be finished. It is like a "tesseract" through *A Wrinkle in Time* toward *A Swiftly Tilting Planet*. It is like a catch tale or a story written on a Mobius strip that goes on and on. It is like the slippers worn by *The Dancing Man*. It should include stories about families from foolish to funny to functioning, from Noodleheads and Stupids and Tub People to Peterkins and Bagthorpes and Austins. It is like an ever-changing colored squiral in the computer language of Logo, combining right angles and straight lines with the "neverendingness" of a spiral. It is all of these things as long as books continue to be written, published, and made available to students on shelves or online through their school library media centers where begins the intellectual journey to middle school and beyond.

Sometimes a whole book is a Literary Caper. Joanna Cole and E. L. Konigsburg are two gifted authors whose deft touches move the reader from fiction to fact or fact to fiction in Quintessential Capers. Teachers are the instrument and model in two such literary gems that connect students, teachers, and books. To know how to make a classroom look alive; how to prepare oral or written reports, do research, or understand classroom types, read Cole and Konigsburg. After 10 years in the classroom and at the wheel, Ms. Frizzle is still driving the bus that takes the reader from fact to fantasy. The points of *View from Saturday* differ. The Newbery awarding adults chose Mrs. Olinsky and her Souls because of a masterfully complex plot; artfully drawn characters—main and secondary; well presented information—about sea turtles nesting, acronyms, New York history, retirement life in Florida, and, wryly, education theories, educators, and school rules. Literary allusion—to Caryatids and Humpty Dumpty and the Cheshire Cat—and metaphor—each person's journey and 15 questions with 36 answers—are tucked in with "what every fifth and sixth grader should know." "But," the young kridics say, "We don't know any kids who talk like that. It's totally a grandmother's voice." Still, when kids from classes like Ms. Frizzle's and Mrs. Olinsky's go to the library media center, they'll find, written across the security arch in the best computer fonts, the same welcoming sign that graced the door of Mister Peale's Museum (fig. 11.3):

"Whoso would learn, let him enter here!"
to
"Diffuse a knowledge of the wonderful works of creation."

WHOSO WOULD LEARN, LET HIM ENTER HERE.

HOMER

THE GLOBAL LIBRARY

GUTENBERG

What do you think are the great discoveries of the world? What would you include if this were your museum?

ideas...

literature, art, music...

events...

artifacts...

inventions...

people and places?

Fig. 11.3. Mr. Peale's Museum.

BIBLIOGRAPHY

Aardvarks Disembark. Ann Jonas. New York: Greenwillow Books, 1990.

All Times, All Peoples: A World History of Slavery. Milton Meltzer. New York: Harper & Row, 1980.

All Us Come Across the Water. Lucille Clifton. New York: Holt, Rinehart & Winston, 1973.

Amadeus Mozart. Iby Lepscky. Woodbury, NY: Barron's Educational Series, 1992.

Anastasia's Album. Hugh Brewster. New York: Hyperion Books for Children, 1996.

Anni's India Diary. Anni Axworthy. New York: Whispering Coyote Press, 1992.

The Ark. Marie Angel. New York: Harper & Row, 1982.

The Ark. Margot Benary-Isbert. New York: Harcourt, Brace & World, 1953.

The Armadillo from Amarillo. Lynne Cherry. New York: Gulliver/Harcourt Brace, 1994.

Around the World in Eighty Days. John Burningham. London: Cape, 1972.

Aunt Harriet's Underground Railroad in the Sky. Faith Ringgold. New York: Crown, 1992.

The Ballot Box Battle. Emily McCully. New York: Alfred A. Knopf, 1996.

Bard of Avon: The Story of William Shakespeare. Diane Stanley and Peter Vennema. New York: Morrow Junior Books, 1992.

Bear's Heart: Scenes from the Life of a Cheyenne Artist of One Hundred Years Ago with Pictures by Himself. Burton Supree. Philadelphia: J. B. Lippincott, 1977.

Before the War: 1908–1939: An Autobiography in Pictures. John S. Goodall. New York: Atheneum, 1981.

The Ben Franklin Book of Easy and Incredible Experiments. New York: John Wiley, 1995.

Ben's Book of Virtues: Ben Franklin's Simple, Weekly Plan for Success and Happiness. Karen Greene, ed. New Hope, PA: New Hope Press, 1994.

Ben's Dream. Chris Van Allsburg. Boston: Houghton Mifflin,1982.

Beyond the Western Sea. 2 vol. Avi. New York: Orchard Books, 1996.

Black Is Brown Is Tan. Arnold Adoff. New York: Harper & Row,1973.

The Bobbin Girl. Emily McCully. New York: Dial Books for Young Readers, 1996.

A Book of Americans. Rosemary Benet and Stephen Vincent Benet. New York: Holt, Rinehart, & Winston, 1933.

The Boston Coffee Party. Doreen Rappaport. New York: HarperCollins, 1988.

Boy of the Painted Cave. Justin Denzel. New York: Putnam/Philomel, 1988.

Brendan the Navigator: A History Mystery About the Discovery of America. Jean Fritz. New York: Coward, McCann & Geoghegan, 1979.

The Buck Stops Here. Alice Provensen. New York: Harper & Row, 1990.

Can't You Make Them Behave, King George? Jean Fritz. New York: Coward-McCann, 1982.

Canterbury Tales. Adapted by Barbara Cohen. New York: Lothrop, 1988.

Canterbury Tales. Geraldine McCaughrean. Chicago: Childrens Press Choice, 1985.

The Canterbury Tales of Geoffrey Chaucer. A. Kent Hieatt and Constance Hieatt, eds. and comps. New York: Golden Press, 1961.

Chanticleer and the Fox. Barbara Cooney. New York: Crowell Junior Books, 1982.

Charles Dickens's OLIVER TWIST. Abridged by Lesley Baxter. New York: Dial, 1996.

Charles Dickens: The Man Who Had Great Expectations. Diane Stanley and Peter Vennema. New York: Morrow Junior Books, 1993.

Child of the Silent Night. Edith Hunter. Boston: Houghton Mifflin, 1963.

Children in the Holocaust and World War II: Their Secret Diaries. Laurel Holliday. New York: Pocket Books, 1995.

The Children's Homer: The Adventures of Odysseus and the Tale of Troy. Padraic Colum. New York: Macmillan, 1982.

The Children's Shakespeare. E. Nesbit. New York: Random House, 1968.

A Child's History of America. Edward J. McGrath. Boston: Little, Brown, 1975.

A Child's Portrait of Shakespeare. Lois Burdell. Windsor, Ontario: Black Moss/Firefly, 1996.

Childtimes: A Three Generation Memoir. Eloise Greenfield and Lessie Jones Little. New York: Thomas Y. Crowell, 1979.

Coming to America: The Story of Immigration. Betsy Maestro. New York: Scholastic, 1996.

Commodore Perry in the Land of the Shogun. Rhoda Blumberg. New York: Lothrop, Lee & Shepard, 1985.

Crusaders for Freedom. Henry Steele Commager. New York: Doubleday, 1962.

The Day Gogo Went to Vote: South Africa, April 1994. Elinor Batezat Sisulu. New York: Little, Brown, 1996.

A Day of Pleasure: Stories of a Boy Growing Up in Warsaw. Isaac Bashevis Singer. New York: Farrar, Straus & Giroux, 1986.

Dear Dr. Bell . . . Your Friend, Helen Keller. Judith St. George. New York: G. P. Putnam's Sons, 1992.

Deep Down Underground. Oliver Durea. New York: Aladdin Books, 1993.

Did Marco Polo Go to China? Frances Wood. Boulder, CO: Westview Press, 1996.

"The Dog of Pompeii." Louis Untermeyer. In *More Favorite Stories Old and New for Girls and Boys,* rev. ed. Sidonie Gruenberg, ed. New York: Doubleday, 1960.

Drawn from New England: Tasha Tudor, a Portrait in Words and Pictures. Bethany Tudor. New York: Collins, 1979.

El Cid. Geraldine McCaughrean. Oxford, England: Oxford University Press, 1989.

Eleanor. Barbara Cooney. New York: Viking, 1996.

Encounter. Jane Yolen. San Diego: Harcourt Brace Jovanovich, 1992.

Favorite Tales from Shakespeare. Bernard Miles. Chicago: Rand McNally, 1977.

From the Mixed-Up Files of Mrs. Basil E. Frankweiler. E. L. Konigsburg. New York: Atheneum, 1967.

Frozen Snakes and Dinosaur Bones: Exploring a Natural History Museum. Margery Facklam. New York: Harcourt Brace Jovanovich, 1976.

Full Steam Ahead: The Race to Build a Transcontinental Railroad. Rhoda Blumberg. Washington, DC: National Geographic Society, 1987.

Funny Bananas: The Mystery in the Museum. Georgette McHargue. New York: Holt, Rinehart & Winston, 1975.

Gooseberries to Oranges. Barbara Cohen. New York: Lothrop, Lee & Shepard, 1982.

Grand Constructions. Gian Paolo Ceserine. New York: G. P. Putnam's Sons, 1983.

Grandfather's Journey. Allen Say. Boston: Houghton Mifflin, 1993.

The Great Kapok Tree: A Tale of the Amazon Rain Forest. Lynne Cherry. San Diego: Harcourt Brace Jovanovich, 1990.

Great Lives. Simon Broughton. Garden City, NY: Doubleday, 1988.

He Who Saw Everything: The Epic of Gilgamesh. Anita Feagles. New York: Young Scott Books, 1966.

The Heroic Deeds of Beowulf. Gladys Schmitt. New York: Random House,1962.

Home Place. Crescent Dragonwagon. New York: Macmillan, 1990.

Homesick: My Own Story. Jean Fritz. New York: G. P. Putnam's Sons, 1982.

The House on Maple Street. Bonnie Pryor. New York: William Morrow, 1987.

The House on Stink Alley: A Story About the Pilgrims in Holland. F. N. Monjo. New York: Holt, Rinehart & Winston, 1977.

How Many Days to America? A Thanksgiving Story. Eve Bunting. Boston: Houghton Mifflin, 1988.

How My Family Lives in America. Susan Kuklin. New York: Bradbury Press, 1992.

How My Parents Learned to Eat. Ina Friedman. New York: Houghton Mifflin, 1984.

The Human Body. Jonathan Miller and David Pelham. New York: Viking, 1983.

If Your Name Was Changed at Ellis Island. Ellen Levine. New York: Scholastic, 1993.

The Iliad and the Odyssey. Marcia Williams. Cambridge, MA: Candlewick Press, 1996.

Incredible Journey of Lewis and Clark. Rhoda Blumberg. New York: Lothrop, Lee & Shepard, 1987.

The Indians and the Strangers. Johanna Johnston. New York: Dodd, Mead,1972.

A Jar of Dreams. Yoshiko Uchida. New York: Atheneum, 1982.

Journey to Freedom: A Story of the Underground Railroad. Courtin Wright. New York: Holiday House, 1994.

Judy's Journey. Lois Lenski. Philadelphia: J. B. Lippincott,1947.

Kids At Work: Crusade Against Child Labor. Levis Hine. New York: Clarion Books, 1994.

King George's Head Was Made of Lead. F. N. Monjo. New York: Coward, McCann, 1974.

Kon-Tiki for Young People. Thor Heyerdahl. Skokie, IL: Rand, McNally, 1960. Also *Thor Heyerdahl and the Reed Boat Ra.* Philadelphia: J. B. Lippincott, 1974.

The Land I Lost: Adventures of a Boy in Vietnam. Huynh Quang Nhuong. New York: Harper & Row, 1990.

Leaving for America. Roslyn Bresnick-Perry. San Francisco: Children's Book Press, 1992.

Leonardo Da Vinci. Ibi Lepscky. New York: Barron's Educational Series, 1982.

Leonardo Da Vinci: The Artist, Inventor, Scientist in Three Dimensional Movable Pictures. Alice Provensen and Martin Provensen. New York: Viking, 1984.

Let There Be Light. James Giblin. New York: Harper & Row, 1988. Also *From Hand to Mouth,* 1987. *When Plague Strikes,* 1997.

Letters to Horseface: Being the Story of Wolfgang Amadeus Mozart's Journey to Italy, 1769-1770, When He Was a Boy. F. N. Monjo. New York: Viking, 1975.

The Life I Live. Lois Lenski. New York: Walck, 1965.

Little Rascal: A Memoir of a Better Era. Sterling North. New York: E. P. Dutton, 1965.

A Little Schubert. M. B. Goffstein. New York: Harper & Row, 1972.

Lives of the Artists. M. B. Goffstein. New York: Farrar, Straus & Giroux, 1981.

Lives of the Artists: Masterpiece Messes (and What the Neighbors Thought). Katherine Krull. New York: Harcourt Brace, 1993.

Lives of the Athletes. Katherine Krull. New York: Harcourt Brace, 1997.

Lives of the Musicians: Good Times, Bad Times (and What the Neighbors Thought). Katherine Krull. New York: Harcourt Brace, 1993.

Lives of the Writers: Comedies, Tragedies (and What the Neighbors Thought). Katherine Krull. New York: Harcourt Brace, 1994.

Lost and Found. Jill Paton Walsh. London: A. Deutsch, 1984.

Lost in the Museum. Miriam Cohen. New York: Dell, 1983.

Lucy's Bones, Sacred Stones, and Einstein's Brain: The Remarkable Stories Behind the Grand Objects and Artifacts of History, from Antiquity to the Modern Era. Harvey Rachlin, New York: Henry Holt, 1996.

Lumberjack. William Kurelek. Boston: Houghton Mifflin, 1974.

Lyddie. Katherine Paterson. New York: Lodestar/Dutton, 1991.

Making a New Home in America. Maxine Rosenberg. New York: Lothrop, Lee & Shepard, 1986.

The Man Who Loved Books. Jean Fritz. New York: G. P. Putnam's Sons, 1981.

The Many Lives of Ben Franklin: Written Down and Illustrated. Aliki. Englewood Cliffs, NJ: Prentice-Hall, 1977.

Many Thousands Gone: From Slavery to Freedom. Virginia Hamilton. New York: Alfred A. Knopf, 1993.

Metropolis: Ten Cities/Ten Centuries. Albert Lorenz and Joy Schleh. New York: Harry N. Abrams, 1996.

Michelangelo and His Times. Frederic Theule. New York: Henry Holt, 1996.

Mince Pie and Mistletoe. Phyllis McGinley. Philadelphia: J. B. Lippincott, 1959.

Minty: A Story of Young Harriet Tubman. Alan Schroeder. New York: Dial Press, 1996.

Mister Peale's Mammoth. Sam Epstein and Beryl Epstein. New York: Coward, McCann and Geoghegan, 1977.

Molly's Pilgrim. Barbara Cohen. New York: Lothrop, Lee & Shepard, 1983.

Mother Jones: One Woman's Fight for Labor. Betsey Kraft. New York: Clarion Books, 1995.

Museum People. Peggy Thompson. Englewood Cliffs, NJ: Prentice-Hall, 1977.

Museums: A Book to Begin. Suzanne De Borhegy. New York: Holt Rinehart, 1962.

My Fellow Americans: A Family Album. Alice Provensen. New York: Harcourt Brace, 1995.

My Noah's Ark. M. B. Goffstein. New York: Harper & Row, 1978.

Noah's Ark. Gail Haley. New York: Atheneum, 1971.

Noah's Ark. Peter Spier. New York: Doubleday, 1977.

The Not-So-Jolly Roger. Jon Scieszka. New York: Viking, 1991.

Now Let Me Fly: The Story of a Slave Family. Delores Johnson. New York: Macmillan, 1993.

Odysseus and the Cyclops. Retold and illustrated by Warwick Hutton. New York: McElderberry Books, 1996.

Oh, What an Awful Mess! A Story of Charles Goodyear. Robert Quackenbush. Englewood Cliffs, NJ: Prentice-Hall, 1980.

The Olympians: Great Gods and Goddesses of Ancient Greece. Leonard Fisher. New York: Holiday House, 1984.

On the Day Peter Stuyvesant Sailed into Town. Arnold Lobel. New York: Harper & Row, 1971.

On the Frontier with Mr. Audobon. Barbara Brenner. New York: Coward, McCann and Geoghegan, 1977.

One Small Blue Bead. Byrd Baylor Schweitzer. New York: Macmillan, 1992.

One Wide River to Cross. Barbara Emberley, adapter. Englewood Cliffs, NJ: Prentice-Hall, 1966.

Our Earth. Huck Scarry. New York: Messner, 1984.

People. Peter Spier. New York: Doubleday, 1980.

Peter Pitseolak's Escape from Death. Peter Pitseolak. New York: Delacorte Press, 1977.

Pinchpenny John. Lee Lorenz. Englewood Cliffs, NJ: Prentice-Hall, 1981.

A Place Called Freedom. Scott Russell Sanders. New York: Atheneum, 1997.

Poor Richard in France. F. N. Monjo. New York: Holt, Rinehart and Winston, 1973.

Poor Richard's Almanack. Benjamin Franklin. Mt. Vernon, NY: Peter Pauper Press, n.d.

A Prairie Boy's Summer. William Kurelek. Montreal: Tundra Books, 1975.

Professor Noah's Spaceship. Brian Wildsmith. London: Oxford University Press, 1980.

Quick, Annie, Give Me a Catchy Line! The Story of Samuel F. B. Morse. Englewood Cliffs, NJ: Prentice-Hall, 1983.

Quotations from Shakespeare. Boston: Plays, 1971.

Remarkable Voyages of Captain Cook. Rhoda Blumberg. New York: Maxwell Macmillan International, 1991.

Roosevelt Grady. Louise R. Shotwell. New York: Philomel, 1963.

Sam Ellis's Island. Beatrice Siegel. New York: Four Winds Press, 1985.

Scenes from Childhood. Mary Bruce Sharon. New York: E. P. Dutton, 1978.

Scornful Simkin. Lee Lorenz. Englewood Cliffs, NJ: Prentice-Hall, 1980.

Self-Portrait: Eric Blegvad. Boston: Addison-Wesley, 1979. Also in series: Trina Schart Hyman and Margot Zemach.

Shake Hands with Shakespeare: Eight Plays for Elementary Schools. Albert Cullom. New York: Citation Press, 1968.

The Slave Dancer. Paula Fox. Scarsdale, NY: Bradbury Press, 1973.

The Snowman. Raymond Briggs. New York: Random House, 1978.

Somewhere in the World Right Now. Stacey Schuett. New York: Alfred A. Knopf, 1995.

A Special Bravery. Johanna Johnston. New York: Dodd Mead, 1967.

Stories from Shakespeare. Marchette Chute. New York: World, 1956.

Starry Messenger: A Book Depicting the Life of a Famous Scientist, Mathemetician, Astronomer, Philosopher, Physicist, Galileo Galilee. Peter Sis. New York: Farrar, Straus & Giroux, 1996.

Tales from Chaucer. Eleanor Farjeon. Newton Centre, MA: Charles T. Branford, 1959.

Tales from Shakespeare. Charles and Mary Lamb. New York: Macmillan, 1963.

Talking Walls. Margery Burns Knight. Gardiner, ME: Tilbury House, 1992.

Taste of Chaucer: Selections from the Canterbury Tales. Ann Malcolmson, ed. New York: Harcourt Brace, 1964.

This Is Historic Britain. Miroslav Sasek. New York: Macmillan, 1974. Also *This Is London.*

Three Cheers for Mother Jones. Jean Bethell. New York: Holt, Rinehart, 1980.

To Be a Slave. Julius Lester. New York: Dial Press, 1968.

Toussaint L'Ouverture: The Fight for Haiti's Freedom. Walter Dean Myers. New York: Simon & Schuster, 1996.

Twenty-One Balloons. William Pene Du Bois. New York: Viking, 1947.

Victorians Abroad. John Goodall. New York: Atheneum, 1981.

Voyage of the Beagle: Darwin's Journals. Millicent Selsam, ed. New York: Harper, 1959.

The Wall. Eve Bunting. New York: Clarion Books, 1990.

What Is Papa Up to Now? Miriam Anne Bourne. New York: Coward, McCann & Geoghegan, 1977.

Where Did Your Family Come From? A Book About Immigrants. Melvin Berger and Gilda Berger. Nashville, TN: Ideals Children's Books, 1993.

Where the Forest Meets the Sea. Jeannie Baker. New York: Greenwillow Books, 1988.

Where Will This Shoe Take You? A Walk Through the History of Footwear. Laurie Lawlor. New York: Walker, 1996.

The Whistle. Benjamin Franklin. Minneapolis, MN: Lerner, 1974.

Who Were the Founding Fathers? Two Hundred Years of Reinventing American History. Steven Jaffe. New York: Henry Holt, 1996.

Why Noah Chose the Dove. Isaac B. Singer. New York: Farrar, Straus & Giroux, 1973.

Will's Quill. Don Freeman. New York: Viking, 1975.

The Witch of Fourth Street and Other Stories. Myron Levoy. New York: Harper & Row, 1972.

Wolferl: The First Six Years. Lisl Weil. New York: Holiday House, 1991.

Women Themselves. Johanna Johnston. New York: Dodd, Mead, 1973.

The World in 1492. Jean Fritz. New York: Henry Holt, 1992.

Young Mozart. Rachel Isadora. New York: Viking, 1997.

Zekmet, the Stone Carver: A Tale of Ancient Egypt. Mary Stolz. San Diego, CA: Harcourt Brace Jovanovich, 1988.

Twelve

Mindsets to Mindstorms Through Mindscapes

The word mindstorms is not yet in *Webster's Unabridged Dictionary*; however, the words mindset and brainstorm are. A mindset is "the direction of one's thinking; a fixed state of mind." To brainstorm is "to practice a conference technique by which a group attempts to find a solution for a specific problem by amassing all the ideas spontaneously contributed by its members."

The two words influenced gifted programs, not always to the advantage of the children. The mindset of gifted program planners too often seemed to be that process and product mattered more than high caliber communication of important knowledge. The mindset of gifted students too often was "Divergent thinking is fun," without clear, concise articulation of what they were thinking about. Both words downplayed the need for planning, organization, and content. Brainstorming outside of a context of informed relevance may not be the best technique for creative, productive, critical, or evaluative thinking and problem solving. Maybe the time was ripe for a new combination: *mind* with *storm*.

Mindstorms are the dynamic interactions between children and powerful ideas. The concept is the creation of Seymour Papert, the inventor of the Logo computer language for children. Mindstorms represent the easy movement between the intellectual territories of the humanities and sciences and the actively growing minds of the young. Papert, who once worked with Piaget, sees "children as the active builders of their own intellectual structures. But to say that intellectual structures are built by the learner rather than taught by a teacher does not mean that they are built from nothing. On the contrary, like other builders, children appropriate to their own use materials they find about them, most saliently the models and metaphors suggested by the surrounding culture" (Papert 1980). Papert sees the educator as the anthropologist working to understand which cultural materials are relevant to intellectual development. In his recent writings and lectures, however, he rethinks the role of schools as agents for change. Papert believes that the computer has opened up the movement toward a "family learning culture." He calls children *bricoleurs,* or tinkerers. Children themselves, as they "tinker" with computers, will make

195

the connections. They, not Ms. Frizzle, will drive the Magic School Bus to Papert's future world, where information is measured in tetrabytes of one trillion bytes each, and by the year 2047, it is predicted, computers will be 10 billion times more powerful.

CUES suggests that a school library media center is an immediately available cultural model, metaphor, and material that teaching adults can help children appropriate to their own use. An analogy to the computer is not just an abstraction; the computer has concrete applications in a library media-centered program for the gifted. It is a database for input that helps children improve their thought processing even as it shapes their output. Early programs for the pioneer Apple IIE meshed well with the CUES scope and sequence for the upper grades in those lessons entitled "Exploring the World of Language," "Information? Please! But Help Wanted," "Miscellany Matters," and "Literary Capers." Logo offered a way to use words to draw geometric configurations that defined concepts—movement from the concrete to the abstract. Word processing programs from Bank Street Writer to Appleworks simplified editing and revising, thus encouraging children to write more. Databases codified the way to gather, arrange, and store information for later use. Quiz or question shell program formats were a way of applying miscellany from many sources for entertainment and edification. Tracking Carmen San Diego around the globe via computer or television series, interfacing with networks and webs, interactively sharing data from all sorts and levels of information sources are all second nature now as software and applications become more complex and suave.

Who would have imagined that in February 1997 the Secretary of State of the United States visiting in Moscow would answer questions online from children in hundreds of schools all over the world? Or that 292 years after his birth, Ben Franklin's autobiography, published in 1791, would rate four stars as a net site for kids to surf? The computer and the library media center strengthen their partnership for mindstorming, together supplying young builders with the materials they need for Introduction to Information Gathering 101. In the same year that a committee of the American Library Association searched 50,000 websites to find 700 to recommend as great for kids, the Round Reading Room at the British Library was closing. Lost is its history of great minds who read there, as its 12 million books were moved from the shelves. Mindstorms—the word does indeed apply to all that is on the shelves and in memory storage between the 000s and the 999s, powerful ideas, powerfully expressed by 1999 for the year 2000 and beyond.

EDUCATIONAL TRENDS

A livelier perspective on educational direction sometimes comes from looking at popular trends rather than from studying the research. Consider the progression of educational trends over the past 15 years. In 1982 when this book was first written, the money barrels were emptier for things educational than they had been for many years, yet the state of schools and teaching were said to make us a "nation at risk." The personal computer replaced *Time* magazine's usual Man of the Year. There was concern that we were becoming an A-literate society, one where people can read but opt not to read. Nonbooks about cats and quiche were best-sellers for kids and adults alike. In 1983, Jim Trelease made reading aloud respectable once again. Parking lots at public library story hours were jammed. Audiences were not just preschoolers; infants in backpacks and school-aged children book browsed within listening distance. The year 1983 brought trivia into the cabbage patch with whole classes of children, the gifted included, carrying Cabbage Patch Dolls and Ewoks around the school as they discussed who did or did not own Trivial Pursuit. In 1984, Latin and the classics experienced a revival. By the late 1980s parents were warned lest superbabies become hurried children, unfairly deprived of time to relax and be children who need time to pause and smell the flowers, to catch up on childhood pastimes like reading and being read to. Many parents waited the extra year for maturing before entering their late-year birthday children in kindergarten so they would be the oldest, not the youngest in the class. The world of children's books exploded, and bookstores that now sell them seem like community centers, always open and lively. Scholastic's stock plunged in 1996 because of the slump in the sales of *Goosebumps* books, a relief no doubt to those who despair that horror fiction will ruin young minds.

Vernacular expressions of change are reflected professionally. These include "Effective Schools," "Essential Schools," "Core Knowledge Schools," "Inclusive Schools," "Blue Ribbon Schools," and "charter schools." Educators hear about effective teaching, domains of knowledge, thinking as a teachable skill, writing as a lead-in to thinking. The National Commission on Teaching and America's Future, reporting in September 1996, deplored the state of teacher training, calling it inadequate for the demands of the information age. The message reiterated the earlier 1983 reports of "A Nation At Risk," warning in 1989 against "the rising tide of mediocrity." "Goals 2000" urged that this country offer the world's best math and science education. It suggests that the training of future teachers should include a heavy dose of liberal arts, more practice in the classroom, and a content specialty.

In the transition from card catalog to the Internet, information science jobs have become more technologically oriented. As vast amounts of information move outside the library walls, so do more information science graduates work outside traditional library settings, an image upgrade that attracts more men to jobs entitled Webmaster, Graphic Multimedia Designer, Knowledge Navigator, or Database Manager. But who will catalog the World Wide Web? Despite new terminology, job expectations, enhancing technology, and diminishing traditional roles, the organization and distribution of knowledge continues to be a valued function.

Technological trends have implications for gifted programs: for changes in the way we teach and children learn about *communication* and *multimedia*; and for consideration of funding, elitism, and gender equity issues. "Why are there more boys than girls on the *It's Academic* teams?" and "Let's go back to all-boys or all-girls schools or multiage classrooms." As the twentieth century natural resource-fueled society gives way to the brainpowered high-tech society of the twenty-first century, the library media center must have an acknowledged new role.

Paradigms and Protocols

Not only are there new names for jobs in information, there is also a new vocabulary in gifted education. Students have become facile with it. Paradigms, rubrics, and HOIS are part of this lexicon. A paradigm, from the Greek word for patterns, is a program model or example. A rubric, once the heading of a chapter or discourse done in red, now is a ground rule or authority. A protocol now means a procedure long established. HOIS is an acronym for higher order thinking.

Joseph Renzulli and his associates offer a complete paradigm for a gifted program with the intertwining of the Revolving Door Identification Model (RDIM) for grouping with the Curriculum and Instruction Model of their Enrichment Triad (Renzulli 1977). CUES is a rubric, a protocol of this paradigm to help students make Connections for Understanding and Enrichment of School Subjects through the library media center.

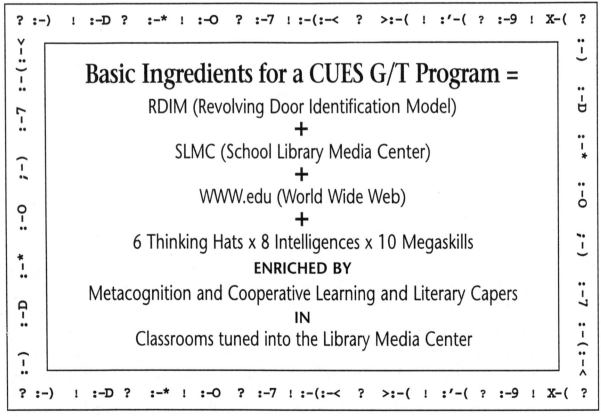

Fig. 12.1. CUES Rubric for G & T.

Pendulums

Diane Ravitch wrote "Bring Literature and History Back to Elementary Schools" as a statement that "education is debased when the curriculum is stripped of its content and when skills, free of any cultural literacy, or historical content are all that is taught." Ravitch worried that our children "have no 'furniture' in their minds, no vocabulary of historical persons or events to draw upon, no reference to the ordinary literary images that fifth graders once imbibed in every common school in the nation" (Ravitch 1984). Although this is less true now, the philosophical and educational dilemma of the 1990s remains: the dichotomy between the progressives and the conservatives about the way to improve our schools and save our children. In 1997, the year which celebrated both the centennial of the electron and John Dewey's pragmatism, articles were written about the dumbing down of our schools manifested in new subject area standards that water down content. These were opposed by articles emphasizing that the process, including a role for self-image, should be the thrust.

In *The Culture of Education*, Jerome Bruner balances two views of the way the mind works: computationally, through information processing and culturally through interpersonal relationships (Bruner 1996). "Going meta" is the active process of education within a philosophy of "neural humanism"—mental development in a collaborative environment. This may answer the perennial question asked by those who have been teaching children during the back and forths of the pendulum: Why does it have to be either—or, when it should be whatever works for the children?

FRONTIERS

Other frontiers exist. Each day some new discovery or new light on enigmas we thought were solved appears in the newspaper or media to be included in a loose-leaf curriculum for further investigation. Scientific discoveries postulate new cosmologies and new theories about the power of nothing, quantum electrodynamics, mathematical laws and evolution, and snowballs in space. A chemical laboratory will fit on a chip in the twenty-first century. Anthropological and archeological findings since January 1997 suggest that human societies emerged earlier than previously thought with the discovery of 400,000-year-old spears in a German coal mine. Stone tools in Siberia indicate the presence of humans there 300,000 years ago. Traces of human habitation exist in south Chile from 12,500 years ago, a millenium before previously thought. Ruins of a "Central American Pompeii" have been excavated. The Ice Maiden of Peru, the Iceman of the Alps, alien-like two-headed clay figures unearthed in Jordan dating from 6500 B.C., and dinosaur eggs and stomach content remains are all documented artifacts.

Who reached the North Pole first—Admiral Perry or Dr. Cook? Expedition diaries shed new light on the great polar controversy. Travel is possible through "Smelly Old History" with Oxford University Press's series of scratch and sniff books. A bioethical problem centers around the fate of the many lab chimps no longer needed for biomedical research. With a life span of 50 years, they reside in a New Mexico compound, whiling away their time playing with toys, watching National Geographic shows on TV, and learning how to use tools. They also enjoy seeing people argue, according to a recent *New York Times* story. Fascinating subjects all for more literature of fact yet to be written!

Youth in Action

Beyond academic performance, a new dimension of social concern inspires many gifted children to action through involvement with the community and the world, and through cyberspace. A *Sixty Minutes* segment spotlighted the Canadian boy who became so concerned after reading about the prevalence of child labor in the world that he began a worldwide crusade to ban it. A 12-year-old girl sold $20,000 worth of lemonade for a center for the homeless. Walking in the shoes of others, even vicariously through books, is creating a new generation of young heroes and heroines. The Partnering Initiative is allied with ASCD, NEA, and other educational policy influences to support the idea of "Civil Education," linking learning to the world beyond the classroom. In many states, community service credits are a requisite for high school graduation. Social service—with the environment, the elderly, and the poor—should be considered an addition rather than a detraction from the basics of education. Youth in Action, a network site, guides teachers and children who care about the environment or human rights to learn, communicate, then take action toward making the world a better place. Will software help us to a brave new "SIM:World"?

Wires and Bridges

Wiring the World

Teachers and students work daily with technology as a speed-up tool and with knowledge as building blocks. At the end of 1996, the size of the World Wide Web was measured at a terabyte of one trillion bytes of data. The Library of Congress, with about 20 million volumes, equals 20 terabytes.

Using the simple wiring of battery-operated devices, an 11th grader invented a "Harmony Helper," allowing singers to check whether they are on key. "Baby-Safe" sounds an alarm when a car seat is not correctly secured. "Grocery Identifier" reads a bar code and speaks the product name for those who cannot read. A high school student patents a laptop-sized eye-testing device. At a technology magnet school in Kansas, 10- to 13-year-olds are in the website design "business," expert in building World Wide Web pages for their school and their community.

To widen its audience and underscore the plight of books in translation, a complete book—*The End of the Rainbow* by Bjarne Reuter, part of the trilogy of Buster—for fourth graders and up appears free on the Internet. Homework help is available via phone line (Dial-A-Teacher) and online (Internet). Yet to be solved are the issues of verifiability. Who screens the answered information for accuracy? American Association of School Librarians' ICONnect service for kids, KidsConnect, is staffed by school librarian volunteers to answer questions and make referrals by e-mail within 48 hours. Students can also access Ask-A-Teacher, Look-It-Up, "discuss it" websites and Just for Middle Schools CD-ROMS.

Bridging the Centuries

In the 1996 presidential campaign, President Clinton envisioned a bridge to the twenty-first century with every child able to read by third grade and with computers available to every child. The bridge building from now to then is in progress. April 19, 1997, was Net Day when volunteers wired schools all over the country. The goal of this grassroots initiative is access to the Internet for all children in American schools by 2001.

Library bridges are not new. Bridges from the library media center to lifelong learning are crossed for the young when *Norman the Doorman* opens the doors to the Majestic Museum, Petrini *The Pet of the Met* sings at the Opera, and *The Dallas Titans Get Ready for Bed* after they exercise their bodily kinesthetic intelligences. Teachers in training at Boston University School of Education analyze *Frog and Toad* in the context of Aristotle's view of bravery as they link children's literature to classical thought. Museum visits with children connect literature and the visual arts. Pippi is almost 50 years old. There were 65,000 birthday cards were sent in celebration of the Cat in the Hat's 40th birthday. For each card received, Random House contributed a book to the National Center for Family Literacy. The role of bridge builder fits in with what library media specialists have been trained to do. Even with the addition of the technological competence needed to work with computers and other media technology, the old roles of inspirer and disseminator still hold sway, with a new job title added, mindscaper. More than 70,000 elementary library media centers staffed with library media specialists, continue to create a MINDSCAPE, an environment that is

- a cornucopia for browsers;
- a habit and a habitat;
- a database;
- a catch-up or wake-up place; and
- a place for transforming the *reception* of information into the *discovery* of the universe of human knowledge.

In this place, it is hoped that each child will sense that "where we go to school each day, Indian children used to play." Though others have passed this way before, every child's journey is unique and exciting. That this does happen is expressed by the children themselves in their conversations, actions, writings, and other creations. It is expressed when

Matias analyzes how he worked with his peers as a computer graphics tutor: "This is not my fast way. This is my teaching way."

Samantha's sixth grade dramatizes their original *satyr* plays based on Greek mythology, enabling them to greet an early Greek sculpture of a satyr as an old friend.

Fifth- and sixth-grade Renaissance Rascal class members publish Shakespearean sonnets.

Third graders show their slide/tape based on their own "Cut-outs in the Matisse Style."

Sara says of the pre-kindergartner to whom she read *Tops and Bottoms*, "He enjoys the story, but he doesn't *get* it."

Jeremy decides that his third-grade drawing skills would not capture the theme powerfully enough, so adapts Gerald McDermott's African geometric technique to illustrate the life of Martin Luther King Jr.

Christopher, age 11, reviews the Civil War novel, *Shades of Gray*, for the local newspaper.

Steven says he both loves and hates "cliffhangers and continueds."

Joe uses two wires, a battery, and a lightbulb as an Electric Tester connecting famous quotes to their authors.

And in some final comments on giftedness and school library media centers: Angela's poem in the style of Shel Silverstein

G & T

I lost 2 school books . . .
But that's Okay
I'm Gifted

I lost 5 pencils . . .
But that's Okay
I'm Gifted

I lost three reports . . .
But that's Okay
I'm Gifted

When the end of school came around
You wouldn't believe what I found!
AND I'M STILL GIFTED

NO PICTURE DUE TO
LOSS OF CRAYON.

Brendan's analysis of his reading metamorphosis:

Fig. 12.2. Triptych Picture.

Anna's metacognitive summary of some literary highlights of her elementary school years:

> In first grade word, we did picture word books. I liked my drawing for "thump" (see figure 12.3).
>
> In second grade, I compared the voyages and rescues at sea and the feelings of the boat people from Cuba and the people on the Titanic.
>
> In third grade, I learned about folktales and biomes and raps for telling about them.
>
> This year, in fourth grade, I read library books about the Amistad rebellion, Anastasia, and Polar, the Titanic bear. It was fun to discover these things before movies made them popular.

THUMP   **Fig. 12.3.**

And an unsolicited testimonial to library media centers from Carrie, Grade 2.

Fig. 12.4. The IMC for the G and T.

REFERENCES

Bruner, Jerome. 1996. *The Culture of Education.* Cambridge, MA: Harvard University Press.

Papert, Seymour. 1980. *Mindstorms: Children, Computers, and Powerful Ideas.* New York: Basic Books.

Ravitch, Diane. 1984. Bring Literature and History Back to Elementary Schools. *Education Week 3* (January 11): 24.

Renzulli, Joseph S. 1977. *The Enrichment Triad: A Guide for Developing Defensible Programs for the Gifted.* Mansfield Center, CT: Creative Learning Process.

BIBLIOGRAPHY

Communication: Means and Technologies for the Exchange of Information. Piero Ventura. Boston: Houghton Mifflin, 1993.

The Dallas Titans Get Ready for Bed. Karla Kuskin. New York: HarperCollins, 1986.

Multimedia: The Complete Guide to CD ROMS, the Internet, the World Wide Web, Virtual Reality, 3-D Games, and the Information Superhighway. London: Dorling-Kindersley, 1996.

Norman the Doorman. Don Freeman. New York: Viking Penguin, 1953.

The Pet of the Met. Lydia Freeman. New York: Puffin Books, 1988.

Polar, the Titanic Bear: A True Story. Daisy Spedden. New York: Madison Press/Little, Brown, 1995.

Index

AASL. *See* American Association of School Librarians
Academic competitions, 131-32
Active teaching, 11-12
AECT. *See* Association of Educational Communications and Technology
Affecting a group, 57-62
Almanacs, 127
Alphabets, 132
American Association of School Librarians (AASL), 25-26
American Library Association, 152
Arks, 173
Arrangement of information, 32. *See also* Classification
Art, 160-63
The Art of Teaching (Highet), 11, 38, 39-40
Association for Supervision and Curriculum Development, 14
Association of Educational Communications and Technology (AECT), 25-26
Ausubel, David, 11
Authors, 89, 95, 151-52
Autobiography, 177-79

Bees (Competitions), 131-32
Beyond Fact: Nonfiction for Children and Young People (Carr), 30
Bible stories, 173-74
Bibliographies, 37, 132, 134
Bibliotherapy, 56
Biography, 176-82
Bloom, Benjamin, 3-4
Blume, Judy, 3-4
Book Links, 29
Books of lists, 134
Braille, 80
Breaking the ice, 57-58
Bruner, Jerome, 7-9, 199

Calendars, 133
California State Department of Education, 30
Card catalogs. *See* Library catalogs
Carr, Jo, 30
Cartoons, 154-57
Censorship, 152-53
Chaucer, 172
Children's Books and Their Creators, 37
Chronologies, 133
Classics, 148-49
Classification
    Dewey decimal, 32, 110-113, 117-18
    Library of Congress, 117-18
    subject, 115
Cognitive Research Trust, 14
Coles, Robert, 10
Collages, 157-58
Collection
    development, 36-37
    easy books, 87-98
    of information, 32
Collective biography, 179
College of William and Mary, 30
Comfortable Polite Research Group, 48-51
Communication of information, 32-33
Competitions, 131-32
Controversial literature, 152-53
Cooperative
    competitions, 131-32
    learning, 15-16
Core Curriculum Series Books, 4
CoRT Thinking Program, 15
Countries, 117
CPRG. *See* Comfortable Polite Research Group
Cultural literacy, 144-63
Culture of Education, The (Bruner), 8-9, 199
Cultures, 117
Curriculum, 146-47
    differentiating by, 11-14
    language arts, 67-81
    liberal arts, 160-63
    media-centered, 23-34
Cybrarians, 5

De Bono, Edward, 14, 15-16, 17-18
De Bono's Thinking, 15
Dewey decimal classification, 32, 110-113
Diaries. *See* Journals
Dictionaries, 124-25
Differentiating
   by curriculum, 11-14
   by grouping, 14-15
   by instruction, 11-14
   by strategy, 15-20

Easy collection, 87-98
Education. *See also* Instruction; Learning;
     Teaching
   frontiers, 199-204
   process of, 7-9
   trends, 196-99
Elementary School Library Collection, The
     (ESLC), 36
Emerson, Ralph Waldo, 36
Emoticons, 60
Emotional intelligence, 55-62
Emotional Intelligence (Goleman), 10, 55
Emotions, 59-62
Encyclopedias, 125-27
Epic poetry, 174
ESLC. See The Elementary School Library
     Collection
Etymology, 73-75
Exhibits, 158-59
Exposition, 93-95

Feelings, 59-62
Feldman, Ruth Duskin, 43-44
Fiction, 174-76
Field guides, 129
First Amendment, 152
First Dictionary of Cultural Literacy, A, 144
Folklore, 149-51
Foreign languages, 73-75
Frames of Mind (Gardner), 9-10
Frontiers in education, 199-204

Gallagher, James, 3
Games, 131
Gardner, Howard, 9-10
Gates, Bill, 185
Geography, 117, 168-70
Geometry of thinking, 13-14

Gifted
   programs, 10
   students. *See* Students
Global understanding, 61-62
Goleman, Daniel, 10, 55
Gowan, John Curtis, 3
Grammar, 71-73
Graphic organizers, 18
Graywolf Annual Five: Multicultural Literacy
     (Simonton), 144
Green, Grahame, 36
Group Investigations procedures, 15
Grouping, 47-64
   differentiating by, 14-15

Handbooks, 129
Hass, Robert, 4
Higher-level thinking, 13-14
Highet, Gilbert, 11, 38, 39-40
Historical fiction, 174-76
History, 116, 133
Human relations, 57-62

Ice breaking, 57-58
ICONnect, 29
Illustrators, 89
Immigration, 170-72
Improvisations, 79
Independent
   learning, 109-110
   study models, 51-53
Information
   power, 25
   processing, 11-12
   science, 197
   seeking, 103-119
   skills, 31-34
Instruction. *See also* Education; Learning;
     Teaching
   differentiating by, 11-14
   models, 11-14
   textbook, 30-31
Intellectual property, 153
Intelligence, 9-10
   emotional, 55-62
Interest, 8
Intuition, 8
Issues, 152-53

Johnston, Johanna, 144
Journals, 168-70
Joyce, Bruce, 11
Junior Great Books, 14
Juvenile biography, 176-77

Kaplan, Sandra, 10, 41-42, 146
Keller, Helen, 37-38
Key Ingredients of Effective Programs (Goleman), 55
Knowledge As Design (Perkins), 12

Labels, 57-59
Language arts, 67-81
Latitudinal group models, 54
Learners. *See* Students
Learning, 9. *See also* Education; Instruction; Teaching
cooperative, 15-16
independent, 109-110
Liberal arts, 160-63
Librarians. *See* Media specialists
Library
catalogs, 113-15
information skills, 31-34. *See also* Information
media center. *See* Media center
media specialists. *See* Media specialists
Library of Congress classification, 117-18
Lists, 134
Literacy, 144-63
Literature, 29-34
controversial, 152-53
Location of information, 32
Logos, 57-59
Longitudinal group model, 48-51

Magazines. *See* Periodicals
Mammoths, 182
Management by objective, 3
Mechanical books, 158
Media, 149
centers
curriculum, 23-34
definition, 3
programs, 25-26
student use of, 26-27
specialists, 4-5, 28(fig.), 33-34, 40-41
MegaSkills (Rich), 38-39
Metacognition, 18

Migration, 170-82
Mindstorms, 195-96
Miscellany, 130
Models
independent study, 51-53
instruction, 11-14
latitudinal group, 54
longitudinal group, 48-51
Models of Teaching (Joyce and Weil), 11
Moods, 59-62
Moral Intelligence (Coles), 10
Multicultural literacy, 144
Multiple intelligences, 9
Museums, 182-86
Music, 162-63
Mythology. *See* Folklore

Narration, 89-93
National Commission on Teaching and America's Future, 197
Nonfiction, 103-119
easy, 95-98
series, 129-30

O'Neill, Mary, 73
Odyssey of the Mind, 14
On Teaching Thinking, 14
Online-Offline, 29
Oratory, 80

Painting. *See* Art
Papert, Seymour, 195-96
Paradigms, 198
Parents, 38-39
Parnassus on Wheels (Morley), 1-2
Payne, Tom, 16-17
Pennsylvania Department of Education, 40
Penny theatres, 157-58
Periodicals, 135-36
Perkins, David, 12, 18
Philosophy for Children, 14
Piaget, Jean, 11, 13
Picture books, 88-98
Pictures, 154-57
Plagiarism, 153
PMI, 18
Poetry, 174
Polette, Nancy, 30
Pop-ups, 157-58

Pritchard, Florence, 12
Problem-solving skills. *See* Skills
Process of Education, The (Bruner), 7-9
Protocols, 198
*Providing Programs for the Gifted and
    Talented: A Handbook* (Kaplan), 10
Punctuation, 72-73

Question answering, 136-37. *See also* Research
Questioning, 16-17
Quotations, 136-37

Rath, James, 25
Ravitch, Diane, 199
Read-Aloud Handbook, The, 37
Readers theatre, 87-79
Readiness, 8
Reading Rainbow, 4
Recesstory, 78
Reference Books for Children, 144
Reference resources, 123-39
Renzulli, Joseph, 15, 198
Renzulli-Hartman Behavioral Scale, 41
Research, 117-19. *See also* Reference resources
Resources, 123-39
Retrieval of information, 32
Revolving Door Identification Model, 15, 28,
    47-54, 198
Rich, Dorothy, 38-39
Rituals, 57-59
Ruffin, Reynolds, 73
Rules, 57-59

Sarnoff, Jane, 73
Searching, 117-19, 137-38
Semantics, 70-71
Sensitivity, 59-62
Serendipity searches, 137-38
Series books, 95, 129-30, 155
Setting a group, 57-62
Seven Wonders, 138-39
Shakespeare, William, 172-73
Shurkin, Joel, 48
Sign language, 80
Simulations, 131
Singer, Isaac Bashevis, 36
Skills
    human relations, 57-62
    information, 31-34

library, 31-34
literature, 31
megaskills, 38-39
Social service, 200
Sources
    of information, 32
    reference, 123-39
Speaking, 80
Special reference books, 128-29
Speechgiving, 80
Storybooks. *See* Picture books
Storytelling, 77-81, 151-52
Storythinking, 79
Strategy, differentiating by, 15-20
Structure, 7-8
Student Team Learning techniques, 15
Students, 41-44
    use of media centers, 26-27
Subject classification, 113-15
Sullivan, Annie, 37-38
Sweet Words So Brave, 144

Tales, 149-51
Teach Your Child to Think (De Bono), 15
Teachers. *See* Media specialists; Teaching
Teaching, 37-41, 197. *See also* Education;
    Instruction; Learning
    active, 11-12
Teams, Games, and Tournaments (TGT), 131
Technology, 197, 200-201
Television, 149
Terman, Lewis, 48
Terman's Kids (Shurkin), 48
Textbook instruction, 30-31
TGT. See Teams, Games, and Tournaments
Theater, 157-58. *See also* Readers theatre
"Think Trix," 16, 18
Thinking, 13-20
    clubs, 17
    geometry of, 13-14
Time travel, 170
Timetables, 133
Titcomb, Mary Lemest, 2
Torrance, E. Paul, 3
Transition curriculum, 146
Travel, 168-70
Trends in education, 196-99
Trivia, 130

United States geography, 117

Vail, Priscilla, 145
Venn diagrams, 18
Vocabulary, 68-71

Web sites, 154-57
Weil, Marsha, 11
Whatever Happened to the Quiz Kids? (Feldman),
    43-44
Who Found America? (Johnston), 144

Whole language, 4
Words, 68-77
Words (Sarnoff and Ruffin), 73
Words, Words, Words (O'Neill), 73
World history, 116, 133
Writers' workshops, 81
Writing, 75-77, 151-52

Youth in Action, 200